FROM COLONIA
TO COMMUNITY

D0950718

Latinos in American Society and Culture
Mario T. García, Editor

FROM COLONIA TO COMMUNITY

The History of Puerto Ricans in New York City

VIRGINIA E. SÁNCHEZ KORROL

UNIVERSITY OF CALIFORNIA PRESS
Berkeley   Los Angeles   London

University of California Press
Berkeley and Los Angeles, California

University of California Press, Ltd.
London, England

© 1983 by Virginia E. Sánchez Korrol
Preface and Chapter 7 © 1994 by The Regents of the University of California

This book was originally published with the title *From Colonia to Community: The History of Puerto Ricans in New York City, 1917–1948,* by Virginia E. Sánchez Korrol, as No. 9 in the Greenwood Press series, Contributions in Ethnic Studies (Greenwood Press, Westport, Conn., 1983). Copyright © 1983 by Virginia E. Sánchez Korrol. This edition by arrangement with Greenwood Publishing Group, Inc. All rights reserved.

The Jesús Colón Papers at the Center for Puerto Rican Studies have been made available through Benigno Giboyeaux for the Estate of Jesús Colón and the Communist Party of the United States of America.

Library of Congress Cataloging-in-Publication Data
Sánchez Korrol, Virginia.
   From colonia to community : the history of Puerto Ricans in New
York City / Virginia E. Sánchez Korrol.
     p.   cm.
   Includes bibliographical references and index.
   ISBN 0-520-07900-0 (pbk. : alk. paper)
   1. Puerto Ricans—New York (N.Y.)—History—20th century. 2. New
York (N.Y.)—History—1898–1951. I. Title.
F128.P85S26   1994
974.7′1004687295—dc20   94-6452
                                             CIP

Printed in the United States of America

9 8 7 6 5 4 3 2 1

The paper used in this publication meets the minimum requirements of American National Standard for Information Sciences—Permanence of Paper for Printed Library Materials, ANSI Z39.48–1984. ⊚

In Memory of
Antonio Sánchez Feliciano
My Father — My Friend
For Chuck
and for Pam and Lauren,
our future

Contents

Plates

Tables

Maps

Figures

Preface: From Margin to Mainstream?

Frequently, in an effort to inspire an appreciation for history in my students, I tell them the story about the boy who borrowed heroes because he had none of his own. A few years ago, six elementary school children were invited to participate in a daylong conference on diversity and multiculturalism, and they had the opportunity to speak to a gathering of college students, faculty, and other interested members of the community. Questioned by the audience about their particular idols or role models, all the students selected a figure of their own gender and race or ethnic background who represented someone they were proud of and would like to emulate. All, that is, except the Puerto Rican fifth-grader, who responded that since he knew of no Puerto Rican who was famous, he "borrowed" the baseball player Darryl Strawberry.

Within the context of the U.S. Puerto Rican and Latino experience, the tale reverberates on several levels. The fact that the hero is black is almost to be expected; that he comes from the world of sports, and not science, literature, or the arts, is a fact of life. All too often, sports figures are synonymous with success in barrio culture. But the striking point of the story is that the boy had no knowledge of the history of his people. He had reached fifth grade without having been taught anything about the historical contributions of his people to the making of the United States. After I recount the fifth-grader's story, the question my students seldom fail to ask is, If the boy is not reflected in this nation's past or present, will he be inclined to invest in its future?

In the ten years since the publication of the first edition of *From Colonia to Community*, I find much has changed but also much remains to be done. Enormous strides have been made to raise the level of awareness about the political, economic, sociocultural, and historical reality of the Puerto Rican diaspora, yet publications on the subject have not found a broad readership, and they appear only sporadically on college reading lists. For the most part, the misinformation, misinterpretations, and omissions in school text-books remain uncorrected. Policymakers, educators, and others in the public sphere typically despair over what they consider a paucity of information, even though Puerto Ricans are one of the most studied groups in American society.[1] At another level, aca-demic gatekeepers have tended to devalue the seriousness of the scholarship on Puerto Ricans, although the literature is meant to generate enlightenment and intellectual exchange. Even the field of Puerto Rican studies is subject to disdain, perceived as too narrow, superficial, or "off the mark," or as a "potential threat" to the fundamental principles of American society.[2] As the edu-cator Jesse M. Vázquez observed, "If American scholars study American culture and society through American Studies, that is considered serious scholarship. However, when a Puerto Rican researcher studies Puerto Rican culture—any aspect of it—it is not seen as quite scholarly enough."[3]

Thus I welcome the opportunity to publish this revised edition of *From Colonia to Community*, which brings the historical nar-rative into the present in a new closing chapter that describes the demographic and organizational evolution in New York's Puerto Rican community since 1948, the end point of the first edition. In addition, this preface gives me a chance to review recent events and developments that underscore the dynamism within the Puerto Rican community and its members' interactions with others in Amer-ican society. Finally, this preface permits me to situate the book within a productive body of literature that persistently seeks to mediate and articulate the Puerto Rican experience in the United States.

The last ten years have witnessed a renaissance in Puerto Rican studies. If ethnic studies is not yet in the mainstream of academia, it is no longer on the margins. Such areas of inquiry, and Puerto Rican studies is no exception, trace their genesis to organized intellectual efforts that challenge absorption into an ethnocentric common culture which had denied—and rendered invisible—linguistic, racial, and national communities.[4] Puerto Rican studies affirms ethnocultural survival and supports, in the words of Edna Acosta Belén, a "U.S. society in which diversity, differentiation, and multiethnic interaction constitute its true cultural nucleus."[5] The field includes an agenda for dispelling stereotypes that not only enlists a revisionist stance about the diaspora but also sets the terms of inclusion into the wider society. The field incorporates inter- and multidisciplinary perspectives, research and advocacy, alternative theoretical frameworks, and accountability to its constituent communities. It is important to note that many of the underlying tenets in Puerto Rican studies resurfaced in the philosophical underpinnings of America's prevailing response to diversity, the multicultural movement.

Extraordinary demographic shifts within our national borders have resulted in part from unprecedented increases in the migration and immigration of people from Asia, the Caribbean, and Central and South America. In response, various scholars and activists have sought to redefine the meaning of diversity in a pluralistic society. The concept of the melting pot gave way to cultural pluralism, as more accurate, inclusive delineations, based on the incorporation of new scholarship and multiple perspectives, began to illuminate alternative paradigms for comprehending diversity and global interdependence. Such concepts have broadened our historical references to meaningfully incorporate the silent, often forgotten voices of those marginal to the mainstream.

Shaped by the transformative climate of the 1960s and 1970s, new scholarship originated, primarily from revisionist or deconstructionist elements in the academy, that validated the inclusion of race, gender, class, and ethnicity as legitimate tools of analysis and postulated a "bottoms up" approach for understanding our past. The coming-of-age of Puerto Rican studies, and other fruitful inter- and multidisciplinary areas of study, also meant joining praxis with intellectual pursuit. Moreover, the field advocates the application of academic resources toward the resolution of community issues and concerns. No longer novelties on university campuses, such academic units reaffirm identity and multiple loyalties, promote equitable intergroup relations, and infuse curriculum with diverse perspectives that continue to inform the cultural discourse.

The challenge of incorporating a wide range of new knowledge and concepts, combined with the rapid demographic changes taking place in the United States, has generated a variety of reactions, but nowhere has the debate been more pronounced than in the continuing public controversies over culture and curriculum. If a primary focus of teaching history is "to foster mutual understanding and respect among people of different backgrounds and conditions,"[6] we must be prepared to situate that objective within the realities of the twenty-first century. We must recognize and affirm the complementarity of our nation's unity and diversity.

The process of imaging ourselves as one nation composed of many peoples brings an urgency to documenting the Puerto Rican experience in all of its particulars, an urgency that is even more pressing today than it was ten years ago. As the second largest Latino group in the United States, Puerto Ricans currently comprise about 1 percent of the total population. But, as policy analyst Angelo Falcón observes, Puerto Ricans constitute "5 percent or more of the populations of six major states that combined represent 118, or 21.9 percent, of total votes in the Electoral College."[7] Clustered in the nation's urban areas, in states that could determine the winner in presidential elections, Puerto Ricans represent a significant voting potential. And if the present rate of population increase continues through the end of this decade, Puerto Ricans living in the states and in Puerto Rico will exceed 7 million individuals by the turn of the century.[8]

A relatively young community, Puerto Ricans continue to place great emphasis on education and struggle to surmount socioeconomic indicators that have prompted some researchers to cast the group into a nether status stigmatized as the "underclass."[9] The strength and potential of this community clearly lie in its youth, and it is here that scholar-activists are held most accountable. At the core of our responsibility as researchers is the planting of the seeds of a historical memory that rests not on "distorting" or "rewriting history," as some traditionalists have charged, but on setting the record straight. Such knowledge should certainly strive to transmit historical accuracy and civic responsibility, but also validation that ensures inclusion and inspires potential for leadership in all young people.

The experience of Puerto Ricans, both in the island and in the United States, has figured prominently in the new scholarship. Marked by a flourish of research activity that has sparked rigorous reevaluation across the disciplines, this literature appears in print as journal articles and essays, monographs, anthologies, and dissertations. In addition, many studies have been generated by research centers, such as the City University of New York's Centro de Estudios Puertorriqueños, the Hispanic Research Center at Fordham University, the Inter-University Program (IUP) for Latino Research (a consortium of university centers throughout the United States), and the Latino public policy research arm of the Social Science Research Council. Recent topics include race relations, identity, poverty, female-headed families, cultural citizenship, the underground economy, voting, health, education, and migration.

Several national research projects in Latino studies also include a strong Puerto Rican focus. Among these are the Recovering the U.S. Hispanic Literary Heritage project located at the University of Houston, designed to rescue and disseminate primary literary sources written by Hispanics in those geographic regions that now constitute the United States. The development of the Ibero-American Heritage Curriculum, spearheaded by the New York State Department of Education, corresponds to the growing needs of public school teachers to instruct about the Latino role in the shaping of America.

As Clara E. Rodríguez puts it, all Puerto Ricans have been "born in the U.S.A." since 1898.[10] But I have limited the following brief overview of the literary output of the past ten years to work on the stateside diaspora. I have chosen not to include numerous journal articles and book chapters nor to cite anthologies on Latinos and Hispanics in the United States, even though these usually include substantive essays or creative literature on the Puerto Rican experience. However, the noticeable increase in doctoral dissertations on Puerto Rican topics is worthy of mention, for it indicates continuity and new directions in research. In the past ten years, over thirty dissertations have explored the status and condition of stateside Puerto Rican women,[11] and at least a dozen more have been written about women in Puerto Rico or about the diaspora in general. At least three of the dissertations convey new historiography: the work of Norma Carr on the history of Puerto Ricans in Hawaii, 1900–1958; the study of music and musicians in New York, 1915–1940, by Ruth Glasser (forthcoming from University of California Press); and the research on Boston's Villa Victoria by Mirén Uriarte Gastón.[12]

In terms of booklength monographs and anthologies, four broad categories predominate: history and migration, work and gender, politics and economics, and literature and sociolinguistics.

Groundbreaking documentation of the struggles and contributions of pre-World War II migrants provides the focus for two important primary sources of the early Puerto Rican community. The first, which has already earned the status of a literary classic, is *Memoirs of Bernardo Vega,* compiled by César Andreu Iglesias and translated into English by Juan Flores. In this memoir, Vega, a tobacco worker, recalls and records historical events and achievements of the pioneer generation. The second key source is the anecdotal writings of Vega's prolific contemporary, Jesús Colón. Collected in two volumes, Colón's commentaries touch upon innumerable aspects of the human experience; they were originally published in a number of newspapers and journals from 1923 to 1971.[13]

Both Colón and Vega understood the harsh, exploitative nature of the migration and the urgency of preserving the history of Puerto Ricans, especially from the perspective of the working class. The investigations of the Oral History, Cultural Studies, and other task forces at the Centro de Estudios Puertorriqueños have extended and expanded that quest, producing valuable documentation and analysis, including *Extended Roots: From Hawaii to New York*; *Affirming Cultural Citizenship in the Puerto Rican Community: Critical Literacy and the El Barrio Popular Education Program*; and *Stories to Live By: Continuity and Change in Three Generations of Puerto Rican Women.*[14]

Stories to Live By begins to question the intergenerational dimensions of the migration and, along with several other studies about Puerto Rican women, reconnects the ties that bind island and mainland women. Viewed through the lens of feminist study, the work of Edna Acosta Belén offers similar opportunities for comparative insights, and for understanding Puerto Rican women in two-world contexts. Altagracia Ortiz's anthology on gender, work, and migration follows a corresponding rationale but uses the interconnections between work and migration on both sides of the ocean as the organizing unit of analysis. Intergenerational feminist constructs of identity, multiple loyalties, and cultural citizenship form the framework of the powerful prose and poetry of Aurora Levins Morales and Rosario Morales.[15] The implications of a divided nation in opposition to the concept of one people split between two distinct geographic-cultural contexts, and issues of identity, self-definition, and the formation of an ethnic consciousness are addressed by Felix Padilla, Asela Rodríguez de Laguna, and Juan Flores.[16]

The scholarship on the diaspora has attained new levels of energy and intellectual sophistication during the past ten years, characterized by a broad sweep of academic investigation combining comparative, quantitative, and qualitative methods of inquiry. Predominantly revisionist in design, the studies incorporate the premise that to understand the uniqueness of the Puerto Rican situation, one must understand (1) the context in which Puerto Ricans migrated, (2) that in which they presently live, (3) the cyclical and structural factors affecting the economically based migration, (4) and the diverse nature of the communities they established throughout the United States.[17] Within such locales, the intersection of race, class, and ethnicity, conditioned by mainstream cultural and social variables, has propagated distinctive patterns in assimilation, labor force and political participation, language usage, religious beliefs and practices, and education. The study of such patterns forms the core of much of the literature of this period.

In 1984 a small interdisciplinary volume of literary and critical essays, *The Puerto Rican Struggle: Essays on Survival in the U.S.,* went into a second printing.[18] The collection addressed cultural and academic issues generally ignored in the mainstream press, with essays on gender and employment, race within ethnicity, voting patterns, traditional and non-traditional religion, community empowerment, music, the Young Lords, and social science methodology. Among the general concepts to emerge from the collection was that of self-definition and validation. The collection also foreshadowed scholar-activists' attempt to define the diaspora for themselves as insiders and outsiders. As one of the editors points out, "It was no accident that nearly all involved with this collection were second-generation Puerto Ricans or had experienced life in U.S. Puerto Rican communities."[19]

The works by Joseph Fitzpatrick, Felix Padilla, James Jennings and Monte Rivera, Clara Rodríguez, and Julio Morales are similarly comprehensive.[20] In general, this literature revises previously held notions about Puerto Ricans, citing new demographic evidence and analysis, and interpreting class-based racial and ethnic identity, gender roles, politics, education, and community building. Fitzpatrick's *Puerto Rican Americans* is especially interesting in this regard because the second edition, published in 1987, sixteen years after the first, modifies conventional ideas about Puerto Rican assimilation, evoking a pluralistic future for the group, that, in turn, intersects with ethnoracial evolution in the United States. While all five studies touch upon similar topics, they vary in focus and emphasis. Jennings and Rivera, Rodríguez, and Padilla offer broad historical and political analyses of politics in the barrio, from community empowerment to electoral participation. Padilla and Fitzpatrick provide insightful interdisciplinary overviews of the establishment of the Chicago and New York communities, and both authors interweave chronological narrative and contemporary creative literature. Studies by Gloria Bonilla-Santiago and by J. Figueroa situate their subjects in specific geographic locales, New Jersey farms and the New York underground economy, respectively. Andrés Pérez y Mena addresses religion, and María E. Sánchez and Antonio M. Stevens-Arroyo trace the evolution of Puerto Rican studies in the university.[21]

Finally, it would be remiss to overlook the steady flow of literary prose and poetry that has characterized our communities since their inception. As second-generation writers have continued to forge new language and images that interpret their own reality, Nuyorican writing has become a distinctive literary genre that enriches the literature of both Puerto Rico and the United States.

During the eighties, the surge in the articulation of gender perspectives and feminist ideology included creative works by Nicholasa Mohr, Judith Ortiz Coffer, Aurora Levins Morales and Rosario Morales, and Carmen de Monteflores.[22] The feminist perspective often augmented and overlapped with themes resonant in earlier creative expression and current social science research: issues of identity, language usage and linguistics, and ethnoracial and national consciousness. Against the theoretical debate that continues to rage over the "pure" definition of Puerto Ricanness, the poetry of Tato Laviera, Sandra María Esteves, and younger voices like that of Martín Espada add new range to the cultural canon.[23]

From Colonia to Community was written within this broad and diverse tradition, so illustrative of the literature on Puerto Ricans on this side of the ocean. I hope this book may also engender collective heroes and heroines along the way.

Notes

1. Edna Acosta Belén, "Beyond Island Boundaries: Ethnicity, Gender and Cultural Revitalization," *Callaloo* (Johns Hopkins University Press, Baltimore) vol. 15, no. 4 (1992), pp. 979–998. See also Sonia Nieto, "'Losers,' 'Outsiders' and 'Leaders': A History of the Education of Puerto Rican Students in U.S. Mainland Schools," in J. A. Banks and C. M. Banks, eds., *Handbook of Research on Multicultural Education* (Macmillan Press, forthcoming), and, in the same volume, Clara E. Rodríguez, "Puerto Ricans in Historical and Social Science Research."

2. Jesse M. Vázquez, "Embattled Scholars in the Academy," *Callaloo* vol. 15, no. 4 (1992), p. 1044.

3. Ibid., p. 1043.

4. Josephine Nieves et al., "Puerto Rican Studies: Roots and Challenges," in María E. Sánchez and Antonio M. Stevens-Arroyo, eds., *Toward a Renaissance of Puerto Rican Studies: Ethnic and Area Studies in University Education* (Highland Lakes, N.J.: Atlantic Research and Publications, 1987), pp. 3–12.

5. Acosta Belén, "Beyond Island Boundaries," p. 986.

6. Statement of the Executive Board of the Organization of American Historians, cited by Dr. Thomas Sobol, Commissioner of Education of the State of New York, in remarks to the Eighty-Fifth Annual Meeting of the OAH, Chicago, April 4, 1992, p. 19.

7. Angelo Falcón, "The Puerto Rican Community: A Status Report," *Diálogo* (The National Puerto Rican Policy Network, New York) no. 7 (Summer 1993), p. 10.

8. Ibid., p. 5.

9. Most recently, Linda Chávez, *Out of the Barrio: Toward a New Politics of Hispanic Assimilation* (New York: Basic Books, 1991) has so stigmatized Puerto Ricans. For a positive viewpoint see José Hernández, "Latino Alternatives to the Underclass Concept," *Latino Studies Journal* (DePaul University Press, Chicago) vol. 1, no. 1 (January 1990); Rina Benmayor, Rosa M. Torruellas, and L. Juarbe, *Responses to Poverty Among Puerto Rican Women: Identity, Community, and Cultural Citizenship* (New York: Centro de Estudios Puertorriqueños, 1992).

10. Clara E. Rodríguez, *Puerto Ricans: Born in the U.S.A.* (Boston: Unwin Hyman, 1989).

11. See Edna Acosta Belén, Christine E. Bose, with Anne R. Rochelle, *Albany PR—Womenet Database: An Interdisciplinary Annotated Bibliography on Puerto Rican Women* (New York: SUNY at Albany, Center for Latin America and the Caribbean, Institute for Research on Women, 1991). An extensive collection of dissertations is housed in the library of the Centro de Estudios Puertorriqueños at Hunter College, City University of New York.

12. Norma Carr, "The Puerto Ricans in Hawaii: 1900–1958" (University of Hawaii, Ph.D. Dissertation, 1989); Mirén Uriarte Gastón, "Organizing for Survival: The Emergence of a Puerto Rican Community" (Boston University, Ph.D. Dissertation, 1987); Ruth Glasser, "Que vivío tiene la gente aquí en Nueva York: Music and Community in Puerto Rican New York, 1915–1940" (Yale University, Ph.D. Dissertation, 1991).

13. César Andreu Iglesias, ed., *Memoirs of Bernardo Vega*, Juan Flores, trans. (New York: Monthly Review Press, 1984); Jesús Colón, *A Puerto Rican in New York and Other Sketches* (New York: International Publishers, 1982); Jesús Colón, *The Way It Was and Other Writings*, Edna Acosta Belén and V. Sánchez Korrol, eds. (Houston: Arte Público Press, 1993).

14. Oral History Task Force, *Extended Roots: From Hawaii to New York* (New York: Centro de Estudios Puertorriqueños, 1986); Rosa M. Torruellas, Rina Benmayor, Anneris Goris, and Ana Juarbe, *Affirming Cultural Citizenship in the Puerto Rican Community: Critical Literacy and the El Barrio Popular Education Program* (New York: Centro de Estudios Puertorriqueños, 1991); Rina Benmayor, Ana Juarbe, Celia Alvarez, and Blanca Vazquez, *Stories to Live By: Continuity and Change*

in Three Generations of Puerto Rican Women (New York: Centro de Estudios Puertorriqueños, 1987).

15. Edna Acosta Belén, *The Puerto Rican Woman* (Westport, Conn.: Praeger Press, 1986); Altagracia Ortiz, ed., *Puerto Rican Women in the Twentieth Century: New Perspectives on Gender, Labor and Migration, 1900–1990* (Philadelphia: Temple University Press, forthcoming); Aurora Levins Morales and Rosario Morales, *Getting Home Alive* (Ithaca, N.Y.: Firebrand Books, 1986).

16. Felix Padilla, *Latino Ethnic Consciousness: The Case of Mexican-Americans and Puerto Ricans in Chicago* (Notre Dame, Ind.: University of Notre Dame Press, 1985) and *Puerto Rican Chicago* (Notre Dame, Ind.: University of Notre Dame Press, 1987); Asela Rodríguez de Laguna, *Images and Identities: The Puerto Rican in Two World Contexts* (New Brunswick, N.J.: Transaction Books, 1987); Juan Flores, *Divided Borders: Essays on Puerto Rican Identity* (Houston: Arte Público Press, 1993).

17. See Rodríguez, "Puerto Ricans in Historical and Social Science Research," and Acosta Belén, "Beyond Island Boundaries."

18. Clara E. Rodríguez, V. Sánchez Korrol, and José Oscar Alers, eds., *The Puerto Rican Struggle: Essays on Survival in the U.S.* (New York: Waterfront Press, 1984).

19. Rodríguez, "Puerto Ricans in Historical and Social Science Research," p. 35.

20. Joseph P. Fitzpatrick, *Puerto Rican Americans: The Meaning of Migration to the Mainland* (Englewood Cliffs, N.J.: Prentice-Hall, 1971; 2d ed., 1987); James Jennings and Monte Rivera, eds., *Puerto Rican Politics in Urban America* (Westport, Conn.: Greenwood Press, 1984); Julio Morales, *Puerto Rican Poverty and Migration: We Just Had to Try Elsewhere* (Westport, Conn.: Praeger Press, 1986); Padilla, *Latino Ethnic Consciousness* and *Puerto Rican Chicago;* Rodríguez, *Puerto Ricans.*

21. Gloria Bonilla-Santiago, *Organizing Puerto Rican Migrant Farmworkers: The Experience of Puerto Ricans in New Jersey* (New York: Lang, 1988); J. Figueroa, *Survival on the Margin: A Documentary Study of the Underground Economy in a Puerto Rican Ghetto* (New York: Vantage Press, 1989); Andrés Pérez y Mena, *Speaking with the Dead: Development of Afro-Latin Religion Among Puerto Ricans in the U.S.* (New York: AMS Press, 1991); Sánchez and Stevens-Arroyo, *Toward a Renaissance of Puerto Rican Studies.*

22. Nicholasa Mohr, *Rituals of Survival: A Woman's Portfolio* (Houston: Arte Público Press, 1986); Judith Ortiz Coffer, *Terms of Survival* (Hous-

ton: Arte Público Press, 1987) and *Silent Dancing: A Partial Remembrance of a Puerto Rican Childhood* (Houston: Arte Público Press, 1990); Levins Morales and Morales, *Getting Home Alive;* Carmen de Monteflores, *Cantando Bajito / Singing Softly* (San Francisco: Spinsters / Aunt Lute, 1989).

23. Tato Laviera, *AmeRican* (Houston: Arte Público Press, 1985) and *La Carreta Made a U-Turn* (Houston: Arte Público Press, 1981, 1992); Sandra María Esteves, *Tropical Rain* (New York: African Caribbean Poetry Theater, 1984); Martín Espada, *Trumpets for the Island of Their Eviction* (Tempe, Ariz.: Bilingual Press, 1988).

FROM COLONIA
TO COMMUNITY

Introduction

In the early decades of this century, a significant number of Puerto Ricans from the countryside and urban centers of the island began to migrate to the northern metropolises of the United States. Although small groups of political exiles had emigrated throughout the last third of the nineteenth century, it was not until after the North American occupation of the island in 1898 that critical social, political, and economic transformations in Puerto Rico triggered an increase in the numbers of people leaving for continental shores. Through the creation of infant enclaves on the mainland, Puerto Rican migrants set about establishing communities which reflected in many ways those they left behind. As early as 1910, over one thousand Puerto Ricans resided in the United States. American citizenship granted via the Jones Act of 1917 stimulated the freedom of movement between the island and the United States. By 1920, forty-five states reported the presence of Puerto Rican-born individuals, with all forty-eight doing so in succeeding censuses. In short, the decades before the onset of World War II witnessed a progressive increase in the numbers of Puerto Ricans living in the United States, a migration slowed only by the Depression, which would peak in the decades of the fifties and sixties.

In New York City and the surrounding metropolitan areas, the Puerto Rican presence became most noticeable just after the Second World War. About that time, the first systematic surveys depicting the plight of the Puerto Ricans in the city began to appear in print. In 1947, for example, a pictorial essay in *Life* magazine chronicled the migration to the United States as the first airborne diaspora in history. Such news stories coincided with investigative reports of various social service agencies highlighting the health, housing, and employment problems of the city's newest migrants. Within a decade, monographs like the Columbia University Study, the Welfare Study, and the New York City Board of Education surveys focused attention on Puerto Ricans in an effort to inform the dominant non-Hispanic society about this group.[1]

While literature on Puerto Ricans during the fifties centered on the economic, social, or racial assimilation or adjustment problems of the post-World War II migration, relatively few studies emphasized the community structure of the Puerto Rican New York settlements throughout the decades before the war. Social scientists like Daniel P. Moynihan and Nathan Glazer blatantly denied the existence of an early Puerto Rican community and failed to perceive the relationship between early support systems or coping institutions and the later migration.[2] Indeed, these particular authors based their ideas on the notion that the process of community building never existed on the island proper and therefore could not be translated to the New York settlements. Thus the experience and resettlement patterns of the larger migration at mid-century were frequently viewed and analyzed in a vacuum without reference to earlier community development or to the forces which motivated the original displacement. The experiences of the pioneer migrants in New York settlements who laid the groundwork for the "great migration" of the later decades had clearly been overlooked.

This study proposes to fill the gap. It explores the development of the Puerto Rican settlements, or *colonias,* in New York City during the first four decades of the century and demonstrates the existence of an identifiable migrant community during that period. Originating soon after the turn of the century, pioneer *colonias* charged with the responsibility of translating the Puerto Rican way of life to unfamiliar territory generated a visual and intrinsic presence which would greatly influence future settlement patterns between the island and the mainland. It was to those *colonias,* vividly Puerto Rican with their *bodegas* (grocery stores), Hispanic boarding houses, or restaurants, formal and informal support networks and organizations, that migrants came.

Focusing on the community's organizational networks, structured and unstructured coping institutions, settlement patterns and migrants' occupations, the study revises heretofore accepted interpretations of the Puerto Rican experience away from the island and builds on pioneer works, such as those of Joseph P. Fitzpatrick, Lawrence R. Chenault, and C. Wright Mills. Moreover, I intend to expand on current scholarship, particularly the research of the Center for Puerto Rican Studies, CEREP (Centro del estudio de la realidad Puertorriqueña), and the Puerto Rican Migration Research Consortium.[3]

Several issues integral to the migratory process will be dissected. How and why, for instance, did Puerto Ricans come to New York City during the first decades of the present century? What kinds of communities did they establish and what institutions or practices emerged to meet migrant needs? How did the settlements in different New York boroughs relate to one another, to issues concerning Puerto Ricans on the island, and to the dominant non-Hispanic or host society? Above all, who were the early migrants and how did they carve a definable community in the city?

Research for this book was divided into two phases. The first consisted of an investigation of United States government documents and publications, census materials, archival collections, newspapers, periodicals, and journals to determine the size and scope of the early *colonia*. Most of this research was executed while I served as a member of the History Task Force of the Center for Puerto Rican Studies, Graduate Center of the City University of New York. In conjunction with this group, an official but untabulated census, The New York State Manuscript Census of 1925, was coded and computed for 7,322 Spanish-surnamed individuals living in Manhattan's Sixteenth, Seventeenth, Eighteenth, and Nineteenth Assembly Districts. Yielding variables including the sex, age, race, and occupation, length of residence in New York City, country of origin, place in and composition of Hispanic households, the census formed the basis for an analysis of the mid-1920s Spanish-speaking community.

Moreover, while participating with the History Task Force, I was

introduced to an autobiographical manuscript detailing Puerto
Rican life in the United States, especially in New York City, dating
from the final decades of the nineteenth century up to and including the 1950s. This material, *Memorias de Bernardo Vega,* edited
by the Puerto Rican writer César Andreu Iglesias, was subsequently
published by Ediciones Huracan.[4] The most comprehensive study
on the subject to date, *Memorias* provided the leads to many
Puerto Rican associations in operation throughout the early
decades, newspapers and journals in existence, community issues,
and leadership. Once the information became confirmed and cor-
roborated, an investigation of the organizational charters on file in
the New York City County Clerk's Office, Supreme Court Building
became possible. Archival collections such as the Vito Marcantonio
Papers and the Arturo Schomberg collection in the New York Public Library also yielded valuable insights on this theme.

While archival materials, census information, and publications
provided important perspectives for an historical reconstruction of
the pre-World War II settlements, oral interviews and popular culture also added major dimensions. The second research phase centered on tracking down appropriate oral history collections and in-
terviewing migrants who had lived through the migration experience within the first four decades of the century. The Columbia
University Oral History Project and the Brentwood Multilingual
Assessment Program on Long Island housed limited collections on
Puerto Rican settlers. The first concentrated on individuals recognized for their contributions in building the Hispanic community in
general. These were mostly community leaders, writers, or both.
The interview with folklorist Pura Belpré is representative in both
of these areas. The second also focused on better-known persons
such as Elizabeth Guanill, commissioner of Human Rights for Suf-
folk County, and others active in establishing the Hispanic Long
Island community. The Long Island Historical Society, however,
offered a fine, extensive, and varied collection of interviews with
pioneering, working-class migrants in the Brooklyn *colonia.* This
set focused on early settlement patterns, community and organizational structure, leadership, and the relationship between the Manhattan and Brooklyn settlements. Numbering close to seventy taped
interviews, half of which have been transcribed, Puerto Rican life-

styles, attitudes, work experience, family structure, and migration processes have all been recorded.

Furthermore, from June 1977 until June 1978, a grant from the Ford Foundation, "Movements of People in the Caribbean," enabled research on return migrants currently living in Puerto Rico. During this period a series of interviews was conducted with retired, working-class individuals cognizant of the New York experience between the two world wars. Their references regarding the formation of the early settlements proved essential to the overall theme, since secondary sources have been so limited in this area. Close to twenty hours of transcribed tapes and an additional twenty-five conversations were gathered with migrants in Puerto Rico and in New York City, augmenting the interviews in other collections. Moreover, as women comprised a significant percentage of the interviews collected, a description of their specific role in the development of the pioneer *colonias* became possible for the first time.

Finally, the second research phase concluded with an investigation of popular culture, particularly the music and songs which so often expressed feelings, attitudes, and concerns of the migrant population rarely found in the literature. Themes of popular songs not only set forth strains of nostalgia for the migrants' absent homeland, but also expressed nascent feelings of incompatability with the alien New York environment.

The book has been organized in the following manner. Chapter 2 describes the background of the migration to New York City, analyzing the factors which encouraged Puerto Ricans to leave the island as well as those which drew the migrants to the city and other parts of the United States. Indicating the migration occurred in response to complex and extensive continental considerations, many of these economically based, the chapter explains how and why Puerto Ricans became concentrated in the metropolitan area throughout the decades before the Second World War.

Chapter 3 explores the concept of community as described in the literature on Puerto Ricans in the mainland. It evolves to demonstrate the existence of an active, energetic, and structured Puerto Rican community which coalesced around various characteristics. These included Puerto Rican settlement patterns, increases in the

size of the *colonia* as well as in commercial and professional establishments, use of Spanish as the language of communication, and
common interests and attitudes expressed in popular culture.

Chapter 4 concentrates on the role of Puerto Rican women in the
structure of the early community. Comprising almost half of the
migrant population throughout the period of this study, women
persisted in maintaining traditional sex and family roles in spite of
their steady integration into the mainland work force. Faced with a
disintegrating and sometimes hostile environment, women devised
practices and customs designed to maintain an intact family structure while shouldering their share of familial responsibilities.
Often, women added supplementary or, in some cases, primary
incomes to the households. Practices such as taking in boarders and
child care expanded to strengthen communal bonds at a time when
the *colonia* was most vulnerable. Thus the practices which emerge
to meet migrant needs in this aspect of settlement are considered
informal coping institutions.

Chapter 5 investigates the formal (incorporated) social, cultural,
civic, and economic organizational structure and the leadership
which these groups engendered. Neighborhood clubs, brother-
hoods, federations, and professional and educational groups played
pivotal roles in defining and reinforcing the *colonia hispana*. Here
we trace the development of three organizational models over several decades, outlining the group's relationship to the community,
to Puerto Rico, and to the dominant non-Hispanic host society.
While the organizational objectives of many such groups appeared
in their certificates of incorporation, these often failed to convey
the full scope of a group's actual functions and operation. By describing the activities and concerns of several representative
groups, the chapter attempts to fill this void.

Chapter 6 examines the functions of political organization and
participation among Puerto Rican migrants. During the early
decades political participation among this group was far more prolific than previously assumed. Political units numbered among the
earliest associations within the *colonia* and these concerned themselves with the social or political issues affecting the community,
relations between the early settlements and with the wider non-
Hispanic society, and with Latin American issues in general. Above
all, these were the groups which sought to serve the migrant *colonia*

as power brokers both within the Spanish-speaking settlements and with the non-Hispanic population.

Chapter 7 serves as summary. Without doubt the study of immigration, migration, and its aftermath forms an integral part of the histories of the Americas. As a Latin migration, the Puerto Rican experience and its efforts to build pioneer settlements should serve as a basis for comparisons with other Latin population movements or with Puerto Rican communities outside of New York City. Inasmuch as changes within federal immigration regulations continue to encourage and stimulate population movements from Latin countries to northern urban centers, an understanding of the Hispanic reality remains critical. New York City, in particular, continues to receive a substantial amount of legal and undocumented immigration. The problems faced by recent arrivals, whether social, in the job market, or in the community, closely parallel the Puerto Rican experience. It behooves us, therefore, to learn as much as possible about their migratory processes and resettlement patterns in order to understand other Latins in the United States.

Notes

1. Among the surveys published between 1947 and 1957 were the following: C. Wright Mills, Clarence Senior, and Rose Goldsen, *The Puerto Rican Journey: New York's Newest Migrant* (New York: Harper & Bros., 1950), based on the findings of the Columbia University Applied Social Research team on the Puerto Rican community in New York City, 1948; New York City Board of Education, Bureau of Educational Program Research and Statistics, *Teaching Children of Puerto Rican Background in New York City Schools* (1953): J. Cayce Morrison, director, *The Puerto Rican Study,* 1953–1957 (New York City Board of Education, 1957); The Welfare Council of New York City, *Puerto Ricans in New York City* (1948); Welfare and Health Council of New York City, *Population of Puerto Rican Birth and Parentage* (1950); Welfare and Health Council of New York City, Brooklyn Council for Social Planning, "Report on Survey of Brooklyn Agencies Rendering Services to Puerto Ricans" (June 1953).

2. Adalberto López, "Some of the Literature on Puerto Rico and Puerto Ricans in English," in Adalberto López and James Petras, eds., *Puerto Rico and the Puerto Ricans: Studies in History and Society* (New York: Schenkman Publishing, 1974), pp. 471–480; Nathan Glazer and Daniel Patrick Moynihan, *Beyond the Melting Pot* (Cambridge, Mass.: MIT Press, 1963); History Task Force, Centro de Estudios Puertorriqueños,

Labor Migration Under Capitalism: The Puerto Rican Experience (New York: Monthly Review Press, 1979), pp. 144–45; U.S. Commission on Civil Rights, *Puerto Ricans in the Continental United States: An Uncertain Future* (October 1976).

3. Lawrence R. Chenault, *The Puerto Rican Migrant in New York City* (New York: Columbia University, 1938; reissue, Russell and Russell, 1970); Joseph P. Fitzpatrick, *Puerto Rican Americans: The Meaning of Migration to the Mainland* (Englewood Cliffs, N.J.: Prentice-Hall, 1971); History Task Force, *Labor Migration.*

4. César Andreu Iglesias, ed., *Memorias de Bernardo Vega* (Rio Piedras, Puerto Rico: Ediciones Huracan, 1977).

Background of the Puerto Rican Migration to New York City

The pre-World War II Puerto Rican settlements in New York City continued various social and economic processes originating in Puerto Rico during the nineteenth century. As time passed—and particularly toward the end of the nineteenth century—changes in the island's economic structure increasingly led to both internal and external emigration to the mainland. Instigated by a poorly integrated labor force, Puerto Rican men, women, and children left their homes. Prior to the Spanish-American War, three migratory patterns existed from the island to the United States. Each had direct or indirect bearing on the emigration and settlement patterns of the twentieth century. Early Puerto Rican settlers came as merchants and students, as adventurers and revolutionaries, and as field and factory workers. The first migration based on commercial factors served as a rehearsal for the next two, which were more politically and economically motivated.

In the beginning, migration was influenced by a commercially oriented pattern which emerged from growing trade relations between Puerto Rican and Anglo-American colonists. Originating in the mid-eighteenth century, commerce between the two initially meant smuggling and clandestine barter, conducted despite Spanish mercantilist policies. This flourishing trade, based on the exchange of Puerto Rican sugar and molasses for basic food staples which Spain failed to provide, enriched the purses of New York, New

England, and Pennsylvania merchants. Early contacts intensified
when the Spanish Crown sanctioned the entrance of ships flying the
stars and stripes into Latin colonial ports during war times.[1]
Commercial movements were inevitably accompanied by the transfer of people as well as commodities.

By 1830, trade between Cuba, Puerto Rico, and the Middle Atlantic states, along with resultant population shifts, reached large
enough proportions to warrant the establishment of a Spanish
Benevolent Society in New York City (Sociedad Benéfica Cubana y
Puertorriqueña), composed of merchants from the islands. These
merchants promoted trade exchanges between the islands and the
mainland, a connection virtually unsevered throughout the century
in spite of subsequent political or economic fluctuations.[2] More
important, the formation of the Spanish Benevolent Society indicated positive expectations regarding the degree of commercial
interaction between Puerto Rico and the United States that was to
follow throughout the nineteenth century.

During the last third of the period, Puerto Rican molasses and
sugar production depended on North American markets to such an
extent that the volume of purchases made by the United States far
exceeded the volume purchased by the mother country, Spain. A
study by Angel Quintero Rivera revealed that 68.6 percent of the
island's sugar was exported to the United States while only 0.8 percent was sent to Spain in 1870. A decade later, 57.0 percent was
exported to northern metropolises, but only 2.0 percent was sent to
Spain; and finally in 1897, the year before the Spanish-American
War, 60.6 percent of Puerto Rican sugar exports went to the United
States, compared with 35.4 percent exported to Spain.[3] Furthermore, the expansion of commercial activity between these points
becomes more significant when we consider that almost all of the
island's molasses exports were destined for the United States. In
return, the United States, along with several European industrial
countries, provided Puerto Rican *haciendas* with the machinery
necessary for planting and harvesting the island's major crops:
coffee, sugar, and tobacco.[4] These commercial interactions involving primarily the island's merchant and creole *hacendado* class
opened the way and influenced to a great extent the selection of the
United States as one entrepot for the immigration of the sons and

daughters of this class. Some would come as students and others as political exiles.

It was this latter group which characterized the second migratory pattern from Puerto Rico during the island's struggle for independence. Attempts to shed Spanish rule had appeared since the beginning of the nineteenth century, reaching a climax in 1868 with the unsuccessful revolutionary attempt known as *El Grito de Lares*. Immediately after this aborted lunge for independence coupled with the failure to establish a Puerto Rican republic, and throughout the last decades of the century, many activists involved in the island's separatist or independence movement were forced to emigrate from Puerto Rico. Arriving in the United States, they rapidly organized into political units. From New York sanctuaries they dedicated themselves to a series of activities furthering the cause of independence; uniting other Puerto Rican exiles; and promoting propaganda campaigns and writing political manifestos directed toward the indoctrination of their compatriots in Puerto Rico. Joining forces with Cuban exiles and other Latin Americans also struggling in their countries' internal revolutions, they published newspapers such as *Patria, La Revolución,* and *El Porvenir* in support of Spanish Caribbean liberation.

By 1895 Puerto Rican political exiles in New York formed a branch of the Cuban Revolutionary Party's governing body and motivated the establishment of various socially and politically oriented associations all dedicated to the theme of Antillean independence.[5] These constituted the first Puerto Rican organizations to operate in New York City. They appealed not only to the political founding exiles instrumental in their creation, but to the trickle of skilled and unskilled Puerto Rican workers who began to make their homes in the city during the first decades of the twentieth century. Among this latter group some individuals had come as contracted agricultural or factory workers; others as skilled artisans; and still others had followed a pattern of migration originating within the island's internal population movements from rural to urban sectors, which culminated in emigration. While we have no way of knowing the exact numbers of migrants who came via this route, we can nevertheless trace the events in Puerto Rico which set these emigrations into motion. Predominantly composed of work-

ing class individuals and rooted in social and economic changes,
this migratory wave was the largest of the pre-Spanish-American-
War period. Most "common laborers" emigrated in reaction to
transformations in land-usage and landholding patterns, a situation which would accelerate under United States domination.[6]

If the last third of the nineteenth century, characterized by the
growth of commercial cultivation, marked the transition from an
hacienda to a plantation system in the island, it was also a period
when the increased production of coffee necessitated changes in
land usage and in the structure of the work force.[7] By 1870 the creation of the island's first sugar refineries motivated an increase in
commercial sugar cultivation, but this situation proved contradictory since it placed Puerto Rican sugar in competition with the
Peninsula's. Spain sporadically encouraged the island's cultivation.
Without a firm technological or financial foundation, and as long
as Puerto Rican sugar competed with the metropolis, *hacendados*
dependent on Spanish markets were inhibited in increasing their
production. Moreover, an increase in the island's sugar growth
meant agricultural expansion based on favorable tariff structures,
available credit, technological improvements, secure markets, and
a larger labor force, none of which existed for Puerto Rican sugar
hacendados at that time. Thus, within a decade the combination of
an uneven growth pattern and the general economic crisis of
1878-79 placed the Puerto Rican sugar industry in jeopardy.

During the same period, Puerto Rican coffee cultivation for
European export surpassed sugar production, with various repercussions. Among these were the concentration of land devoted to
coffee, the expropriation of small farms, the consolidation of large
haciendas, and the stimulation of external and internal migrations.
Since coffee production required less land and fewer workers than
did sugar cultivation, the transformation from the predominance
of one crop over the other necessitated changes especially in the
structure of the labor force.[8] By 1873, the abolition of slavery and
of laws restricting the geographical mobility of free workers in the
island encouraged freedom of movement between Puerto Rican
agricultural sectors. Some cane workers, for example, would migrate to the mountain coffee regions during the sugar crop's "dead
season," returning to coastal areas in time for the new harvest. But
the decline in the sugar industry released numerous workers who

now migrated to the coffee sectors but could not be incorporated into that crop's smaller production on a steady basis.[9] Former slaves previously employed in skilled jobs or crafts in the *ingenios* also migrated to the island's urban centers. In time, the labor force of these towns provided the basis for the creation and development of large-scale cigar factories based on wage labor.

By the last decades of the century, an internal migratory wave emerged from the coastal sugar regions to the interior and western sectors of the island, which were the traditional coffee-producing regions. Equally important, internal population movements within Puerto Rico would in time give way to external emigration to other parts of the Hemisphere. Many former landowners reduced to day-worker status, along with growing numbers of landless peasants, regarded emigration as contract laborers as the solution to their unemployment problems. These early migrations were seemingly composed of workers from the sugar cane growing region and adjacent areas. That these migrations were well structured and carefully manipulated is suggested by the fact that ships expressly chartered for this purpose by neighboring Caribbean *hacendados* regularly picked up contingents of laborers in the island's southern ports.[10] Responding basically to the nonintegration of a growing work force into the island's existing relations of production, potential migrants also reacted to high taxes imposed on foodstuffs, a prevailing coin shortage, and a marked decrease in subsistence farming. All of these factors, including emigration from the island, would accelerate under North American auspices. The direct colonial relationship between the United States and Puerto Rico would further aggravate the changing social and economic processes already in operation at the close of the epoch, culminating in even larger movements of people (see Map 1).

Thus we can conclude that the migratory waves in operation before the onset of the twentieth century linked the island to the mainland in bonds which would solidify after 1898. The migration patterns in effect before the Spanish-American War brought various Puerto Rican groups into contact with New York and other industrial centers. Many of them remained in the places of their original destinations, establishing footholds in several cities. As if reenacting predestined scenarios, turn-of-the-century migrants continued to form infant enclaves, the basis for the more extensive

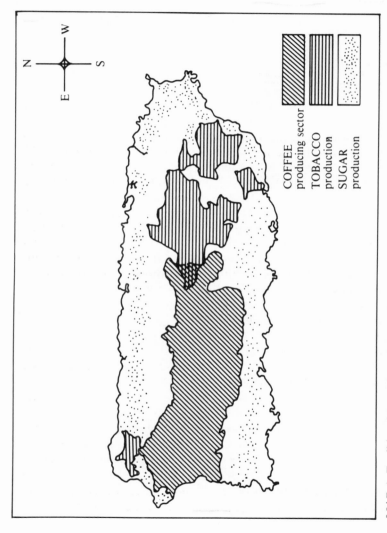

MAP 1 Traditional Land Use in Puerto Rico

COFFEE
producing sector

TOBACCO
production

SUGAR
production

migration that would follow. This was the case, for example, with the early New York settlements, shaped predominantly by tobacco workers, and with the San Francisco community composed of agricultural workers enroute to or from Hawaii.[11]

Emigration from Puerto Rico—The Early Decades of the Twentieth Century

After the Spanish-American War and particularly during the early decades into the century, Puerto Rican working-class emigration increased while the migration of political exiles was eliminated by the changes in the new colonial situation which relegated the island to the status of a United States possession. To facilitate the influx of United States capital and the establishment of North American corporations after 1898, the island's educational, monetary, legal, and economic systems also underwent modifications. American currency superimposed and undervalued Puerto Rican currency based on the Spanish peso; roads, bridges, and schools were built; new curriculums intended for rapidly Americanizing the island's work force were instituted. Moreoever, improvements in health and sanitation radically reduced mortality rates aiding in the process in augmenting the population at a time when changes in production methods, land usage, and land ownership could no longer incorporate them into the work force.[12]

If the patterns of emigration before 1900 emerged in response to social, political, or economic transformations under Spanish colonialism, what were the underlying causes of emigration in the twentieth century? Stated in other words, what were the factors which "pushed" Puerto Ricans to migrate after the United States occupation? At least two major theories propose to answer this question. The first, postulated by researchers like Lawrence R. Chenault and Oscar Handlin, maintained the island was plagued by an excess population, partly resulting from health and medical improvements made under United States policies, whose basic needs could not be met by the island's limited resources. The second theory, set forth in in-depth analyses of migration conducted by research centers such as the Center for Puerto Rican Studies and CEREP (Centro de estudios de la realidad puertorriquena), maintained that population movements from Puerto Rico throughout the Western Hemisphere and especially to the United States occurred in two patterns and for very different reasons: the structural movement of contracted factory and agricultural workers (such as the workers contingents recruited by neighboring Caribbean *hacendados* before 1898), and the nonstructured migration of noncontracted, working-class Puerto Ricans. Both situations responded to an acceleration of the island's nineteenth-century economic transformation, which intensified after the Spanish-American War and resulted in the creation of a marginal population. At the same time, changes in production and land ownership created a surplus working class prepared to migrate wherever it was most needed within the North American capitalist orbit. We will explore both theories in the order in which they were introduced.

The causes for emigration had been traced to overpopulation and the inefficient use of agricultural resources as early as 1901. One newspaper article of the time stated:

> The excess population [of Puerto Rico] is another obstacle to industrial development. There are only two ways to overcome it. One is emigration and the other is the establishment of agricultural stations where laborers can be taught how to grow the food needed for their own subsistence. . . . Emigration is a temporary but valuable measure. The existing population is too dense taking into account the country's ability to provide for its people. This is the case even though the island's resources can significantly support one million inhabitants and afford them comfort at least as it is understood in the tropics.[13]

The premise that Puerto Rico's economic problem was rooted in overpopulation convinced United States government officials charged with the island's responsibility to repeatedly recommend emigration as a temporary measure. In 1917 for example, a memorandum addressed to the United States Secretary of War, entitled "Excess Population in Porto Rico," recommended bringing between fifty thousand and one hundred thousand individuals to labor on farms as agricultural workers. If that was not possible, then similar work requiring manual labor might be arranged.[14] Along with the same communication, a confidential note addressed to the island's Governor Yager proposed: "Would it be possible to secure fairly good Porto Rican laborers to be brought to the United States for work requiring manual labor. How many men could be secured without interfering with Porto Rican industries and would you anticipate great difficulty, transportation being arranged from this end."[15]

By mid-1930s, the overpopulation theory continued to be proposed as the underlying cause of outmigration. In his study on the Puerto Rican migrant in New York City, Chenault said:

> During a period of about thirty-six years from the time of the census of 1899, or from about one year after the American occupation to December 1, 1935, the population of Puerto Rico increased more than eighty percent. For the approximate period of thirty years prior to 1930, the increase per decade was approximately eighteen percent. In the period from the census of 1930 to the census of 1935, however, a period of five and two-thirds years, there was an increase in number of over eleven and one-half percent.[16]

And almost thirty years later, yet another study reported:

> Puerto Rico's central problem since its annexation to the United States has been over-population. A birth rate that was always high and a lower mortality rate that has been declining steadily since 1930 have combined to more than double the population of the island in a half-century.[17]

However, the countertheory to the overpopulation premise, according to the History Task Force of the Center for Puerto Rican Studies, contended that while the island's population did in fact nearly double between 1899 and 1940, the yearly rate of increase rose only slightly. During that time, migration was hardly instrumental in keeping numbers down. Until the 1940s, death rates on the island declined slowly, and it was not until the forties that the island experienced an impressive escalation in population coinciding with the expansion of health and sanitary services into rural areas.[18] Therefore, the propensity for Puerto Ricans to remain on or leave Puerto Rico was not solely influenced by excess population coupled with limited resources, but rather by the effects of structural economic changes on the island's working class.

From 1898 to 1940, for example, the formation and decline of a capitalist plantation system in Puerto Rico conditioned the growth, employment, and emigration of Puerto Rican workers. The major branches of production—cane cultivation, sugar manufacturing, tobacco, and needlework—experienced a varying degree of relative overpopulation, precipitating both internal migration and external emigration.[19] In addition, since 1900 high unemployment predominated among men in general, but the phenomenon increased dramatically after the 1920s. During the same period, women became incorporated into the work force, particularly in manufacturing and the needle trades, and constituted a majority of undersalaried tobacco workers by the 1920s. These conditions impacting upon the island's labor force directly coincided with changes in land usage and production.

Within the first decades of the North American occupation, sugar emerged once again as the island's single most important crop. By the twenties, the concentration of arable land under the domination of four absentee-owned North American corporations and the transition from an *hacienda* to a plantation type economy was well established. In 1899, for instance, 26.2 percent of the acres under cultivation with the three major crops were devoted to sugar cane, while 71.6 percent and 2.2 percent produced coffee and tobacco, respectively. By 1929, however, sugar cultivation covered 49.3 percent, while coffee was grown in 39.7 percent and tobacco in 11.0 percent of the acres under cultivation (see Table 1). Moreover, from 1899 to 1929 there was a 230 percent increase in the amount of land under cultivation, which dramatized the enormous growth in sugar production over a thirty-year period. Astutely linking production and migration, one researcher proposed that the latter was stimulated both legally and indirectly through the passage of laws such as the Foraker Act (1900), the Second Organic Act (1917), and the Federal Statute of Relations with Puerto Rico Act (1944). Tacitly supporting the nonenforcement of the Sherman Anti-Trust Act in the island, these laws boosted the spread of sugar monopolies and indirectly encouraged thousands of small farmers to leave their farms.[20]

TABLE 1

Acreage under Cultivation with Puerto Rico's Major Crops

	1899		1929		1939	
Sugar	72,000	(26.2%)	237,758	(49.3%)	229,750	(52.3%)
Coffee	197,000	(71.6%)	191,712	(39.7%)	181,106	(41.2%)
Tobacco	6,000	(2.2%)	52,947	(11.0%)	28,584	(6.5%)
Total acreage under cultivation for major crops	275,000	(100.0%)	482,417	(100.0%)	439,440	(100.0%)

Between 1889 and 1929 the total acreage devoted to sugar production increased 230 percent, going from 72,000 acres to 237,758 acres. Tobacco acreage also increased dramatically by 780 percent but coffee remained essentially unchanged. In all, the overall increase in land under cultivation with the Island's three major crops increased by 75.4 percent for the same period.

Source: Puerto Rico Census by Agriculture, 1940.

The complete transformation from coffee *hacienda* to sugar plantation was viewed from another dimension by Angel Quintero Rivera. In 1895, before the United States' occupation of the island, the sugar industry yielded $4.4 million in exports. Two decades after the war, it had produced $74 million, representing 6 percent of the total value of exports. Conversely, whereas the United States imported close to 85 percent of the sugar it consumed before the acquisition of Puerto Rico and the other sugar islands (Hawaii, Cuba, and the Philippines), only 0.4 percent was imported by 1932. Moreover, the effects these changes in production had on Puerto Rico's internal migration and the labor force in general paralleled the changes produced by the ascendency of coffee and the decline of sugar in the last decades of the nineteenth century. But now the migration shifts were from a declining coffee sector, with its vestiges of pre-capitalist relations including non-wage employment, to a mechanized, technologically advanced plantation system designed to generate high profits. Professors Campos and Bonilla referred to this phase when they stated: "Although it maintained a high rate of profit the cultivation and processing of sugar cane was incapable of generating sufficient employment. The result was chronic unemployment that found its social expression in intensive strike activity and in the emigration of thousands of Puerto Rican workers."[21]

Agrarian workers who in the past customarily moved from one agricultural sector to the next depending on employment opportunities, now found their options limited because the concentration on a mechanized capital-intensive sugar industry displaced more workers than it incorporated into the system. During the crop's "dead season," workers who were unable to make ends meet continued to leave the island.

Contrary to the expansion of sugar cane cultivation, coffee production, whose principal markets were in Europe, and to a lesser extent the cultivation of tobacco, also underwent severe crisis after the North American occupation. New taxes, credit limitations, and the undervaluation of the Puerto Rican currency forced many former coffee *hacendados,* small independent farmers, and peasants to give up their land holdings or see them repossessed or sold on the auction block. The situation for the workers in those regions became more acute due to the rapid decline in the acreage dedicated to subsistence farming. By the 1920s, for example, the average acreage reserved for staples in the sugar cane farms fell to less than 0.076 percent per average family unit. The peasant population of the central areas, former coffee workers, and remaining small farmers unable to survive hard times began to move to sugar-connected municipalities in search of jobs.[22]

Between 1899 and 1940 the traditional coffee-producing central western mountain region extending from Moravis to Mayaguez (see Map 2) experienced a relative depopulation, but the northeastern non-coffee-producing mountain region increased in population. Cane-growing municipalities on the coast also grew along with the urban San Juan-Rio Piedras region, emerging in time as the main urban concentrations in Puerto Rico. The decade from 1930 to 1940 alone found fifty-four of the seventy-seven municipalities decreased in population. Thirty-three lost 10 percent or more of their 1930 population and six lost 20 percent or more.[23]

Furthermore, with the exception of San Juan, all of the islands' municipalities had five unemployed laborers for each available unskilled position. The job shortage partly motivated the movement of 71,000 individuals from the island between 1909 and 1940. In the opinion of one researcher, these internal migratory interludes were merely stepping stones toward eventual external emigration. Professor Maldonado-Denis believes:

> The social result of this process of progressive deterioration of Puerto Rico's agriculture has been the mass exodus of the peasant population to the cities (of Puerto Rico) and to the North American ghettos. . . . Many of the displaced *campesinos* that flocked to the urban areas did so as an intermediate step towards migration to the mainland.[24]

The traditional patterns of family life and land ties were also callously eroded by all of these transformations. Each individual displacement altered extended family values, creating among its members a propensity to move in adverse situations rather than to stay. Thus the connections between internal population movements and the subsequent emigrations to the mainland become clear. Puerto Rican workers became conditioned to traverse the island in search of better job opportunities. In time, internal movements also ended

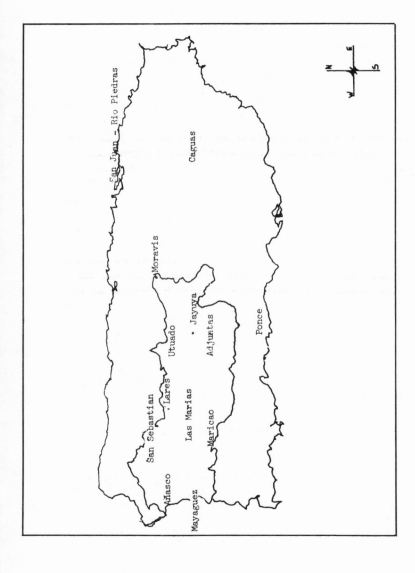

MAP 2 The Coffee Region in Puerto Rico

in frustration since the conditions motivating migration continued to be in operation throughout the island. Of equal importance, the colonial relationship between Puerto Rico and the United States discouraged the formation of native industry or internal markets which might have provided an anchor for urban workers.

The penetration of United States capital into the Puerto Rican economy since 1898 virtually destroyed the traditional pattern of individual land ownership and consolidated the dominance of large continental corporations. Almost all of the major foreign corporations, 103 out of 107, in operation on the island by 1922 were American owned. Large-scale American investments stimulated the supremacy of a one crop economy based on sugar production. Within a decade after the United States occupation, four American corporations produced 50 percent of all of the sugar cultivated in Puerto Rico. Put into other words, Puerto Rico's economy depended upon an agrarian system in which 2 percent of the island's sugar farms controlled 65 percent of all land devoted to that crop.

Moreover, the development of substantial trading outside of United States markets was virtually impossible. By the mid-twenties the United States accounted for over 95 percent of the island's exports and approximately 90 percent of its imports. Inclusion within the continental Coastwise Shipping Act meant the United States enjoyed a monopoly over Puerto Rican commercial activities. American capital investments were not limited to agrarian enterprises. Corporations performed a major role in the tobacco and fruit industries, were the major investors in public utilities, and, along with Canadian interests, owned a significant share of all Puerto Rican bank resources by 1929.[25]

By 1920 sugar cane and tobacco processing, which constituted Puerto Rico's main industries along with a growing cottage-based needlecrafts industry, increased production without an increase in the work force. From 1910 to 1934, sugar production increased from 347,000 tons to 1,114,000, but the total employment in that sector remained almost the same. The sugar workers numbered 87,643 and increased to 92,398 during that period. While 25.3 percent of the agrarian labor force were needed to produce 100 tons of sugar in 1910, only 8.3 percent were employed in this area in 1934. And tobacco production experienced a 12 percent increase in production, but suffered a 26 percent reduction in employment between 1910 and 1920.[26]

At the same time, artisans and independent craftsmen such as shoemakers or carpenters underwent a similar process of transformation in the urban centers. Threatened by an increase in the surplus work force and confronted with competition from United States manufactured goods, skilled craftsmen, unable to make ends meet, flocked to work in tobacco factories. This was then the only industrial sector which enjoyed some degree of prosperity. The numbers of cigar makers increased by 197 percent from 1899 to 1910 and the acreage under tobacco cultivation also increased during this period. In 1910, 74.6 percent of all cigar makers were working in factories of over one hundred employees; a decade later in 1920, 82 percent were employed in factories of over five hundred workers. By 1920, North American interests controlled almost all of the processing and marketing facets of this industry, and while only 4.4 percent of the island's total production was exported at the turn of the century, 19.3 percent was exported two decades later.[27] By the mid-1920s, cigar makers suffered a setback motivated by mechanization in the industry, the growth in the popularity of cigarette smoking and the decade of the Great Depression.

By the mid-twenties the effects of the Depression were deeply felt in Puerto Rico. This critical time signaled a period of contraction in the agricultural sector directly related to a decline in the trade-exchange terms, with serious effect on Puerto Rican incomes. But while the income reduction in the sugar industry was 32 percent from 1929 to 1939, tobacco incomes had already decreased by 51.9 percent in the period 1920–1930. By 1939, the tobacco industry in Puerto Rico was virtually nonexistent.

Second, the period fostered greater dependency on the United States for basic commodities at a time when the population had increased by 21.1 percent but employment had only increased by 1.7 percent, causing one commentator to point out:

> In an index where the prices between 1910 and 1914 are defined as 100, the price of Puerto Rican exports in 1937 was 92.5 and the price of Puerto Rican imports 126. . . . In order to maintain the same level of imports in terms of gross product without

inflicting a negative turn in the balance of trade, the Puerto Rican economy had to increase its gross export production to 36.2 percent.[28]

By 1939, the situation of both the rural and urban worker had changed minimally. Wage laborers received from sixty to eighty cents a day. From 1930 to 1940, the per capita incomes of Puerto Ricans declined from $126 to $120.

The situation in general led to an increase in structural unemployment, as well as an increase in the growth of a marginal work force reduced to working part-time or in miscellaneous employ (chiripeo). Many families were forced to depend precariously on poorly paid female work such as home-based needlecrafts. This was a disastrous turn of events because women's labor had always been considered supplementary and therefore viewed as less valuable than men's. Home sewing, as a case in point, was well known for its miserable salaries and inadequate work conditions. In addition, women generally occupied the lowest paying jobs in all of the industries where they were employed.[29]

To make matters worse, women were often employed in declining sectors. Domestic service which had employed 78.4 percent of all females in the labor force in 1899 declined to 27.7 percent in 1930 and decreased drastically after 1940. The tobacco industry, where women came to represent 53 percent of all workers as strippers and classifiers of tobacco leaves, also diminished about the same time. Between 1930 and 1935, including the period of the Depression, unemployment continued to increase and emigration continued to present an attractive alternative.

Clearly, the movements of people from Puerto Rico to the United States responded basically to economic conditions on the island which in turn created a marginal population outside of the stable work force. The search for economic opportunity once again became the motivating factor propelling numbers of Puerto Ricans to migrate, first to the island's urban centers and then across the ocean. The internal migrant in Puerto Rican cities often became part of a pool of unskilled labor working for low wages, and family earnings were frequently supplemented by women's work. Chronic unemployment seasonally rose to alarming levels. The pressure of a labor surplus created a group geared for emigration among some Puerto Ricans—those with resources, ambition, and a lack of opportunity within the island's existing structure. Although migration incorporates a wide range of causes and consequences both for the sending and the receiving societies, there are two components which are outstanding: those factors, already discussed, which encouraged the migrant to leave his or her homeland; and those factors which attracted the migrant to new destinations.

THE PULL FACTORS

Job opportunities, congressional legislation, and favorable transportation routes combined to influence personal motives for emigration. For Puerto Ricans, the attraction of New York City was largely economic. Job opportunities, above all, loom as the single most important factor encouraging potential migration. While some scholars caution against divorcing the "push" from the "pull" forces inherent in the migratory experience, others insist one factor outweighs the other. Several researchers, among them C. Wright Mills and Harvey S. Perloff, for example, viewed the "economic pull" forces as the stronger variable in analyzing the Puerto Rican case. Demonstrating the relationship between the migrants' personal employment goals and migration as well as the correlation between the Business Activity Index in New York City and the levels of migratory participation, Mills concluded that close to 90 percent of the migrants came in response to employment possibilities.[30]

As a mobile labor force within the North American economic system, migration certainly fluctuated according to business cycles and the requirements of the labor market. While in the first decade of this century only 554 or 37 percent of all Puerto Ricans in the United States were domiciled in New York City, by 1920 an estimated 7,364 or 62 percent lived there. Within ten years this figure rose to 44,908, or 81 percent, according to some counts, and in 1940 it increased to 61,462, or 85 percent, but these figures were disputed by Hispanic groups as undercounts.[31] By 1920, forty-five states reported the presence of Puerto Rican born persons and all forty-eight did so in succeeding censuses. Thus the twenties appear as the turning point for increased immigration. Significantly, while it was a period of declining employment on the island, it represented a time of increased opportunity on the mainland.

During the First World War a shortage of semiskilled and unskilled labor in the United States activated the "pull" forces of migration from the island to New York City. Followed by a demand for labor during the prosperous period, 1922–1929, Puerto Rican migrants were faced with the opportunity to work in factory positions formerly held by newly arrived European immigrants. A potentially growing labor force, Puerto Ricans became entrenched in garment manufacturing and light factory work, hotel and restaurant business, cigar making, domestic service, and laundries within a short time.[32] Based on the 1925 census tabulations for four Harlem Assembly Districts heavily populated by Hispanics, almost all of the Puerto Ricans worked in light industries with smaller contingents represented in the commercial and service sectors and a fraction in public service employment (see Table 2). Almost a decade later Chenault observed:

> One is apt to find a Puerto Rican in some form of building service, acting as a waiter, working in a laundry or employed in a factory. Even in the prosperous years before the Depression employment was one of the major problems if not the major one, of the Puerto Rican in New York. Because of the great demand for labor, however, in the early years before the Depression, the majority of the workers from the island found it comparatively easy to secure work of some sort. The two largest employers of Puerto Rican labor in New York City were a large biscuit company and a pencil factory.[33]

Two factors were especially important for the growth of Puerto Rican employment throughout this decade. The first, the passage of the Second Organic Act or the Jones Act of 1917, created a double impact on migration: it conferred American citizenship on Puerto Ricans changing among other characteristics their status from immigrant to migrant and sanctioning population moves between the island and the mainland as if they were merely relocations across state lines; and it required obligatory military service in the armed forces of the United States. The latter provided a seg-

TABLE 2

Occupations of Hispanics in 1925 Based on the Enumerations Reported in the Census of 1925, Assembly Districts 16, 17, 18, 19 in Harlem

PRIVATE SECTOR	A.D. 16		A.D. 17		A.D. 18		A.D. 19	
Owners & supervisors	9	1.5	66	1.8	35	1.8	44	4.3
Workers in production	164	27.0	1188	31.7	558	28.8	279	27.4
Workers in commerce	14	2.3	358	9.6	104	5.4	110	10.8
Workers in services	80	13.2	233	6.2	156	8.0	79	7.7
PUBLIC SECTOR								
Supervisors	—	—	2	.1	—	—	—	—
Workers in production	—	—	—	—	1	.1	—	—
Workers in commerce	—	—	3	.1	1	.1	—	—
Workers in services	2	.3	60	1.6	16	.8	18	1.8
EXCLUDED FROM WORK FORCE								
Housewives	145	23.8	781	20.9	415	21.4	194	19.0
Children & students	187	30.8	903	24.1	576	29.7	253	24.8
Retired, not employed	4	0.7	40	1.1	48	2.5	32	3.1
N.A.	3	.5	108	2.9	28	1.4	11	1.1
TOTAL	608	100.1	3742	100.1	1938	100.0	1020	100.0

Source: New York State Manuscript Census, 1925, Assembly Districts 16, 17, 18 and 19.

ment of the Puerto Rican male population, those who served in the military, an opportunity to familiarize themselves with life, customs, and opportunity in North America. The Jones Act, therefore, significantly encouraged migration. Between 1909 and 1916, for example, the largest group of Puerto Ricans to leave the island for the United States consisted of 7,394 individuals. But in 1917, the year of the citizenship act, 10,812 Puerto Ricans left in almost all cases, en route to North America.[34]

The second factor favoring immigration was the passage of the Johnson Act of 1921. Radically curtailing European immigration, this act contributed to the expansion of job opportunities during the post-World War I period. The laws indirectly resulted in job vacancies for unskilled workers, fostering a series of positions destined to be filled by the available black and Puerto Rican work force. Signed into law by President Harding, the Johnson Act limited the number of aliens to 3 percent of the number of foreign-born of that nationality already residing in the United States based on the census of 1910. The revised Johnson Act of 1924 curtailed immigration even more by admitting only 2 percent of each foreign-born group resident in the United States in 1890. A third act in 1929 fixed the total annual quota at 150,000. With minor exceptions such as the favoring of displaced persons from Europe and alloting minimum quotas to Asian and African countries, these immigration laws remained in effect until 1964.

The correlation between population movements from Puerto Rico and the requirements of the labor market in the United States, and in particular New York City which continued to draw a significant share of the migration, was demonstrated once again during the Depression period. Formal and informal avenues of communication between Puerto Ricans in New York City and relatives on the island (referred to as the "family intelligence network"), kept potential migrants abreast of the insecurities of the Northern job market.

From 1931 to 1940 there was a decrease in the annual average net migration traced directly to employment decline. In his study on migration, Clarence Senior, one-time director of the Social Science Research Center of the University of Puerto Rico, demonstrated that there were fourteen years of high unemployment in the United States in which the net return flow to the island has been greater than the out-migration. These included the years 1921 to 1922 and 1931 to 1934, periods in which job opportunities decreased in the mainland. Demographer Vázquez Calzada addressed this very issue when he remarked, "Between 1930 and 1934 there was a return migration of almost ten thousand people, which is equivalent to 20 percent of the Puerto Rican population in the United States at that time."[35]

Those Puerto Ricans who remained in New York, fortunate enough to be gainfully employed remained concentrated in the unskilled, semiskilled, blue-collar areas working at jobs basically similar to those held by immigrant groups during the past decade. But whereas during the twenties migrants were filling positions previously slated for newly arrived European immigrants, the decade of the Depression found Puerto Ricans competing with unemployed individuals for jobs as dishwashers, countermen, laundry workers, or in maintenance. Resulting from the unusually high unemployment affecting all sectors of the labor force, workers scrambled for any available job. Workers of other ethnic groups, more experienced with the English language and United States customs, who had progressed up the occupational ladder into skilled positions now found themselves unemployed and desperately competing for menial jobs.

That Puerto Ricans continued to hold blue-collar jobs is further demonstrated by the types of jobs available during the thirties. Because of the drastic effects of the Depression in the Puerto Rican New York residential areas, the island's Department of Labor established an office in the heart of the Latin community on 116th Street in an attempt to place the unemployed migrants in jobs. Agency records for the period of its operation, 1930 to 1936, indicate the majority employed were hired in blue-collar positions (see Table 3). Of 1,977 individuals placed by the branch office, 23.4 percent were hired as laborers and in construction; 16.2 percent were placed in laundries; another 12 percent in factories; and 6.4 percent in the hotel business. The rest were employed in restaurants, garages, and in miscellaneous jobs.

Similar employment patterns continued during the forties when once again migration responded to the demands of the United States labor market. During the years of the Second World War,

TABLE 3
Jobs Secured by Puerto Ricans through the New York Based Department of Labor of the Office of Puerto Rico, 1930–1936

OCCUPATION	NUMBER OF INDIVIDUALS PLACED
Laborers and construction	402
Laundry	321
Factories	238
Porters	157
Hotels	126
White collar (clerks, sales, etc.)	121
Janitors, handymen, watchmen	110
Carpenters, painters, plumbers	109
Tailors, garment workers	75
Restaurants (waiters, countermen, etc.)	74
Garages, auto mechanics, electrical workers	67
Cigarmakers and cigarettes	53
Clerks, groceries and shipping	32
Farmworkers	11
Shoemakers	8
Miscellaneous	73
TOTAL	1,977

Source: Chenault, *The Puerto Rican Migrant in New York City* (New York, Colombia University Press, 1938; re-issued, Russell & Russell, 1970), pp. 74–76.

migration was limited along with all movements to and from Puerto Rico. However, immediately following the war, migration increased again in proportion to the availability of work. In the early years of the forties the North American economy went from bust to boom. Whereas unemployment in American cities exceeded the official rates in Puerto Rico in the early months of 1940, by mid-1943 the United States had achieved full employment. As had been the case in past epochs when cheap immigrant labor provided the means of expanding cities and establishing manufacturing centers, the early years of the 1940s saw a return to labor recruitment in the United States. Minorities and women were actively sought for factory and farm work. Unskilled labor was solicited from rural to urban areas as well as from bordering countries. The impoverished Americans of the Depression era were now at work.[36] Some scholars argue the labor shortages of the Second World War precipitated the motivating forces behind the large-scale Puerto Rican migrations of the period just before and after the war while others maintain that close to 400,000 foreign contract workers entered the country in response to the requirements of the labor market between 1942 and the end of the war, very few of whom were Puerto Rican. Still others propose that although World War II drew nearly eight million workers into the labor force, it was rather the demobilization of that work force and the departure of workers after the war which created a void on the labor market to which Puerto Rican workers responded. Certainly the opportunities for employment were more numerous and varied in a booming economy than could be found in Puerto Rico during the same period. The joint issues of jobs and wages continued to be ever present and decisive.

But the migration also responded to a more basic reality. This was the colonial relationship between Puerto Rico and the United States. While each influenced population movements from the island, some researchers contended the employment conditions in the United States were of less significance in generating migration than were the critical ties between the island and the mainland. Clara E. Rodríguez, for example, focused on the often neglected colonial situation in her study exploring migration motivations. She proposed:

> Of what significance to migration would these changes in employment and national income be if the colonial ties were not present? Would an increase in national income in the United States provoke migration from Puerto Rico but for the colonial ties? Would those factors that have generally been seen as facilitating the Puerto Rican migration . . . have existed but for the colonial relationship? Why weren't cheap

and easy airfares established to nearby cheap labor pools of French Canadians, Cubans or Appalachians? Would military service and the radio have been similarly perceived by Puerto Ricans but for the colonial tie? But for the colonial relationship, would the "pull forces" have been perceived, responded to, or perhaps even generated? Put bluntly, would Mayor Wagner of New York have gone to Puerto Rico to tell Puerto Ricans about the jobs available in New York?[37]

In many cases migrants were indeed directly recruited from Puerto Rico and encouraged to make the journey through offers of paid transportation and other subsidies. By 1948 the Migration Division of Puerto Rico's Department of Labor in New York City established programs to educate potential migrants about conditions in the city. Between 1947 and 1949 a yearly average of 32,000 individuals constituted the net migration from Puerto Rico, many responding to attractive offers from representatives of New York factories in search of workers for the garment and needle-trade industries. Throughout this period the United States Employment Service cooperated with the island's Department of Labor to discover where work shortages were developing and how Puerto Rican workers could best make a contribution. Vázques Calzada, representative of a group of researchers who have emphasized the connection between government policies and migration states:

> Migration has been considered by some social scientists, as well as by the majority of our government leaders, as the best solution to the demographic problem of the Island. Although publicly it was indicated that the government of Puerto Rico was not fostering migration, its actions showed just the opposite. In the population projections prepared by the Planning Board (in Puerto Rico), one of the first variables always included was massive migration.[38]

While Puerto Rican planners intended to alleviate demographic problems, New York businessmen sought to increase their productivity. So closely did the migration of the fifties remain locked into the city's business cycles that a former director of the Migration

Division of the Commonwealth of Puerto Rico's Department of Labor, observed, "The size of the Puerto Rican migration varies closely with job opportunities in the U.S.; i.e., when job opportunities increase, migration increases; when job opportunities decline, migration declines." The Harvard Study of the New York Metropolitan Region during the same period further underscored the critical role of the Puerto Rican worker particularly in industrial sectors which might have otherwise been endangered:

> The rate of Puerto Rican migration to New York is one of the factors that determines how long and how successfully the New York metropolitan region will retain industries which are under competitive pressure from other areas. To the extent that some of these industries have hung on in the area, they have depended on recently arrived Puerto Rican workers who have entered the job market of the New York area at the rate of about 13,000 each year.[39]

Although Puerto Ricans continued to be concentrated in blue-collar, low skills, low-paying sectors, especially in light industries, restaurants, and hotels for men and in the garment industry for women (see Figure 1), migration was nevertheless almost universally viewed as financially beneficial.

Wages and war-related occupational mobility were key factors in attracting the migrant to the mainland, according to economists Rita M. Maldonado and Lois S. Grey. Professor Maldonado indicated the two essential reasons for migration were (1) if the average wage in the United States was higher relative to that in Puerto Rico and (2) if the job market in the United States was relatively better than that in Puerto Rico.[40] Moreover, Professor Grey concluded migration to the mainland entailed a risk of downward mobility for the highly skilled, but offered the prospect of upward movement for those with lesser skills or work experience. Throughout the fifties migrants with white-collar experience tended to become employed below their skills level in New York, but most migrants, generally from rural areas and experienced in farm labor found mainland jobs in factories thereby moving up the occupational ladder. Indeed, a comparison of average weekly wages in Puerto Rico

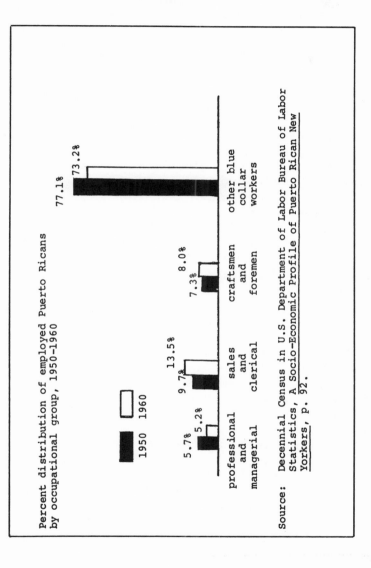

Figure 1 The Occupational Distribution of Puerto Ricans in New York City

over a period of three decades with wages received in New York City demonstrated the migrants were paid higher wages in their first New York jobs than they had received in their last job on the island (see Table 4).[41]

Thus, the correlation between the demands of the labor market through the twenties, thirties, and forties as well as the relative material progress that the move represented—the "pull" factors—and the high unemployment rates in Puerto Rico—the "push" factors—is clear.

TABLE 4
Comparison of Average Weekly Wages in Puerto Rico with Average Weekly Wages in New York City

PERIOD	LAST JOB IN PUERTO RICO	FIRST JOB IN NYC
1920s	$13.00	$19.04
1930s	$12.00	$22.62
1940s	$14.00	$31.43
Post–WW II	$14.60	$28.05

Source: Clarence Senior and Donald O. Watkins, "Toward a Balance Sheet of Puerto Rican Migration," United States-Puerto Rico Status Commission Report, 1966, Washington, D.C, p. 749.

But migration is a complex phenomenon involving the breakup of family units, the determination to succeed in an alien environment, and the ability to create a better existence frequently under hostile conditions. In spite of the underlying causes indeterminately resulting in migrant moves, push-pull factors, and recruitment tactics, in the final analysis, each individual migrant made the decision to leave the island for his or her own constellation of reasons. While the underlying causes for the great majority were economic in nature, migrants commonly responded to other motivations as well. Some migrants were the initiators of the decision to leave while others became the followers. The true story of who these people were and their reasons and methods for coming to New York

City may be told in both statistical terms and in the personal tales of those who migrated.

INDIVIDUAL MOTIVATIONS BEHIND MIGRATION

Who were the Puerto Rican migrants? Characteristics held in common between migrants of the island's internal movements and migrants in New York during the mid-twenties reveal similarities while an additional profile of city migrants during the mid-fifties offers yet another perspective in determining a more accurate portrayal of these individuals. Based on persons tabulated for the 1925 census, migrants were: in their most productive years; slightly more males than females; more of urban than rural origins; more white than black; and because of the internal migrations within the island during the early decades, more likely to fall into skilled or semi-skilled labor groups within a Puerto Rican context. Skilled tobacco workers, for example, were well represented among the earliest Puerto Rican groups in the city, circa 1915 to 1920. The fact that 55.6 percent of the females and 64.2 percent of the males fell into the fifteen through thirty-five-years-old age bracket further defines the migrant as the "cream" of the island population.[42]

An analysis of the migrant characteristics of those who traversed the island during the decade of the thirties concludes these persons were above average in comparison with those who did not move. Professional and semiprofessional individuals were found in the migrant stream far out of proportion to their percentage of the population. While service personnel were also represented to a far higher degree among the migrants, the opposite was true of farm laborers and farmers.[43]

By 1948 migrants in New York closely resembled those who had previously participated in internal movements. These continued to be in their most productive years (between fifteen to forty-four years of age); more educated than the island average (8 years for both males and females as opposed to 6.1 for remaining males and 5.6 for remaining females); more urban than rural (82 percent of the migrants came from the island's three largest cities).[44] Throughout the fifties, migrant characteristics continued to mirror those of earlier periods with one exception. Males and females tended to move to the mainland in much the same numbers as they had done before with males predominating slightly; agewise, 70 percent of those who left the island were between the ages of fifteen and thirty-five; migrants had on the average a higher level of education than those who remained in Puerto Rico; but the later migrations appeared to be of more rural than urban origins.[45]

One migrant who was typical of the skilled tobacco workers of the first two decades was Bernardo Vega. He left Puerto Rico at a time when the cigar industry was overloaded with skilled workers. In his memoirs, Vega unwittingly revealed his personal motives for coming to New York while at the same time offering insights into the expectations of the migrant group as a whole. The following passage recounts conversations with fellow passengers aboard the steamship *Coamo* in August 1916:

> The days passed quietly. Towards the dawn of the first day, the passengers began to act as if they were all family members. We did not hesitate to discover one another's histories. The overriding theme of our conversations, however, was what we expected to find in New York City. With our first earnings we would send for our nearest relative. Later on at the end of several years we would return to the homeland with our savings. We all, more or less, set our sights on the farm we would buy or the business we would establish in our respective hometowns. . . . All of us carried our individual castles in the air.[46]

Another migrant, Homero Rosado, hoped to fulfill his goals of completing his education while working in the city. A native of Ponce, the decision to emigrate was motivated by family hardships. Leaving the island at the age of seventeen, Don Homero arrived in Brooklyn in 1930:

> I lived with my parents, brothers and sisters. We were two sons and three daughters. My parents were poor but they struggled to meet their economic responsibilities towards us. As we completed high school, our father decided the young women would continue their studies in the university but the young men would have to go to work because our father could not continue to support all five of us. For this reason I decided to leave for the United States because I wanted to

continue my education but was unable to do so in Puerto Rico. When I reached seventeen years of age I went to San Juan, borrowed twenty-five dollars for the fare and disembarked on one of the steam ships which sailed weekly, named *Jacinto*.[47]

Similarly, Antonio Rivera Hernández left Puerto Rico during the twenties in search of opportunity and a better future. Coming to New York completely on his own, Rivera Hernández was seventeen when he left the island. His decision to emigrate came after completing one year of college. Neither was he unemployed nor was he representative of the working class. What he was was an ambitious young man who, as so many like him, did not see a future for himself in Puerto Rico. In a personal interview he described the situation at the time of his departure:

Unfortunately at home we were many and I dreamt only of studying law and my father, well, we had no money . . . a poor family. We were many. We lived in an enormous house but we were many and very close in age. Well, my mother and father decided I should study education and prepare myself for the career of a rural teacher. This was an area I could not accept. I studied one year but failed to matriculate for the second. . . . To keep me from a life of decadence, my father gave me the passage to New York City. They made all the arrangements, supervision on board ship, contacts in New York City, never anticipating my shipboard chaperones would succumb to seasickness leaving me very much on my own.[48]

While most migrants failed to realize their ambitions, compromising in many cases for poor working conditions but living wages, Don Antonio proved to be an exception. He availed himself of the educational opportunities in New York City, perfected his command of English and spent over thirty years actively participating in the activities of the Puerto Rican community. Don Antonio became a dental technician, an examiner for the United States Postal Service, and was one of the first Puerto Rican insurance agents employed by the John Hancock Life Insurance Company. He also published and edited several journals catering specifically to the interests of the Puerto Rican community.

One individual whose experiences were more typical for the migrant community was Antonio Sánchez Feliciano. The youngest son of a landowning, sugar-growing family of nine children, Don Antonio saw a limited future for himself in a declining agricultural economy. His older brothers, Carmelo and Emilio, were the first to leave making the trip from the western part of the island to the capital by train, then boarding a steamship to New York City. Another brother, Fernando, had already left as a seasonal agricultural worker to harvest the crops along the mainland's eastern seaboard. Surviving the influenza epidemic of 1918, which left scores of his compatriots buried in Savannah, Georgia, Fernando settled in New York, establishing a beachhead, so to speak, for the other migrants in the family. When Don Antonio decided to migrate, he was following an example set by his brothers before him. Before his sixteenth birthday he had already attempted to stow away three times. He arrived in New York at the age of seventeen in 1926, aboard the steamship *Coamo*. With limited work experience, his brothers had already secured a factory job for him as an unskilled laborer.[49]

Yet another stowaway described an experience which was rather unique among the migrants. This individual left the island at the age of eight or nine years arriving in New York completely on his own in 1919:

> I left home because I used to go around with other bigger fellows than myself and we used to run away; in those days when a child ran away from one town to another one, some people from the police department, they brought us home, no matter how far we were in the island, they brought us home. But this time I ran away to the capital of Puerto Rico which they call San Juan. Over there a fellow, a small fellow like myself, we got into a ship. I came to this country. When we arrived here they apprehended us because we were kids. We didn't know how to run away or anything. So they took us to a ship, I think that was in 25th Street in Manhattan, and they keep us there. And from there we also ran away. We ran away until this day.[50]

One individual whose experiences were reminiscent of the internal and external migratory patterns of the early decades was Mary Geraldino. During her childhood in Puerto Rico, she lived in

Yauco on the eastern part of the island, in Ponce on the south and in Santurce in the northeast. Before settling in New York, she lived in Cuba for eight years. Dona Mary was a "follower," for it was her father who, determined to provide a better life, decided to move the family to Cuba around 1924. When she made the decision to migrate to New York, Dona Mary was almost twenty years of age. She arrived in the city in 1936, directly from San Juan, Puerto Rico, having moved back to the island several years before. Her greatest motivation for migrating was the lure of good paying jobs and a sister who had already made her home in New York.

Another woman who followed relatives on the migration trail described her experiences in the following manner: "My sister and her husband came to visit the island and they talked me into going to live with them in New York."[51] And still another individual responded:

> We were eleven, six females and five males. My father always provided for us selling fruits and vegetables at the *Puente de Balboa.* But we were poor and as the oldest female I was like a second mother. The burden of caring for the younger children was always on me. In 1930, I was invited to go to New York to live with my cousin. I went and I stayed. I was seventeen years old at the time.[52]

During the late thirties and early forties, conditions in Puerto Rico were described by most migrants as deplorable. Typical of the migrants who referred to economic difficulties was Don Rafael de León. At thirty-six years of age, a married man and father of four children, Don Rafael worked sporadically, loading and unloading fruit aboard ships. Twelve hours of work brought three dollars a day. Food was scarce at that time. If rice could be bought, it cost one dollar for 1½ pounds. Multitudes lined up to purchase five cents' worth of milk every day. Work could sometimes be gotten at the United States military base at *Isla Grande,* but there thousands of workers worked eight hours a day for one dollar. These salaries could barely support one individual let alone a family of six. Borrowing fifty dollars for his ship fare and an additional thirty-six dollars for emergencies, Don Rafael set out for New York City on April 25th, 1945, arriving ten days later.[53]

Another migrant with similar problems, Dona Margarita Her-

nández, emphasized the reasons for her exodus rested on lack of
both employment and opportunity:

> Well at that time, no, in '46, look in '46, I tell you things were
> so bad here that my husband was fired from the factory and
> upon his dismissal did not know what to do or where to turn
> to. He could not find where to make a living! The needle-
> trades industry had hit rock bottom—my husband was a
> mechanic in the needle-trades business and at the same time,
> he was the "foreman" over three hundred or four hundred
> women. . . . We were evicted from our home because we
> owed so much money. Our rent was only eleven dollars a
> week and we owed more than one hundred dollars. One day,
> a woman whom he had worked for, asked if he would be in-
> terested in going to work in New York. As you can imagine,
> we accepted, since we didn't have a chance to make a living
> here.[54]

The thirties and forties stimulated many migrants to leave,
although the return migration during the Depression period was
greater than the net out-migration. Individual migrants continued
to base their reasons for leaving on lack of opportunity: "I came to
New York because the food situation was very bad in Puerto Rico
and there was no work. One of my sisters who lived in San Juan,
the capital, went to New York. She sent for my brother first. Later
I came with my father."[55] "There is nothing in Puerto Rico. My
father and two brothers are here. I don't like it here but I hate it
there. Here at least I can live."[56]

It was not unusual for New York City to attract the bulk of the
Puerto Rican migration. The shipping lines connecting the island
and the mainland had their terminus in New York City. The settlements in New York were also older, more established, and as previously discussed, formed the foundation for the infant Puerto Rican
and Hispanic enclaves since the late nineteenth century. The commercial routes between San Juan and New York were well known
and among the most efficient of water routes. Certainly, during the
first decades of the twentieth century, these routes became increasingly available to passenger steamship trade. While the routes
between San Juan and the Gulf of Mexico or the southern ports of

the United States had been in use for contract labor contingents before, these offered a limited, more expensive first-class voyage for the private passenger, often beyond the means of most Puerto Ricans seeking to leave. On the other hand, the sea routes between the island and New York City offered several different class fares, were more efficient, and boasted the best facilities. Throughout the twenties and thirties, fares ranged between twenty-five and fifty-five dollars and travel time covered from three to five days. On faster ships direct travel time between New York and San Juan averaged 3½ days; others required from four to five days. By comparison, voyages undertaken by contract workers to the southwestern, western, or southern parts of the United States involved several stages totalling eighteen or more days.[57]

In 1926, for example, Rosa Roma left her native Mayaguez and headed for New York City completing a variety of transcontinental connections along the way:

> I came from Mayaguez to San Juan by train which cost five dollars and thirty-seven cents at that time in comparison with hiring a private car which was very expensive—twenty dollars. The train was for passengers and it was driven by coal. It left at 12:00 midnight from Mayaguez and arrived at the steamship terminal at 7:00 A.M. There, we immediately boarded the ship. I paid fifty-five dollars for the voyage to New York and the ship was the *Coamo*. We were seasick. I don't remember much about food service. But I do remember I was traveling second-class and there were some students traveling on first—Spaniards. We flirted with them, talked with them—they brought us pastries and fruits from first class.[58]

Fifteen years later, the journey offered more variety. For instance, Margarita Soto was twenty years old in 1940 when she made the trip from Puerto Rico to Cuba, then to Miami, and finally to New York City.

> We left Isla Grande, Puerto Rico by plane and flew directly to Santiago de Cuba. There were no direct flights to New York City at that time. From Cuba we changed planes because that

plane was scheduled to fly to South America. There we waited one day for a flight to Havana. Since we were almost at war, my aunt and uncle decided not to wait for a flight to Havana and instead took a bus. We left for Havana at 3:00 P.M. arriving the next day at 7:00 A.M. and took a flight to Miami. From there we rode a bus to New York.[59]

Around 1947 close to twenty-seven airlines, mostly from Miami, converged on San Juan Airport. With the increases in job opportunities after the Second World War, air travel became one of the greatest assets to the Puerto Rican migration, and regular air service commenced between New York City and San Juan. Many of the smaller wildcat lines originated with Army surplus planes purchased from the War Assets Administration by former G.I. pilots, but the commercial run was initiated by Eastern Airlines. In the late forties Puerto Ricans paid between thirty and fifty dollars, depending on which line they flew, for their trips north. The airplane cost about the same and could accommodate more passengers within a week's time than could the steamships. Moreover, airplanes made a radical improvement over ships as they were able to reach their destination in a matter of six hours. Throughout the late forties and fifties Puerto Ricans landed and departed frequently at the major airports at Newark and Teterboro in New Jersey, at La Guardia field in New York City, and in Miami, punctuating the airplane's contributions to the "great migration" from Puerto Rico.

Conclusion

Thus we have discussed the events which joined forces to push Puerto Ricans from the island and the opportunities which awaited them in New York City. Migration fluctuated according to the requirements of the labor market, drawing those facing critical futures on the island along with the family followers. In the words of the migrants themselves, almost all came in search of opportunity, the chance to make something for themselves and their families. They came on the steamship shuttles between San Juan and New York, ignoring closer destinations because New York represented familiarity and better resources. In time, they came by air, becoming the first airborne migration in history. And when they came, particularly to New York City, they formed communities and settlements frequently reflecting those left behind.

Notes

1. For an excellent account of eighteenth- and nineteenth-century contraband trade see: Arturo Morales Carrión, *Puerto Rico and the Non-Hispanic Caribbean: A Study in the Decline in Spanish Exclusivism* (Rio Piedras: University of Puerto Rico, 1952); and Loida Figueroa Mercado, *Breve historia de Puerto Rico,* 2 vols. (Rio Piedras: Ediciones Edil, 1970).

2. Robert Ernst, *Immigrant Life in New York City, 1825–1863* (New York: Kings Crown Press, 1949). See also Clarence Senior, *Puerto Rican Emigration* (Rio Piedras: University of Puerto Rico, 1948); and C. Wright Mills, Clarence Senior, and Rose K. Goldsen, *The Puerto Rican Journey* (New York: Columbia University Press, 1950).

3. History Task Force, Centro de Estudios Puertorriqueños, *Labor Migration Under Capitalism: The Puerto Rican Experience* (New York: Monthly Review Press, 1979). See also Angel Quintero Rivera, "Puerto Rico 1870–1940: From Mercantilist to Imperialist Colonial Domination" (paper presented at the Latin American Studies Association Conference, Pittsburgh, Pennsylvania, April 1979).

4. Carlos Buitrago Ortiz, *Los orígenes históricos de la sociedad precapitalista en Puerto Rico* (San Juan, 1976).

5. Olga Jimenez de Wagenheim, "Prelude to Lares," *Caribbean Review* vol. 8, no. 1 (January-March 1979), pp. 39–43. See also Figueroa Mercado, *Breve historia de Puerto Rico.*

6. Centro de Estudios Puertorriqueños, *Documentos de la migración puertorriqueña, 1879–1901,* no. 1 (New York: Centro de Estudios Puertorriqueños, Graduate Center, CUNY, 1977). In addition to the Centro's studies, several other groups have given the study of migration top priority. Among them are the Puerto Rican Migration Research Consortium in New York and the Centro del estudio de la realidad puertorriqueña (CEREP) in Puerto Rico.

7. History Task Force, *Labor Migration,* pp. 70–73.

8. Ibid. See also Morris Morley, "Dependence and Development in Puerto Rico"; Adalberto López and James Petras, *Puerto Rico and Puerto Ricans: Studies in History and Society* (New York: Schenkman Publishing, 1974), pp. 215–220.

9. History Task Force, *Labor Migration,* pp. 81–83.

10. Angel Quintero Rivera, "Background to the Emergence of Imperialist Capitalism in Puerto Rico," in López and Petras, *Puerto Rico,* pp. 87–102.

11. Ibid. See also Clarence Senior and Donald O. Watkins, "Towards a Balance Sheet of Puerto Rican Migration," in U.S.-P.R. Commission on Status of Puerto Rico, *Status of Puerto Rico: Selected Background Studies* (Washington, D.C.: Government Printing Office, 1966).

12. Quintero Rivera, "Puerto Rico, 1870–1940," pp. 12–20. See also Marcia Rivera Quintero, "Capitalist Development and the Incorporation of Women to the Labour Force" (paper presented at the Latin American Studies Association Conference, Pittsburgh, Pennsylvania, April 1979).

13. *La Correspondencia de Puerto Rico,* May 11, 1901, cited in Centro de Estudios Puertorriqueños, *Documentos,* p. 37.

14. This information appears in an interoffice memorandum addressed to the Secretary of War, Bureau of Insular Affairs, April 17, 1917.

15. Ibid.

16. Lawrence R. Chenault, *The Puerto Rican Migrant in New York City* (New York: Columbia University Press, 1938; reissue, Russell & Russell, 1970), pp. 28–30.

17. Oscar Handlin, *The Newcomers: Negroes and Puerto Ricans in a Changing Metropolis* (Cambridge: Harvard University Press, 1959), p. 49.

18. History Task Force, *Labor Migration,* pp. 103–106. This is also an important theme in Ricardo Campos and Frank Bonilla, "Industrialization and Migration: Some Effects on the Puerto Rican Working Class," *Latin American Perspectives,* vol. 3, no. 3 (1976).

19. Angel Quintero Rivera, "Puerto Rico 1870–1940," pp. 12–20, 87–110. Marcia Rivera Quintero, "Capitalist Development," pp. 9–11.

20. James Jennings, *Puerto Rican Politics in New York City* (Washington, D.C.: University Press of America, 1977), p. 32.

21. Campos and Bonilla, *Industrialization,* p. 79.

22. Senior and Watkins, "Towards a Balance Sheet," pp. 698–699. Marcia Rivera Quintero, "Capitalist Development," pp. 9–11.

23. Senior and Watkins, ibid.

24. Manuel Maldonado-Denis, *Puerto Rico: A Socio-Historic Interpretation* (New York: Random House, 1972), p. 312.

25. Morley, "Dependence and Development," p. 217.

26. Angel Quintero Rivera, "Puerto Rico 1870–1940," pp. 24–25.

27. Ibid., pp. 17–18.

28. Ibid., p. 23.

29. Marcia Rivera Quintero, "Capitalist Development," p. 23. See also: Caroline Manning, *The Employment of Women in Puerto Rico* (Washington, D.C.: U.S. Government Printing Office, 1934); and Isabel Picó de Hernández, "Estudio sobre el empleo de la mujer en Puerto Rico," *Revista de Ciencias Sociales,* vol. 19, no. 2 (June 1975).

30. Mills et al., *Puerto Rican Journey.* See also Harvey S. Perloff, *Puerto Rico's Economic Future* (Chicago: University of Chicago Press, 1950).

31. Senior and Watkins, "Towards a Balance Sheet," p. 705.

32. U.S. Department of Labor, *A Socio-economic Profile of Puerto Rican New Yorkers* (Bureau of Labor Statistics, Regional Report 46, July 1975), p. 9. See also Senior and Watkins, "Towards a Balance Sheet," p. 701; and History Task Force, p. 109.

33. Chenault, *Puerto Rican Migrant,* pp. 71–72.

34. History Task Force, *Labor Migration,* p. 109. See also: Centro de Estudios Puertorriqueños, Taller de Migración, *Conferencia de Historiografía* (New York: Graduate Center, CUNY, 1974), parts 1–3.

35. José L. Vázquez Calzada, "Demographic Aspects of Migration," in History Task Force, *Labor Migration,* pp. 223–238.

36. Constance M. Green, *The Rise of Urban America* (New York: Harper & Row, 1965).

37. Clara E. Rodríguez, "Economic Factors Affecting Puerto Ricans in New York," in History Task Force, *Labor Migration,* p. 199. See also: *The New York Times,* June 27, 1964.

38. José L. Vázquez Calzada, "Demographic Aspects," p. 231.

39. Rodríguez, "Economic Factors," p. 213.

40. Rita M. Maldonado, "Why Puerto Ricans Migrated to the United States in 1947–73," *Monthly Labor Review,* no. 9 (September 1976).

41. Lois S. Gray, "The Jobs Puerto Ricans Hold in New York City," *Monthly Labor Review,* no. 46 (October 1975).

42. The New York State Manuscript Census, 1925, Assembly Districts 16, 17, 18, and 19.

43. Senior and Watkins, "Towards a Balance Sheet," p. 707. See also: Clarence Senior, "Migration as a Process and the Migrant as a Person," *Population Review,* vol. 6, no. 1 (January 1962), pp. 30–41.

44. Senior and Watkins, "Towards a Balance Sheet," pp. 707–709. Gray, "Jobs," pp. 13–16. U.S. Department of Labor, *Socio-economic Profile,* pp. 16–17.

45. José L. Vázquez Calzada, "Demographic Aspects," pp. 228–230.

46. César Andreu Iglesias, ed., *Memorias de Bernardo Vega* (Rio Piedras: Ediciones Huracan, 1977), p. 40.

47. Interview with Homero Rosado, Brooklyn, New York, October 1980.

48. Interview with Antonio Rivera Hernández, Rio Piedras, Puerto Rico, August 1977.

49. Interview with Antonio Sánchez Feliciano, Aguada, Puerto Rico, July 1977.

50. Interview with Aurelio Cruz, Brooklyn, New York, October 1978.

51. Interview with Julia González, Rio Piedras, Puerto Rico, August 1977.

52. Interview with Elisa Baeza, Mayaguez, Puerto Rico, July 1977.

53. Interview with Rafael de León, Brooklyn, New York, October 1980.

54. Interview with Margarita Hernández, Mayaguez, Puerto Rico, July 1977.

55. *New York World Telegram,* May 1, 1947.

56. Ibid.

57. Centro de Estudios Puertorriqueños, *Conferencia de Historiografía,* pp. 16–19.

58. Interview with Rosa Roma, Santurce, Puerto Rico, August 1977.

59. Interview with Margarita Soto Alers, Aguada, Puerto Rico, July 1977.

Settlement Patterns and Community Development

Without doubt and contrary to the opinions of many researchers, there existed a pre-World War II communal structure within the Puerto Rican settlements, prepared to cushion the impact of the migration experience and to perpetuate essential characteristics designed to maintain that community intact.[1] Articulations in support of Latin customs and traditions coupled with a sense of communal responsibility found expression in more ways than one. Simple indicators of the existence of a Puerto Rican community were the facts that Puerto Ricans resided within clear geographical areas, had a common language, historical and cultural heritage, and shared common interests. Settlements formed on a physical level with the entrenchment and solidification of neighborhoods throughout the city. Through the proliferation of a business and professional sector, and the leadership and stability which these inspired, communities were easily identified as Puerto Rican. Moreover, early migrants continued to speak in Spanish as the language of communication and as the basis for a particular lifestyle in which traditions and customs were expressed.

The Meaning of Colonia

Two observers who identified such characteristics were Lawrence R. Chenault, who wrote of the Puerto Rican migration to New York City during the decade of the thirties, and José Hernández

Alvarez whose studies concentrated on the decade of the fifties. Chenault located the geographic boundaries of the early settlements in East Harlem, South Central Harlem, and in the Borough of Brooklyn, pointing out the main difference between the Puerto Ricans and other groups was that the former tended to come to particular areas of one large city, rather than to several cities.[2] Chenault furthermore demonstrated that these areas formed the heart of the entire Latin community in New York City with an abundance of restaurants, stores, theatres, and organizational activity. He described emerging institutions such as the regional societies and other associations of social and recreational interests.

Hernández Álvarez confirmed settlement patterns similar to those described by Chenault in his monumental study on the movement and settlement patterns of Puerto Ricans during the forties and fifties.[3] His work demonstrated the following:

1. Puerto Rican residents of the United States live in a *colonia* or urban nucleus marked by dense settlements, provision for manifestation of the Puerto Rican social identity and way of behavior and by frequency of internal activity and dependence.

2. These neighborhoods or *colonias* have constituted the primary context for migration and dispersal of the Puerto Rican population in New York City, which was in turn dependent on employment opportunities and the grapevine of information.

3. During the post-war period, 1945–1950, the migration flow from Puerto Rico was almost exclusively toward New York City and the basic social organization of the New York community was forged in the context of this initial movement.

4. Finally, the Puerto Rican migration was highly mobile. Many migrants were likely to return to the island and migrate to the mainland again within a five-year period. This phenomenon was the root of the close links which existed between the island and the mainland communities.

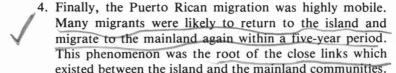

In writing about the *colonias* of the 1940s and 1950s, Hernández Álvarez introduced a model which isolated the distinct characteristics of a typical Puerto Rican community. The *colonias* were geographic, urban centers marked by dense settlement; they provided outlets for Puerto Rican interests, creating institutions which affirmed social identity and fostered internal activities while coping with problems stemming from contacts with the host society. The *colonias,* furthermore, attracted potential migration from Puerto Rico because they offered the migrant a familiar base in which to operate. In short, the migrant looked forward to settlement in an area where the language, customs, attitudes, interests, and traditions were similar to those he or she had left in Puerto Rico.

[handwritten margin note: colonias defined]

[handwritten margin note: Similarity to homeland an attraction]

Although Hernández Álvarez wrote of Puerto Rican migratory patterns at mid-century, his model proved applicable to the earlier decades as well. Chenault had basically observed the same patterns of settlement among the Puerto Rican migrants of the mid-thirties. Indeed as early as the 1910s, there existed identifiable settlements, which not only created institutions and group associations, but kept active links with island society and broached communication on several levels with the non-Hispanic group as well. Moreover, these early settlements were held together by characteristics similar to the Hernández Álvarez model. They were:

1. The geographic location and distribution of Puerto Ricans in New York City.

2. The physical characteristics of Hispanic neighborhoods as evidenced by the growth of professional, commercial, and social enterprises and the types of leadership generated.

3. The persistence of the Spanish language, customs, and habits for the maintenance of a shared identity as Puerto Ricans.

4. Common interests and attitudes towards assimilation as expressed in popular culture.

Location and Characteristics of Puerto Rican Neighborhoods

The development of Puerto Rican neighborhoods coincided with the availability of jobs for Puerto Rican migrants. Thus, the earliest settlements flourished in those areas of the city where employment was readily accessible. The cigar-makers' migration at the turn of the century, for example, founded settlements in Manhattan's Lower East Side and Chelsea sections among Eastern European and Italian immigrants because close to five hundred Hispanic owned and operated tobacco factories located there. The Brooklyn community also developed along the Navy Yard area precisely because jobs along the waterfront were plentiful. During the 1920s, the Greenpoint section of Brooklyn similarly attracted Puerto Ricans.[4] Early settlers of that Borough affirmed the section was densely populated by Puerto Ricans who worked in several area factories such as the American Manufacturing Company, which specialized in making rope from Philippine hemp. Such companies were important to the development of Puerto Rican concentrations not only because they employed migrants already residing in New York City, but also because they directly recruited workers from the island, bringing them to live in the Borough and providing for their basic needs according to contractual agreements.

A case in point was the recruitment of 130 women directly from Puerto Rico by the American Manufacturing Company.[5] Their experiences, perhaps typical for other contractual workers as well, offer further insights into the relationship between settlement patterns and job opportunities.

The group was brought to Brooklyn by steamship, met by company representatives, and placed in company-owned, three-story buildings centrally located on a spacious thoroughfare. The shelters, considered modern for the period, used electric lighting rather than gaslight common in many buildings of the neighborhood. Two chaperones, from "well-known" respected Puerto Rican families looked after the women's welfare and completing the household, another group of four women were hired especially to provide domestic services such as cooking.

The rope factory, moreover, provided free bus transportation to and from work. This vehicle which accommodated forty persons was also available for recreational excursions in exchange for chauffeur's fees and the cost of gasoline. Through all of these company-sponsored activities, Puerto Rican workers had the opportunity to thoroughly familiarize themselves with city neighborhoods, transmitting this information in letters to friends and relatives in Puerto Rico.[6]

In addition, the settlement originally oriented around work opportunities soon attracted small businesses catering to specific

migrant needs, particularly in the area of food consumption. While
the appearance of restaurants, grocery stores, or rooming houses,
the earliest types of commerce in Puerto Rican neighborhoods, was
limited in the Greenpoint section at this time, some businesses were
in operation. Workers employed in the American Manufacturing
Company recalled the first businesses in the neighborhood concerned with the Puerto Rican consumer were *bodegas:*

> There was a small *bodega* on Franklyn Avenue near the factory
> which was owned by friends of mine and they sold hot lunches
> to the factory people. It took close to ten minutes to get there
> but once in a while we (me and my brother Carmito) ran like
> hell, got to the store and sat down to a steaming plate of rice
> and beans which we gulped down to get back to *"Las Sogitas"*
> on time.[7]

If the foundations of the earliest migrant settlements rested on a
work-oriented base, the establishment of subsequent neighborhoods depended equally on cheap housing, good transportation,
and accessible shopping. Motivated by these factors, the expansion
of Puerto Ricans into other geographic areas and the conversion of
these vicinities into *colonias* accelerated during the period of the
late twenties and thirties.

While Puerto Rican *colonias* were simultaneously developing in
various areas of the city, it was the Harlem community which
would assume the lead as the largest and most significant of all the
inter-wars settlements. Among the earliest descriptions of that
neighborhood was that of Bernardo Vega, a young cigar maker
who later committed his recollections to print.

In 1916, the year of Vega's arrival in New York, the section that
was destined to become *"El Barrio,"* or the Spanish-speaking district, provided homes primarily for Jewish and Italian families.
Recently arrived European immigrants mingled with first generations, creating a tapestry of vivid cultures, customs, and languages
which fascinated the young cigar maker. Older, more experienced
immigrant families lived along the spacious tree-lined Saint Nicho-
las and Manhattan Avenues while more recent arrivals occupied the
easternmost section of the district.

The Jewish ghetto extended along Park Avenue between 110th
and 117th Streets east of Madison Avenue. Professional centers

situated along 110th Street complemented the luxury and entertainment enterprises on Lenox Avenue while stores offering poorer
families lesser quality merchandise proliferated in the region east of
Eighth Avenue. Park Avenue also carried reasonably priced goods
in push carts bazaar-laden with bargain items. These formed an
open-air market under the trestle of the New Haven and New York
Central Railroad.[8] Nestled among all this confusion were some
fifty Puerto Rican families.

The *Marqueta,* the open-air market described by Vega, played an
important role in the everyday lives of early migrants because it
constituted the largest shopping center which sold Puerto Rican
items. Its location in the Harlem area in conjunction with available
cheap housing aided in attracting settlers into this region. It was
here that they could obtain essential consumer goods. Caribbean
foods and spices shared shelf-space with other ethnic favorites and
bargain hunters bought seasonal clothing, often irregulars and
second-hand, at a fraction of their original cost at other retail
stores. Early migrants were very familiar with the functionings of
the *Marqueta* and many dated their arrival in New York City
according to whether or not this landmark was indoors or open-air.
Recollections such as those of Raquel Rivera were common among
pioneer settlers.

> In the twenties and thirties the *Marqueta* was almost all Jewish.
> What happened was the Jews began to sell Puerto Rican
> products like *platanos* and other items. Eventually, Puerto
> Ricans took over the stalls but in the early times it was run by
> others, Jews, Italians. . . . Everyone communicated very well.
> I would see the "storekeepers" put your purchases in a little
> basket, weigh it and say, "un dollar" or "two dollars," (holding
> up two fingers) whatever it cost. Actually, I didn't do any
> shopping myself, but I accompanied my aunt who did shop.
> The Jewish vendors always knew a few words in Spanish: *si,
> bueno, barato* and so on.
>   In addition to vegetables and other foodstuffs, everything
> was sold in *la marqueta:* I remember there was an area for
> selling stockings. Another for pocketbooks. Now I remember!
> One side, it was divided, one side, the right was reserved for
> those articles, stockings, pocketbooks, clothing. The left side
> was solely for, and I think it still is, for vegetables.[9]

Interestingly, the Brooklyn community also expanded geographically, but it lagged behind the Manhattan settlement particularly in the commercial and professional sectors. Throughout the first decades of the century, Brooklyn migrants looked towards Manhattan as the mecca for Latin entertainment, shopping, or professional services. Almost all of the important social and commercial institutions catering especially to Puerto Ricans operated in Manhattan. Families in need of medical care traveled to Manhattan, in some cases, forced to pay double fare. Moreover, the Brooklyn Puerto Rican neighborhoods were older, buildings more decrepit than those found in Manhattan. Coupled with inadequate housing conditions, the negative influences of run-down waterfront neighborhoods and related industries posed detrimental or inhibiting factors to that *colonia's* growth.[10] Before long, the leaders of the Brooklyn settlement, acutely aware of the disparities between both *colonias,* addressed themselves to these issues. One such individual angrily remarked:

> Sometimes I get angry with them (meaning the Puerto Rican professionals in Manhattan) because I do not see why when your kind arrives in Brooklyn from Puerto Rico, as soon as they leave the ship (steamships from the island often docked in Brooklyn piers), they run to Manhattan to operate there instead of staying in Brooklyn to help us. You can tell them that we resent their apparent disregard for us. You can tell them whenever you have a chance, that had they stayed in Brooklyn, and put up their businesses, established their law, medical and dental offices here things would have been more advantageous to them and to us. . . . I hope that as soon as possible something can be done to see that Brooklyn is the focal point of all Puerto Rican activities in New York.[11]

Were Brooklyn Puerto Ricans justified in their resentment of the rapid progress in the Manhattan *colonia*? In many ways they were. By 1926 the Porto Rican Brotherhood of America, a Manhattan-based community association, described the enormous geographic and numerical expansion of the city's Puerto Rican population, demonstrating Manhattan's superiority in numbers and resources. As depicted in their souvenir program for that year, the settlements throughout the city remained working class, but a small segment of

the group participated visibly in the commercial and professional
life of the *colonias*.[12] Whereas the migrant group had confined
itself to geographical areas closely determined by work opportunities almost a decade before, neighborhoods now appeared in five
distinct sections of the Manhattan and Brooklyn boroughs. Perhaps of greater significance, the report attempted to determine the
actual numbers of Puerto Ricans living in New York City. The
Brotherhood's report of 1926 estimated Puerto Rican residents
throughout the city numbered close to one hundred thousand individuals—a debatable analysis if one considers the available research on the subject—and these were distributed as shown in
Table 5.

Thus, 60 percent or the majority of the Puerto Rican migrant
population lived in two areas of Manhattan: 90th Street to 116th
Street between First and Fifth Avenues; and 110th Street to 125th
Street between Fifth and Manhattan Avenues (see Map 3). These
areas, recognized by the non-Hispanic as East Harlem and South
Central Harlem, were known as *el Barrio* or *la colonia hispana* by
the Puerto Rican migrants, both nomenclatures synonymous in the
migrant mind.

"In New York City the *colonia hispana* was called Harlem and is
still Harlem today. . . . The Puerto Rican colony . . . Harlem . . .
was composed predominantly of Puerto Ricans and it has grown
enormously throughout the decades," declared one resident. Similarly, others noted the expansion of such enclaves, referring inter-
changeably to the new geographic entities as East Harlem or Spanish Harlem. "The Puerto Rican settlement in the section of New
York City known as East Harlem which covers the northeastern tip
of Manhattan Island, grew up after the First World War," wrote
journalist Dan Wakefield at mid-century.[13] These geographic
boundaries, furthermore, were shared with a steadily diminishing
Italian and Jewish population. Thus, within a decade *El Barrio's*
fifty Puerto Rican families as described by Bernardo Vega in his
recollections, had been joined by several thousands and these filled
the living quarters vacated by other more upwardly mobile ethnic
groups.

Additional insights may be obtained about the Puerto Rican
families living in those areas from census data collected for four
Harlem Assembly Districts for 1925. Of 7,322 individuals living in

1,535 households, practically all who were employed worked as operatives and unskilled workers in light industry, with smaller groups engaged in commerce or business, and a tiny fraction employed in the public service sector. These figures essentially coincided with the analysis of the distribution of Puerto Ricans in the city as reported in the Porto Rican Brotherhood program of 1926.

Moreover, Puerto Ricans in the four Manhattan Assembly Districts cited lived among other ethnic groups, particularly Jews, Italians, Russians, and Irish. These districts were rounded out with a smattering of black residents as well. But while some intermingling of Puerto Ricans and other ethnics within the same apartment house buildings appeared in the census, the incidence of blacks and Puerto Ricans sharing buildings was limited.[14] Finally, the census of 1925 indicated nine in ten heads of households were born in Puerto Rico. An average household evolved around a married couple with children. Lodgers or extended family members almost always completed the households. In short, during the twenties, the Puerto Rican *colonia* was characterized by family-based households, most of which were working class. (See Map 4.)

The thirties found limited changes in the settlement patterns of the Puerto Rican neighborhoods. "In Manhattan," declared Chenault, "Puerto Ricans lived in a district bounded from about 97th Street up to and along 110th around the northern part of Central Park, northward to about 125th Street and approximately from about Third Avenue on the East to Eighth and Manhattan Avenues

TABLE 5
Estimate of Puerto Rican Residents in New York City, 1926

DISTRICT	RESIDENTS
14th Street to 30th Street	10,000
90th Street to 116th Street	
First Avenue to Fifth Avenue	20,000
110th Street to 125th Street,	
Fifth Avenue to Manhattan Avenue	40,000
Washington Heights	5,000
Brooklyn	25,000
TOTAL	100,000

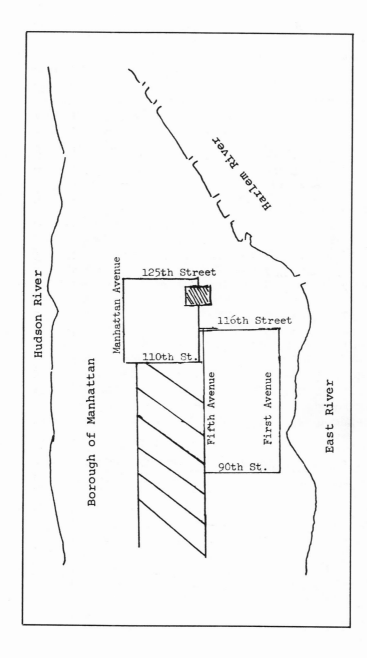

MAP 3 Largest Concentration of Puerto Ricans in Manhattan Based on Report of Porto Rican Brotherhood of America, 1926

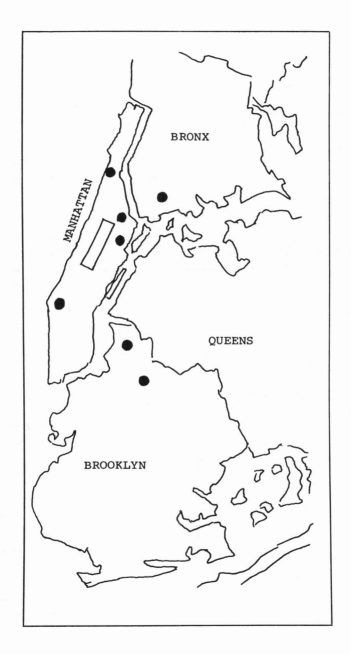

MAP 4 Geographic Location of Puerto Ricans in New York City Based on Report of Porto Rican Brotherhood of America, 1926

on the West.'' The largest concentration continued to develop in
the area around 115th and 116th Streets, further solidifying the
contours of the present-day *Barrio Latino*. At the same time, the
Brooklyn community expanded geographically along the water-
fronts south to the Gowanus Canal, extended inland to about Third
Avenue and included the Greenpoint section.[15]

The actual size of both settlements in numerical terms remained
debatable. As residents of a United States possession, migrant
Puerto Ricans did not figure in immigration counts, and calcula-
tions were based on private studies made by organizations such as
the Porto Rican Brotherhood or Catholic Charities. While the
Brotherhood's report estimated a total of 100,000 individuals in
1926, the *New York Times* and the New York Mission Society
arrived at figures between 150,000 and 200,000 persons for the
same period. By comparison, the growth of a commercial and professional sector in that sizeable community remained somewhat
limited.

The Growth of a Professional and Commercial Sector

If numerical increases among Puerto Ricans and the expansion
of settlement boundaries marked one aspect of community formation, the growth of a commercial and professional sector concur-
rent with a nascent type of leadership more clearly punctuated the
physical characteristics of the *colonia*. By the late 1920s the commercial sector had developed rapidly to include some two hundred
bodegas or grocery stores and about one hundred and twenty-five
restaurants. By 1926 newspaper articles confirmed the "rapid
influx of Latins and West Indians'' who described themselves as
Puerto Rican and initiated the opening of their own businesses,
"patronizing no others.''[16] It was precisely in the proliferation of
commercial and professional establishments—small businesses,
bodegas, botánicas, restaurants and boarding houses—that the
physical characteristics of the Puerto Rican community were most
sharply defined.

Since the early days of the Puerto Rican migration, the backbone
of the pioneer settlements had been formed by businessmen. The
ownership of barbershops and boarding houses represented the
first forms of entrepreneurship among the early settlers. More

important, pioneer enterprises lent an air of solidarity to the community offering consumer goods and services in familiar surroundings tailored to migrant needs. The *marqueta,* the open-air market described by early settlers, continued to supply consumer products but never assumed the "cultural" position of the neighborhood business for at least two reasons: First, the open-air market traded with all the ethnic groups residing in the Harlem area. Second, many of the shopkeepers of *La Marqueta* failed to involve themselves in the communal activities of the Puerto Rican *colonias.* It was in this capacity where many local businessmen and professionals assumed a degree of leadership. The owners of small businesses along with a handful of Puerto Rican professionals firmly held onto the reins of community leadership by spearheading the establishment of neighborhood clubs or organizations and making themselves available for advice or neighborhood activities. It was not unusual for Spanish-speaking customers to seek advice from the Puerto Rican pharmacist or the local *curandero* in health matters, from the neighborhood priest or spiritualist in matters of faith or from the community baker or barber on jobs, apartments, or other negotiations. These local leaders enjoyed a certain status in the community commensurate with their types of businesses or academic background. The pharmacist and the priest, for example, commanded greater admiration than the grocer because the former were better educated, thus more knowledgeable. However, all businessmen depended on the patronage and goodwill of the community. These sought to maintain customers by allowing credit and to attract new ones through advertising their Puerto Rican wares in the local community presses. In this regard, competition for migrant attention was stiff. All vehicles for conveying information were utilized and these included not only the local presses, but newspapers, newsletters, and journals popular within the community.

One hotel for example, *El Hotel Latino* located at 221 West 14th Street featured enticing Spanish foods—*Comidas Latinas*—as its main attraction. Another advertised in *El Heraldo* stressing its convenient location and easy access to public transportation:

I have the pleasure once again of offering my home to my friends and to all travelers from the Antilles, Central and

South America. It is located at 440 West 23rd Street. It is one
of the most centrally located areas and can be reached by all
manner of public transportation. Dining is Creole style.

Ulises del Valle[17]

Throughout the early thirties, a growing number of restaurants
featured creole cuisines and on many occasions Puerto Ricans
patronized community restaurants, even though the home
remained the focal point for family meals. For those who cultivated
eating out as a popular leisure time activity, the choice of restaurants was varied as many continued to advertise in local presses.
The following ads were typical:

El Paraiso

Here you will find rice and *gandules verdes* and spare ribs,
codfish fritters and potatoes.
Open Tuesday and Wednesday, 12 noon to 4 A.M.
211 E. 116th St.[18]

Restaurant "El Louvre"

70 East 111th Street
Antonio Delgado—El hombre del dia
General Chef—Creole and Spanish
Specialty—Chicken and Rice with *mofongo.*[19]

Significantly, both of these restaurants, typical of the period,
addressed themselves to the Hispanic community in general, but
featured distinctive Puerto Rican specialties as their main attraction: *arroz con gandules verdes*—rice with pigeon peas, a dish traditionally reserved for the Christmas season when the peas were
harvested; *mofongo*—a plantain appetizer made with bacon, garlic, and other spices.

In a personal interview, one migrant, niece of a *bodegero* in
Spanish Harlem, described dining out as a pleasant, reasonably
priced social experience:

What I recall most vividly was a restaurant called "Fuentes"
where they made *empanadas* with *tostones* for which they

charged a dollar or $1.25, but these *empanadas* were enormous and the *tostones* exquisite. Do you know it was there I met Tony (her husband to be) with his cousin Juan Antonio Corretjer. We went to eat there one night and I recall we ate very, very well. But observe (*fíjate*) the restaurant was well-known! There was at the time a popular song which referred to Fuentes—well this was the celebrated *mozón* of the restaurant.[20]

This individual was representative of the younger Puerto Rican generation who were particularly active participants in many neighborhood activities. However, restaurants survived not only on the patronage of leisure dinnertime guests. Situated in predominantly working-class neighborhoods and catering primarily to an Hispanic clientele, restaurants often specialized in take-out trade. Hot lunches in three-tiered covered metal containers were prepared and sold to the workers residing in the community who continued to perpetuate the Latin custom of consuming a full midday meal. The containers often carried rice, beans, meat or poultry, salad and Puerto Rican bread—a large lunch by non-Hispanic standards.

Other *Barrio* residents recalled the growth of different types of businesses. Commercial enterprises like Valencia Bakery and Cofresi Travel Agency became synonymous with Puerto Rican business. During the thirties these not only advertised in local presses, but over Spanish-language radio stations as well. Valencia especially appealed directly to the Hispanic consumer by announcing weddings, birthdays, baptisms, and other celebrations over the airwaves for which special cakes were purchased.[21]

In addition to commercial ventures, a handful of Spanish-speaking professionals catered to the health and legal problems affecting the Puerto Rican community. According to the 1925 census, less than 3 percent of the 7,322 Hispanic individuals tabulated were professionals. However, one study proudly reported the professional community numbered about one hundred persons including "two Puerto Ricans engaged as Spanish instructors in the Department of the 'great' Columbia University."[22] Doctors, lawyers, and dentists also advertised their practices in the Hispanic press. For example, one newsletter carried an ad offering the services of a nurse/midwife: María F. Aparicio, *Enfermera y comadrona: gra-*

duada en Puerto Rico; 59 West 115th Street'' (graduated from Puerto Rico). Other ads announced the closing or resumption of specific practices. Such was the case of one physician who announced his return from Europe and his engagement once again in medical practice:[23]

Dr. Carlos G. Armstrong

Announces his return from Europe and the resumption of his medical practice.

Hours	*Telephone*	*Location*
1–2 p.m.	CAthedral 5578–7347	601 West 110th St.
6–7 p.m.		New York City

And another:

My best advertising is a satisfied clientele. Do you wish to be my best announcement? Come to see me and I assure you, you will be. In addition, so you will accept my offer, I'll make a special deal.[24]

By 1923 the listings in the *Guía Hispana,* a guide to the commercial and professional listing of the Spanish-speaking communities, reinforced the importance of Hispanic businesses. First, it made available the names, addresses, and telephone numbers of Spanish-owned businesses in much the same way that telephone directories did for other companies. Second, it advertised their existence. The *Guía* listed some one hundred and fifty professionals including physicians, dentists, and lawyers, and two hundred and seventy-five businesses. About forty restaurants completed the inventory.[25]

Interestingly, the Chenault study on the Puerto Rican migration during the mid-thirties shed doubts on the Puerto Rican commercial and professional entrepreneurship, maintaining that it was difficult to ascribe the ethnic origins of owners or professionals merely on the basis of a Spanish surname. Yet the majority of the Spanish-speaking residents of the city did come from Puerto Rico during the decades of the twenties, thirties, and forties, continuing to do so afterwards as well. The granting of American citizenship in 1917 contributed much to migration from the island without the restrictions necessarily placed on immigration from other Spanish-speaking countries. Furthermore, the census figures for the four sample districts in Harlem confirmed the predominance of Puerto Ricans among the city's Latin population.[26] Perhaps of greater importance, these early migrants were the ones who exerted considerable influence on the development of the commercial and professional sectors, as owners, as professionals, and as consumers. In many cases these individuals emerged in time as internal and/or external leaders within the *colonia hispana*.

Who were the handful of professionals who served the Puerto Rican community? One was Dr. José N. Cesteros, who lived and practiced medicine in his *barrio* apartment. He was equally respected by the Puerto Rican and non-Hispanic community as a physician and for his political activities during the thirties and forties (see Chapter 6). Another was Dr. José Julio Henna, Puerto Rican patriot and physician, one of the founders and deans of the Medical Board of French Hospital in Manhattan. Dr. Henna was born in Puerto Rico in 1853, the son of Joseph Henna of Plymouth, England and María del Rosario Pérez of Puerto Rico. As a young man Henna participated in the cause of Puerto Rican independence alongside Betances and Hostos, leading to his eventual banishment by Spain. The eighteen-year-old exile came to New York City, studied at the College of Physicians and Surgeons and obtained his medical degree in 1872. Following graduation, he traveled abroad, working for a time in Paris, London, and finally returning to New York. From 1880 until his death in 1924, Dr. Henna was one of the leading physicians connected with French Hospital, serving also on the staff of Bellevue Hospital.

Professional activities did not alienate Henna from life in the Puerto Rican settlements of New York nor from concern for events occurring in Puerto Rico. In 1895 he was chosen president of the Revolutionary Party which struggled for independence from Spain. After the Spanish-American War, he was twice elected as a delegate to appear before the Senate and House Committees on Civil Government in the island. Moreover, as founder and president of the Ibero-American Club, Dr. Henna participated at the forefront of many social and cultural activities in the New York *colonia* where he made his home for fifty-five years.[27]

As in the case of Dr. Henna, many individuals active in commerce or the professions participated in neighborhood associations, building a reputation as persons to whom the community could turn in time of need. Some, like Dr. Henna or Dr. Cesteros, were recognized by the host society as leaders or power brokers for the early settlements. Others, like the Colóns, Jesus, Ramón, and Joaquin, politically active community figures of the pioneer settlements of both Manhattan and Brooklyn, were considered leaders primarily within the settlements by the residents of the *colonias.* Thus, leadership operated on several levels. First, leaders were prominent Puerto Ricans recognized by both the Latin and non-Hispanic society as representing the pioneer settlements. Second, leaders were those individuals like the local priest, pharmacist, or *curandera* to whom the early migrants turned in times of stress. Third, leaders were also individuals who distinguished themselves as organizers or power brokers for the settlements, but not necessarily recognized as such by the host society.[28]

In the Brooklyn *colonia,* leadership emerged in much the same way as in Manhattan. One leader, Carlos Tapia, was a storekeeper by trade, but his experience at many different types of jobs and his political involvement brought him into intimate communication with the needs of the early migrants. Recognized as a leader among his people in Brooklyn, Tapia held the distinction of being equally respected by the residents of the Manhattan *colonia* as well. On several occasions he was called upon to aid the migrants of that borough.[29] One incident involved the "Harlem Riot" of 1926, when a group of more established Harlem residents engaged in street fighting, arguments, and bottle throwing, protesting the encroachment of Puerto Ricans and other Hispanics in the Harlem area. Called upon by other Puerto Rican community leaders to avenge the migrants, Tapia and a group of Puerto Ricans were apprehended and dispersed by the police. This incident signaled a critical moment in the life of the pioneer settlements and exemplified without a doubt the role of the community leader. In the minds of the migrants this was especially defined as an individual who placed himself between the *colonia* and the dominant host society. Carlos Tapia fulfilled this role in the opinion of one migrant: "Carlos Tapia helped the Puerto Ricans in every way. He even used to help them physically and economically. By physically I mean any abuse the Puerto Ricans got they used to go to Carlos Tapia. And he and his people would correct everything. They didn't go to the police, they went to Carlos Tapia."[30]

Pura Belpré, folklorist and children's librarian by vocation, represented yet another type of leadership — one which strove to preserve the customs and cultural traditions of the Puerto Rican people, setting them apart as a distinctive identifiable group. The first Puerto Rican librarian in the New York Public Library system, Belpré initiated Latin community projects throughout several branches of the library system as early as 1921. Promoted to chief storyteller at the Seward Park Branch, she also volunteered her time as storyteller in the Union Settlement House, Madison House, and the Educational Alliance, all of which enjoyed considerable Puerto Rican patronage. Touched by the concern for cultural traditions among the early migrants, Belpré established children's programs which emphasized Puerto Rican traditions, games, and folk tales fostering through storytelling the internalization of positive language and cultural values. Under her supervision the Harlem branch to which she was assigned fulfilled community cultural needs by presenting Hispanic exhibitions and programs focusing on the many contributions of Latin writers and artists.[31]

Language as a Reinforcement of Community

As the migrant settlers became entrenched in various neighborhoods of New York City, those characteristics which singled them out as a distinct ethnic group became more visible to the non-Hispanic. Overall, these were (1) the use of Spanish as the language of communication and (2) the perseverance of island interests or customs as expressed in celebrations, close family associations, and attitudes toward assimilation.

Reserved as the language for the work place and business, English was also used as the means of communication with the host society. Spanish, on the other hand, remained in the home and the community. While authoritative institutions placed great emphasis on English language proficiency, these were not always priority concerns among the Puerto Ricans themselves.[32] Among the migrant population some desiring to improve their job prospects availed themselves of night school courses to perfect their command of vernacular English.[33] Others were more intent on structuring their new environments along the lines of those with which they were most familiar and were more concerned with instilling in their children the language and values which formed their cultural heritage. Still others intended to return to Puerto Rico once they had improved their economic situation. While economics and, to a lesser extent, education constituted important stimulae for learning English for the predominantly working-class communities, most Puerto Ricans did not envision themselves spending the rest of their lives as English-speaking "Americans."

The use of Spanish as the language of communication served as a bond which not only welded intercommunity relationships, but also secured the connections with the rest of Puerto Rico and Spanish-America. Puerto Ricans in New York City read Spanish language newspapers; saw Mexican and Argentinian films; listened to Spanish radio stations; formed associations which promoted Spanish language and culture; danced and listened to Latin music.

Since the late nineteenth century, for example, the growth and intellectual diversity of the Spanish-reading population in the city sought and found stimulation in a number of popular journals published abroad, in Puerto Rico and in New York. Among them were *El Buscapie* (1877), *América* (1883), *El Latino-Americano* (1885), *Las Novedades* (1887), *Revista de Literatura, Ciencias y Artes* (1887), *El Avisador Cubano* (1888), *El Economista Americano* (1887), and *La Juventud* (1889).[34] Similarly, novels and related reading material were available to the early migrant settlers during the first decades of the twentieth century. Among periodicals sold in New York were: *Cultura Proletaria,* which represented an anarchist political viewpoint; *El Heraldo,* a bilingual publication edited by the Autonomist leader Muñoz Rivera; and *La Prensa.* The latter began publishing in 1913 as a weekly, appearing on a daily basis by 1918. This newspaper was destined to become the most important journalistic endeavor for the city's Spanish-speaking population.[35]

La Prensa boasted the motto *"único diario español e hispano-americano en EEUU"* (the only Spanish and Hispano-American newspaper in the United States). It did not confine its services to reporting foreign and domestic news, but fully involved itself in community affairs. Besides advertising for local businesses, special sections reported the arrivals and departures of individuals to and from Spanish-America. Classified ads informed the Spanish-reading public of employment opportunities. Calendars of community events merited regular reporting as did the myriad activities of community groups throughout the city's *colonias*. Religious and educational affairs appeared in print including the weekly agendas of the Brooklyn and Manhattan Hispanic churches: *Nuestra Señora de Guadalupe, Nuestra Señora de la Esperanza, La Iglesia del Pilar,* and *La Milagrosa.* Finally, social or cultural news appealing directly to the small commercial and professional sector informed the public of events such as the series of literary seminars held at Columbia University directed by the well-known Spanish novelist Vicente Blasco Ibañez, the merger of two community associations, or a benefit dance for a church held at the Brooklyn Academy of Music.[36]

Direct community involvement centered on the sponsorship of Latin projects or activities appealing to Hispanics in general. In 1919, for example, *La Prensa* cosponsored a gala ball in conjunction with several community groups the proceeds of which were slated for building an Hispanic sanitarium. On another occasion, the paper's director, José Camprubi, participated at the initiation of a newly federated association composed of representatives of numerous neighborhood units. This liaison group proposed to represent the Spanish-speaking in matters relating to the wider non-Hispanic society. Finally, *La Prensa* frequently joined in fund raising for relevant neighborhood causes, concerts, contests, beauty pageants, and *los juegos florales*. The latter, consisting of competitive dramatic recitations, was significant because it perpetuated the cultural traditions of medieval Spain in the New York Latin *colonias*.[37]

Many less ambitious Spanish language *revistas* continued to appear periodically, oriented around fashionable causes or utilizing current fads, but these seldom retained the longevity characteristic of the older tabloids. Some were organs for the many diverse community organizations operating in the *colonia hispana*. Others, philosophically dedicated to the perpetuation of the language and culture, delivered their message to the Latin community in general. One of these was the magazine *Gráfico,* edited by Ramón LaVilla and later by Bernardo Vega. Published in New York City from

1926 to 1931, on a weekly basis, the motto of this worthy journal was "Semanario Defensor de la Raza Hispana," a response to the intrinsic mission of those who placed the preservation of both language and culture uppermost (see Figure 2).

Described by its creators as a satirical, comical, and literary journal, *Gráfico* appealed specifically to a working-class circulation rather than the general Spanish-speaking population which read *La Prensa*. It printed advertisements, an advice column, community organizational news, general essays, and fiction. One typical issue contained an editorial, a novella, a brief biography of the Mexican philosopher José Vasconcelos, an autobiographical essay by the Puerto Rican historian, Dr. Cayetano Coll y Toste, a sports article, a movie review of *The Jazz Singer,* social and cultural news of Puerto Rico, the New York *colonias,* and Spanish America.[38]

The editorial, in particular, was the vehicle for attacking significant issues affecting the Puerto Rican settlements. These covered a wide range of ideas including views on the current political situation in New York, analysis of the meaning of key American holidays to Hispanics, discrimination against Puerto Ricans, and discourses on class consciousness. An excellent example was the editorial of July 8, 1928, where the oppression of the working class, which included most of the magazine's Puerto Rican readers, was compared to the struggle for American independence:

> American people indulge today in celebration of the birth of their freedom forgetting they are no longer masters of their destiny. America is populated by economic slaves. The masters of society are not only depriving their countrymen of their freedom but while engaging in celebration of the Fourth of July, the nation as a whole, is depriving some other unfortunate weak people of their liberty and pursuit of happiness.[39]

Another editorial questioned the value of American citizenship in the protection of Puerto Rican civil rights. Here *Gráfico* broached the subject of discrimination against Puerto Ricans in New York, recommending the creation of a city agency authorized to speak for these disadvantaged residents of the Spanish-speaking settlements in the same manner that foreign consulates protected their nationals:

The most vulnerable group of those which comprise the large family of Ibero-Americans (in New York City) is the Puerto Rican. Truly it seems a paradox that being American citizens these should be the most defenseless. While the citizens of other countries have their consulates and diplomats to represent them, the children of *Borinquen* have no one.[40]

The editorial highlighted, moreover, the inefficacy of the Puerto Rican resident commissioner, a United States congressional appointee charged with representing island interest in the North American congress, and other officials, to deal successfully with the everyday problems of the city's *colonias*. Regardless of how sympathetic they might be, these hard-working individuals fol-

*Weekly Defender of the Hispanic Race

Figure 2 Journal Masthead, *Gráfico,* 1927

lowed a different agenda oriented around island/mainland considerations, duties and obligations. But the problems of most Puerto Ricans, as expressed in the editorial, took place in New York City where they had established homes, faced racial and cultural discrimination daily from other ethnic groups, and dealt with menial, undersalaried employment. *Gráfico's* recommendation was: "For these reasons it is here (New York City) where Puerto Ricans require a knowledgeable individual authorized to represent and advise them in those relationships which, by virtue of the environment in which we, as aliens find ourselves, must be maintained with other social groups." Calling attention to their perception of themselves as "aliens," the editorial issued a direct appeal to the Puerto Rican worker, stressing unity, brotherhood, and understanding. *Gráfico* intended to encourage support for their position on critical issues on two levels: first, within the vertical class structure of Puerto Rican society; second, by fostering an understanding of the workers' struggle based on a one-to-one relationship: "Agruparemos bajo una sola bandera: la de la fraternidad, y con ella en alto, sostener los ideales y prestigios que nos son inherente" (We shall unite under one flag: that of brotherhood and with it on high we shall maintain those ideals and privileges which to us are inherent).[41]

While *Gráfico* exemplified a typical community journal for the period of the late twenties, the *Revista de Artes y Letras* performed a similar function for the community a decade later. Pledged to the development and dissemination of Hispanic culture, this journal also prided itself on a dedication to the preservation of the Spanish language and a continuation of Latin traditions. It focused on important issues relevant to the Spanish-speaking settlements, social or educational affairs, and politics. Founded and edited by a Puerto Rican woman, Dona Josefina Silva de Cintrón, an individual recognized for her involvement in the development of the interwar *colonias,* the monthly journal flourished from 1933 until 1945. *Revista de Artes y Letras* published the writings of major literary figures of Spain and Spanish America including notables like Julia de Burgos and La Hija del Caribe. The former, best remembered for her contributions as a lyric poetess, lived in New York during the thirties and forties, an experience which sensitized her to the particular situation of the migrant settler.

Artes y Letras frequently featured articles on family and child welfare, and its editorials centered on community issues such as the education of Puerto Rican children or the importance of preserving the Latin heritage. Community organizational news, advertising, interviews, and advice columns shared space with literary essays and fiction. The latter comprised close to 80 percent of the journal's format offering important exposure and communication for new Latin writers.

Through its emphasis on culture and literature *Artes y Letras* appeared to direct its efforts towards a more educated segment of the Spanish-speaking population. But while the journal did not openly address the working class as *Gráfico* had done before, *Artes y Letras* nevertheless strongly identified with the community in which it originated. It involved itself in the *colonias* by taking stands on relevant issues through its editorials and by concerning itself with the organizations of the early settlements. Announcements of all types of community activities appeared in print regardless of which groups were sponsoring the events. The political, religious, or social affairs of groups representing a wide range of interests were seldom ignored and as news items, failed to compromise the journal's original commitments to literary ideals.

The editorial of March 1936 signaled another example of the journal's community involvement as well as its preoccupation with the promotion of the Spanish language. Terming it the educational harassment of Spanish-speaking youngsters in New York City schools, the journal launched a crusade against the testing of Harlem school children by the city's Chamber of Commerce (see Chapter 6). Aroused by the journal's position on this issue, neighborhood groups, concerned also with the language issue, banded together to explore the situation.

For some time, migrant families believed their children suffered undue hardships in the school system because they were unable to speak fluent English. Youngsters transferring from Puerto Rico to New York City schools had commonly been placed one or two years behind the grade level previously completed on the island. In other cases, youngsters and secondary school students were assigned to classes for retarded or slow learners since school administrators could not adequately evaluate achievement levels for monolingual Spanish-speaking students. Equally disturbing, the repetition of grades on the secondary level discouraged many students from completing their course of studies.

The Puerto Rican *colonia* stood united on the language education issue, and several organizations spoke out against the city's educational policies. One such group, *Madres y Padres Pro Ninos Hispanos* sought to relieve the situation by offering an alternative. While they were not actively campaigning for the idealogical preservation of language and culture, they struggled for recognition of the Spanish academic achievements of their children. Acting as buffers between the school administrators, faculty and the *colonia's* schoolchildren, they proposed a rudimentary form of bilingual education in which the classrooms would be staffed with liaison-parents as well as teachers. While their ideas were not implemented, an attempt was made nevertheless, to aid the schools in evaluating the educational progress of Puerto Rican students more accurately.[42] Thus, the insistence on the preservation of Spanish as the language of communication emerges as a reaction to the rapid integration desired by the host society as well as a manner by which to keep an intact sense of identity.[43]

The importance of Spanish became apparent in other ways as well. One of these was in the area of entertainment. Movies and movie stars offered the working-class *colonias* Spanish escapism in a pre-television era. Argentina and Mexico, particularly the Mexican Estudios Churubusco, were the chief producers of Spanish comedies, melodramas, musicals, and westerns. The 1940s, termed the golden age of the Mexican cinema, produced between 130 and 140 Spanish language films a year, many under the direction of individuals like Buñuel, Julio Bracho, and Fernando Fuentes, all of whom would achieve international recognition in the coming decades.[44]

A subculture of Latin filmgoers responded to the Spanish cinema and promoted the popularity of such stars as María Felix, Mapi Cortez, Libertad Lamarque, Carlos Gardel, and Pedro Infante. Thrilled by the exploits of Jorge Negrete or Pedro Armendariz in Mexican westerns, audiences also eagerly applauded the comic antics of Cantinflas or Tin Tan. Community presses advertised current films and followed the professional and personal lives of the movie stars. Interviews with personalities like Dolores del Río or Arturo de Córdova, favorites among Latin filmgoers, frequently appeared in journals like *Gráfico* or *Artes y Letras*. Some, like

Dolores del Río, gained fame in American films as well. When this happened, as was also the case with a young Ricardo Montalbán, the Spanish language presses consistently emphasized the performer's Latin roots, as if to reclaim him or her for the community once again.[45]

Interests and Attitudes

The common interests and attitudes which coalesced the Puerto Rican settlements into a community were eloquently expressed in the popular culture of the period. Music proved remarkably vital for internalizing and externalizing the attitudes of the migrant population. As primary vehicles for expression combining Iberian, African, and Taino Indian influences within the Puerto Rican culture, music, song, and dance had undergone a long development on the island and were transported to the mainland along with the migrant settler. Thus, traditional rhythms such as *Bomba, Plena, Aguinaldo, Seis, Danza y Danzón* were found at the center of musical development in New York *colonias* as well as in Puerto Rico. Essentially summarizing the feelings and attitudes of frustration, nostalgia, unrequited love and homesickness of the Puerto Rican migrant, music also provided a crucial bridge between the island and the mainland communities. In the working-class *colonias* of New York, popular culture in many cases expressed migrant sentiments more poignantly than the written word.

Often a song gained popularity in the migrant settlements as well as in Puerto Rico, since it was played on the Spanish-language radio stations, carried back and forth by the migrant population itself, or played by musicians in groups of *trios* or *conjuntos*. Lyricists, arrangers, and musicians were well known to Puerto Rican audiences on both sides of the ocean and seldom did a piece gain popularity without the migrant community crediting the composer, the lyricist, and the musical group with the success of the song. These creative individuals ranked alongside movie stars or politicians in the minds of the people. One composer lyricist idolized on both sides of the ocean whose work evoked memories of Puerto Rico and the plight of the humble peasant was Rafael Hernández.

Owner of Almacenes Hernández, one of the first Puerto Rican music stores in Manhattan, Hernández composed the songs which became synonymous with the migration experience.

In the back of his store there was a piano which his sister, Victoria, used to teach aspiring musicians. Every time a student came for a lesson she would chase Rafael out of the rocking chair near the piano in which he was singing and strumming his guitar. Rafael would take his guitar and a tin can of black coffee out on the sidewalk, sit down near the edge of the curb and with his feet in the gutter, he would tune his guitar and begin to sing and write words to songs on little pieces of paper.[46]

In *Lamento Boricano,* Hernández succinctly captured the peasant's love for his homeland and the economic misfortunes underlying his move from the island. Along with *Preciosa,* another hymn to the island more nationalistic in tone, *Lamento Boricano* assumed the role of an informal national anthem in some circles of the interwar settlements precisely because it expressed wholehearted concern for the burdens under which the island existed. Moreover, migrants in New York identified with its message interpreting the *jibarito's* journey as the voyage from Puerto Rico to New York.

Popular music not only conveyed nostalgia for the lost homeland or concerns with the island's desperate situation; some songs like *Yo Me Vuelvo a Mi Bohío* satirized the difficulties of adjusting to living in New York City. In the song the protagonist comes to New York expecting to progress because things in Puerto Rico are so bad, only to find the situation in New York is worse. "Sometimes the heat and other times the damned cold, sometimes he resembles a mess ice skating through the snow"—the solution is he will return to his Puerto Rican home—his *bohío.*[47]

Still other songs like *¿Alo, Quien Llama?* expressed awareness of the working-class struggles taking place in Puerto Rico and immortalized an actual event which took place in the factories of Mayaguez. Both songs emerged at an important period in the development of the city's *colonias* following the end of the Second World War, when the Latin neighborhoods had increased dramatically in size. While agencies engaged in studies designed to deal with the problems of the city's newest neighbors and attempted to assimilate them into the dominant society, Puerto Ricans poked fun at themselves in their songs, asking if indeed they wanted to integrate into the system.

If gut feelings and reactions found expression in songs, music played other important roles as well. First, it enabled the migrant community to sing, listen to, and play the familiar songs associated with holidays or festive occasions in Puerto Rico. Second, it nurtured a continuation and bonding together of friends and relatives in the celebration of birthdays, weddings, baptisms, and other important life-cycle occasions in the migrant experience. Invariably, neighborhood musicians provided live music for these celebrations while invited guests danced or sang. These activities alternated with dramatic recitations or poetry declamations, all forming a natural part of the evening's entertainment, not unlike celebrations in Puerto Rico. Moreover, *trios* or *conjuntos* complete with vocalists often came together to entertain at weekend parties not necessarily confined to holiday celebration. These gatherings composed of friends, relatives, and neighbors encouraged intergenerational activities, and older participants interacted freely with children, infants, and young adults without friction.

Puerto Rican musicians played at house parties as well. Soon after his arrival, cigar maker Bernardo Vega noted the practice of holding rent parties, particularly in the Harlem settlement where spacious apartments lent themselves to this type of action. These parties were not confined to family participation (although family members frequently shared leisure time activities), but rather designed to attract paying customers. The underlying motive of a rent party was to sufficiently enrich the residents of the apartment so they could pay their rent. Vega observed: "In the more spacious Harlem apartments, the custom of celebrating parties on Saturdays and Sundays became established. These were not family parties but rather dances where people paid to get in."[48] Musicians were paid with profits from the sale of beer, *maví* (a native Puerto Rican soft drink) or Puerto Rican delicacies. Those families fortunate to include musicians as relatives appeared to be more economically secure during periods of hardships since these individuals often found house parties at which to play.

During the 1930s a house party in the *Barrio* was a ball. The apartment and hallway reeked with the spicy aroma of garlic and oregano which emanated from the fresh hams in the oven. Thin slabs of *pernil* accompanied plates of steaming *arroz con gandules.* The elders drank beer that flowed from a wooden keg kept in the kitchen sink on top of a twenty-five cent block of ice. The bathtub, filled with cracked ice, covered several flavors of soda pop that children drank. *Trios* or *quartets* which consisted of a lead vocalist, a maraca player, guitarist and sometimes a trumpeter provided live music in the living room . . . as the evening came to a close each musician was three dollars richer.[49]

As late as the 1950s these customs were still in practice. One young musician recalled similar parties taking place in the apartment which was his home. His mother was often the lead vocalist and music became an intimate, natural part of his upbringing. Live music and the special relationship surrounding musical expression flourished aided by a growing record industry catering to those very interests.

Two decades into the twentieth century *Danzas, Danzóns, Plenas,* and *Aguinaldos* had already been recorded by Columbia and RCA Victor Record Companies, finding a lucrative market of enthusiastic consumers among the city's Latin population. By the 1930s Latin bands played to packed houses in the *Teatro Hispano* or the *Campamor* Theatre at Fifth Avenue and 116th Street in the heart of Spanish Harlem. Dance halls like Hunts Point Palace, Tropicana Park Palace, and the Audobon Ballroom hired popular Latin bands to attract Hispanic dancers. However, record companies, above all, continued to bring popular music into the home.

By the late forties, the Latin music industry was thriving with record companies and labels. The first Puerto Rican-owned company recorded on the Dynasonic label. This was the Spanish Music Center on 110th Street and Fifth Avenue, where neighborhood trios and quartets recorded in the back of the store while records on the Decca or later the Tico labels were sold in the front. In addition to records, the Spanish Music Center sold piano rolls of Latin favorites and musical instruments such as the traditional Spanish guitar.[50]

As a business venture, the small music store spread quickly throughout the *colonia hispana* and came to symbolize the Latin settlements as the candy store had characterized other ethnic immigrant neighborhoods. Emanating from these establishments the rhythms of *el Son, la Guaracha,* Puerto Rican *Plenas* and *Aguinaldos* combined with the romantic *Boleros* and *Danzas* to serenade the Spanish-speaking neighborhoods day and night, nurturing a continuation of vital cultural expressions rooted in Puerto Rico and Spanish America. In time, other recording companies like Ansonia, Seeco, Mercury, and Alba also catered to Latin tastes especially after the enthusiastic response of non-Latin audiences to the introduction of the *Mambo.*[51]

In spite of the popularity of Latin music for the non-Hispanic host society, Latin music continued to be an integral part of the Spanish-speaking community, which not only set it apart, but served also to identify it as a distinctive unit. It was here that Puerto Ricans shared a common interest which more often than not, served as a community base, kept cultural communications open with the island, and even allowed a degree of interaction with the host society. Clearly, Latin music expressed the development of the *colonia* on two levels: The cultural, as an expression of Puerto Rican heritage and creativity; and the physical, as an example of Latin entrepreneurship.

Conclusion

That the pioneer Puerto Rican settlements prior to mid-century constituted communities is indisputable. We have traced the genesis of the Puerto Rican settlements in two dimensions: the geographic boundaries and settlement patterns as well as the physical characteristics emphasizing professional, commercial, and leadership development. Early *colonias,* or migrant neighborhoods, were urban centers marked by dense settlement patterns. Through the proliferation of a business, professional, and social sector, held solidly on a working-class base, settlements were easily recognized as Puerto Rican.

But the migrant settlements formed solid communities in other dimensions as well. These were the persistence of the Spanish language, customs, and habits for the maintenance of a shared identity as Puerto Ricans and a perpetuation of common interests and attitudes as expressed in life-cycle celebrations and popular culture.

Notes

1. Some of the studies which have debated communal development among Puerto Ricans include the following: Oscar Handlin, *The Newcomers: Negroes and Puerto Ricans in a Changing Metropolis* (Cambridge: Harvard University Press, 1959); Nathan Glazer and Daniel Patrick Moynihan, *Beyond the Melting Pot* (Cambridge: MIT Press, 1963); Alfred Kazin, "In Puerto Rico," in *Contemporaries* (New York: Little, Brown & Co., 1960); Daniel J. Boorstein, "Self Discovery in Puerto Rico," *Yale Review,* 1955.

2. Lawrence R. Chenault, *The Puerto Rican Migrant in New York City* (New York: Columbia University Press, 1938; reissue, Russell & Russell, 1970), p. 158.

3. José Hernández Álvarez, "The Movement and Settlement of Puerto Rican Migrants within the United States, 1950–1960," *International Migration Review,* vol. 2, no. 2 (spring 1968), pp. 40–51.

4. Interview with Ramón Colón, The Puerto Rican Oral History Project, 1973–1974, Long Island Historical Society, Brooklyn, New York. See also Ramón Colón, *Carlos Tapia, A Puerto Rican Hero in New York* (New York: Vantage Press, 1976), p. 44.

5. Octavo informe anual del negociado del trabajo, informe sobre la intervención e investigación realizada por el negociado del trabajo en relación con las trabajadores Portorriqueñas contratadas en Puerto Rico por la American Manufacturing Company de Brooklyn, New York (San Juan: Puerto Rico, 1920), pp. 10–18.

6. Ibid., p. 15.

7. Interview with Antonio Sánchez Feliciano, Aguada, Puerto Rico, July 1977.

8. César Andreu Iglesias, ed., *Memorias de Bernardo Vega* (Rio Piedras: Ediciones Huracan, Inc., 1977), pp. 45–46.

9. Interview with Raquel Rivera Hernández, Rio Piedras, Puerto Rico, August 1977.

10. Chenault, *The Puerto Rican Migrant,* pp. 104–107.

11. Colón, *Carlos Tapia,* p. 74.

12. The Souvenir Program of the Porto Rican Brotherhood of America, June 1926.

13. Daniel Wakefield, *Island in the City—The World of Spanish Harlem* (Boston, Houghton Mifflin Co., 1959).

14. The New York State Manuscript Census, 1925, Assembly Districts 16, 17, 18, 19. A partial tabulation of this census was done by the Center for Puerto Rican Studies, CUNY. See also History Task Force, Centro de Estudios Puertorriqueños, *Labor Migration Under Capitalism: The Puerto*

Rican Experience (New York: Monthly Review Press, 1979), pp. 148–151; and Peter Laslett, *Household and Family in Past Time* (Cambridge: Cambridge University Press, 1972).

15. Chenault, *The Puerto Rican Migrant,* p. 128. Handlin, *The Newcomers,* pp. 93–98.

16. *New York Times,* July 30, 1926, p. 29.

17. *El Heraldo,* August 3, 1901, classified ads.

18. *Gráfico,* March 27, 1927, p. 2.

19. Ibid.

20. Raquel Rivera Hernández interview.

21. Interview with Lillian López, New York City, May 1976. Interview with Evelina Antonetty, Columbia Oral History Project, Columbia University, New York City.

22. The Porto Rican Brotherhood of America, program.

23. Ibid.

24. *Gráfico,* February 27, 1927, p. 2.

25. Chenault, *The Puerto Rican Migrant,* p. 71. See also *Guía Hispana* (New York, Guía Hispana Publishing Co., 1934); *Polk's New York City Directory,* 1933–1934.

26. New York State Manuscript Census, 1925; Iglesias, *Memorias,* p. 193.

27. *New York Times,* February 3, 1924, p. 23; Iglesias, *Memorias,* pp. 184–185; History Task Force, *Labor Migration,* p. 83.

28. For an interesting interpretation of leadership in Puerto Rican communities, see John M. Goering et al., "An Examination of the Needs for Outreach Development in the Area of Hispanic Discrimination" (The Graduate School and University Center, CUNY, July 1977, unpublished manuscript). See also John W. Gotsch, "Puerto Rican Leadership in New York" (M.A. Thesis, New York University, 1966).

29. *New York Times,* July 27, 1926, p. 21; and July 30, 1926, p. 29. See also Iglesias, pp. 188–191; Ramón Colón interview.

30. Interview with Pedro Ruiz, Aguada, Puerto Rico, July 1977.

31. Interview with Pura Belpré, Brooklyn, New York, May 1979; and Columbia Oral History Project.

32. The following reports are examples of studies conducted on Puerto Ricans in New York City during the late forties and early fifties: C. Wright Mills, Clarence Senior, and Rose Goldsen, *The Puerto Rican Journey: New York's Newest Migrant* (New York: Harper & Bros., 1950) (this book was based on the Columbia Study of 1948, a research project conducted by the Bureau of Applied Social Research of Columbia University); New York City Board of Education, "A Program of Education for Puerto Ricans in New York City" (1947); New York City Board of Education, Bilingual

Committee of the Junior High School Division, "Tentative Report of the Committee on Classification," Bulletin no. 1 (1959). Welfare Council of New York City, "Puerto Ricans in New York City" (1948).

33. Ramón Colón interview; Raquel Rivera Hernández interview; Antonio Sánchez Feliciano interview.

34. Iglesias, *Memorias,* pp. 106–107. See also Iris M. Zavala and Rafael Rodríguez, *The Intellectual Roots of Independence* (New York: Monthly Review, 1980), pp. 12–30.

35. Iglesias, *Memorias,* pp. 96, 140, 148. Vega also cites the publication of the first Puerto Rican newspaper, *La Voz de Puerto Rico,* in 1874, and *Puerto Rico Herald,* a bilingual publication in 1901, on pp. 88 and 127.

36. Iglesias, *Memorias,* p. 140.

37. *La Prensa,* July 21, 1919, p. 2.

38. *Gráfico,* July 1, 1928.

39. Ibid., March 27, 1927, p. 2.

40. Ibid.

41. Ibid.

42. Interview with Fausta Mercado, Brentwood, New York, June 1976.

43. This information was conveyed in several interviews.

44. Interview with Rosa Roma, Santurce, Puerto Rico, August 1977; *Nuestro,* May 1980, pp. 26–27; *Gráfico,* July 8, 1928; *Artes y Letras,* January 1936.

45. See note 44.

46. Max Salazar, "The Perseverance of a Culture," in Clara E. Rodríguez, Virginia E. Sánchez Korrol and José Oscar Alers, eds., *The Puerto Rican Struggle: Essays on Survival in the U.S.* (New York: Puerto Rican Migration Research Consortium, 1980), pp. 77–78.

47. Miguel Angel Figueroa and Conjunto Típico Ladi, "Yo Me Vuelvo a Mi Bohío" (Verne Recording Corporation, V. 10006B).

48. Iglesias, *Memorias,* pp. 143–145.

49. Salazar, "The Perseverance," pp. 77–78.

50. Max Salazar, "Latin Music's Rivalries and Battles," *Latin New York,* January 1975, pp. 44–46.

51. Ibid., January 1976, pp. 36–38. Bandleader Pérez Prado is credited with introducing the mambo dance craze with his recording of "Mambo No. 5" in 1948.

The Other Side of the Ocean

Women held a special place in the early Puerto Rican settlements of New York City, often providing links between the island and mainland enclaves. Pivotal in retaining ethnicity through the transmission of language, customs, and cultural traditions within familial settings, women also functioned as part of an informal informational network. Referred to as "the family intelligence service" by Clarence Senior, and functioning very much like the Portuguese equivalent of "making a *cunha,*" the network acclimated incoming migrants to the intricacies of the receiving society.[1] Over the factory sewing machines or on apartment house stoops, in the *bodegas* or in the privacy of their own homes, women exchanged information on housing, jobs, folk remedies, the best places to shop, their churches, and their children's schools. What has usually been classified as idle female chatter provided in essence the tools for handling the unfamiliar situation.

The women of the Puerto Rican *colonias* were charged with yet another responsibility—that of contributing to the creation of a Puerto Rican community rooted on traditional family units. This entailed maintaining Hispanic family values in the midst of an alien

An earlier version of this chapter appeared in *Caribbean Review,* January-March 1979, Vol. VIII, no. 1.

New York environment, establishing settlements where customs
and institutions mirrored those previously adhered to in Puerto
Rico, and within this context, contributing to the financial support
of the family.

Migrant Profiles

Who were the women of the *colonias*? A partial tabulation of
four Assembly Districts in the 1925 New York State Manuscript
Census revealed a modified social profile of the Puerto Rican
female migrant. The 1925 census enumerators listed all male and
female heads of household, children, extended relatives, and
boarders. Their ages, occupations, and lengths of stay in the United
States were also provided, indicating a partial but precise view of
the socioeconomic conditions of the early female migrants. Since
the Assembly Districts selected for tabulation were generally considered to shelter heavy Spanish-speaking concentrations, we can
speculate that the information provided in the census presented a
fairly typical profile for other boroughs as well as Manhattan. Out
of 7,322 Spanish-surnamed individuals living in Manhattan's Sixteenth, Seventeenth, Eighteenth, and Nineteenth Assembly Districts, almost half (3,496, or 47.7 percent) were female, leaving
3,815, or 52.1 percent, males and 11, or 0.2 percent, as unclassified
(see Table 6).[2]

The bulk of the female population was composed of housewives
and children; 1,474 or 52.2 percent of the females living in that area
listed their occupation as "housewife" in the manuscript census;
28.5 percent or 997 were female children, many of them students;
with the remaining 29.3 percent adult participants in the work
force. The group isolated under the categories of housewives and
children, furthermore, had spent a relatively short period residing
in the New York settlements. Forty-five percent of these had been
in the United States less than three years. Almost twenty-three out
of every one hundred women had been in the United States from
four to six years; 11 percent listed their term of residence at between
seven and ten years and about 6 percent admitted to eleven or more
years in New York City (see Tables 7 and 8). The majority of the
female population, 78.9 percent in the four sample districts, was
under thirty-five years of age; moreover, in the over-forty-five age
group, women substantially outnumbered men and there were ten

times as many grandmothers as grandfathers.[3] In short, the women migrants of the twenties and thirties were comparatively young, had not been residing in New York City for any length of time, and frequently listed their occupations as "housewives" in the census's occupational category.

TABLE 6
Gender Distribution of Hispanics in Assembly Districts 16, 17, 18, 19

	16		17		18		19	
	#	%	#	%	#	%	#	%
Female	294	48.1	1,770	47.3	928	48.0	504	48.6
Male	317	51.9	1,962	52.5	1,003	51.9	533	51.3
N.A.*	—	—	8	0.2	2	0.1	1	0.1
TOTALS	611	100.0	3,740	100.0	1,933	100.0	1,038	100.0

*No information available

Total Hispanic Population in Index Districts = 7,322.
Source: New York State Manuscript Census, 1925.

TABLE 7
Number of Years in United States as Reported by Hispanics in Assembly Districts 16, 17, 18, 19

YEARS	NUMBER	%
0–3.9	3,231	44.1
4–5.9	1,634	22.3
7–10.9	1,001	13.7
11–18.9	293	4.0
19	267	3.6
N.A.	896	12.2
TOTAL	7,322	100.0

Source: The New York State Manuscript Census, 1925.

TABLE 8
Number of Years in the United States by Gender Reported by Hispanics
in Assembly Districts 16, 17, 18, 19

YEARS IN U.S.	FEMALE		MALE	
	#	%	#	%
0–3.9	1,576	45.0	1,655	43.4
4–5.9	824	23.6	810	21.2
7–10.9	416	11.9	583	15.3
11–18.9	129	3.7	164	4.3
19	110	3.1	154	4.0
N.A.	445	12.7	449	11.8
TOTALS*	3,500	100.0	3,815	100.0

*Note: The total of 7,311 persons excluded the eleven individuals in Table 6 for
which gender information is unavailable.

Source: The New York State Manuscript Census, 1925.

With the exception of labor force participation, the male migrant
population compared favorably with the female. Of 3,815 individuals, 70.5 percent or 2,688 men were employed in the work force;
911 or 23.9 percent were listed as minors—children and students—
and 216 or 5.7 percent were retired, not working or not available
(see Table 9). Whereas 45 percent of the female migrant group had
resided in the United States for three years or less, 43.4 percent of
the males had lived in the mainland for that period of time.
Twenty-one male migrants out of every one hundred had been here
four to six years, and 15.3 percent estimated their residence at
between seven to ten years.

 A homogeneous population such as that comprised by the
migrant group was extremely important for the perpetuation of traditional family patterns, which in turn would form the basis of the
early colonias. By comparison, it was somewhat different for the
Black West Indian immigrant population, for example, which also
came into the Harlem area about the same time. This immigration
followed the common European patterns in that West Indian males
outnumbered women in all but one (fifteen-to-twenty-four) adult

TABLE 9

Occupational Categories of Hispanics by Gender in Assembly Districts 16, 17, 18, 19

	FEMALE		MALE	
	#	%	#	%
PRIVATE SECTOR				
Owners, supervisors	16	.5	137	3.6
Production	600	17.2	1,604	42.1
Workers in circulation	118	3.4	466	12.2
Workers in services	156	4.5	390	10.2
PUBLIC SECTOR				
Supervisors	—	—	—	—
Production	—	—	1	—
Commerce	1	—	3	.1
Services	8	.2	87	2.3
OTHER				
Housewives	1,474	42.2	—	—
Children and students	997	28.5	911	23.9
Retired or not employed	55	1.6	126	3.3
N.A.	71	2.0	90	2.4
TOTALS	3,496	100.1	3,815	100.1

Source: The New York State Manuscript Census, 1925.

age bracket.[4] The relatively equal sex ratios among the Puerto Ricans, furthermore, encouraged the extension of island family composition patterns in the mainland settlements. These reflected an attempt in the pioneer settlements to preserve a traditional family structure where the male was the household head and the female's dominant role was reproduction, childcare, and household management.

Nevertheless, numerous migrant women were determined to combine jobs with traditional family life and initiated modifications in community living with this end in mind. One group composed predominantly of young wives and mothers, cherishing Hispanic family traditions which dictated women's place in society, preferred to remain in the home. Others formed an important segment of the city's labor force. Faced with the economic realities confronting the overwhelmingly poor, working-class *colonias,* this group found ways to combine traditional family life with gainful employment outside of the home. Finally, a small group found fulfillment participating in community affairs, in volunteer organizations, and working as professionals or in white-collar capacities. Based on census information and oral interviews, the majority of the migrant women fit into the first category.

THE TRADITIONALISTS

In New York, at least two factors unconsciously influenced Puerto Rican thinking in terms of women's roles. First, women were expected to fulfill their traditional role as wives and mothers in the new *colonias* as they had previously done in their island home. The fact that male and female migrant numbers remained relatively equal and stable in almost all age brackets, with the exception of the over-forty-five group, throughout the migration encouraged this dimension of community formation. Second, although women migrants in New York participated in a series of community and work-related enterprises, they remained conditioned to believe that motherhood and marriage expressed their primary functions in life. Those who did work for a living did so only because it was essential for their individual or collective survival. One migrant articulated typical sentiments regarding women's place in the work force when she stated:

> I do not criticize working outside the home because I did it myself in New York out of necessity and if it had not been out of necessity I would have never worked outside the home because I wanted to be with (to raise) my children. . . . If the husband earns enough to support his home, the wife *must* not work.[5]

However, the necessity to work in the home or outside of the home became such an integral part of Puerto Rican survival in general, both on the island and in the New York settlements, that women compromised and accepted wage-earning responsibilities as a natural extension of the homemaker role.

Clearly, the term "housewife" as it appeared in the census occupational category was misleading or open to interpretation when applied to Puerto Rican women. For while migrant females thought of themselves as *mujeres de la casa,* the traditional lady of the house, many found ways nevertheless to participate in activities designed to supplement and in some cases provide primary family incomes.

As necessity begets invention, many home-centered, money-making ventures emerged in response to the very real economic family needs of the working-class settlements. Among these, piecework ranked as one of the major forms of home enterprises. In New York this included the making or decorating of lampshades, hats, artificial flowers and jewelry, embroidery, crocheting, and garment sewing. Women commonly secured a work load or a "lot" from a local contractor or subcontractor for which the worker received payment per completed portion, virtually the same procedure practiced in Puerto Rico.

Women workers in Puerto Rico and in the New York settlements for the most part recognized the values and disadvantages of piece-working. This included an awareness that piecework, particularly home-based needlework, exemplified an exploitative enterprise designed to enrich the purses of the contractor, subcontractor and factory owner at the expense of the worker.[6] Moreover, piecework in Puerto Rico established a precedent for the forms it would take in New York *colonias.* Initially a cottage industry in Puerto Rico, wages in this economic sector were remarkably low. By 1934 a United States Department of Labor report on the employment of women on the island revealed the extent to which some workers were exploited in a number of industries, especially the home needlework area:

> Women worked extremely long hours, days and evenings. Hourly earnings in needlework were extremely low: for 31.4 percent of the women they were less than one cent, for 31.1 percent they were one and under 2 cents, and for 31.4 percent they were 2 and under 4 cents. . . . Unfair practices in home

needlework included payment in groceries, payment in keep; delays in supplying work and payment, retention by agent of wage increases.[7]

Since women's salaried labor was traditionally thought to be merely supplementary and since any salary was better than none at all, other benefits or conveniences were sought as compensation by those who did piecework. Consequently, this type of work gained popularity in New York precisely because of other adjustments: it could be done in the home at one's own pace; made use of traditional sewing skills; and virtually eliminated the need for English language proficiency or commutation throughout a strange city.

Not surprisingly, sewing and home piecework ranked among the earliest and most popular work experiences of many women migrants.[8] A significant number preferred this type of work rather than securing outside employment because they had young children who needed a mother's care. Some combined it with factory work especially during critical periods such as the Depression. Others turned to it sporadically, when faced with dependent family situations, language barriers, or simply the notion that women belonged in the home. One woman, Doña María, ran a household in *El Barrio* which included four children, elderly grandparents, and a husband. Her major responsibilities, while the children were young and her husband worked in the cigar industry, lay in the home. There she made lampshades and other piecework items for several years, but as her children matured, she began working in a local factory, eventually becoming plant forelady.[9] Another migrant, Doña Elisa, came to New York as a domestic, specifically to care for the young children of a cousin. As the relative assumed personal responsibility for Doña Elisa's welfare, the young woman was charged with childcare and household duties in exchange for room and board. But Doña Elisa, requiring some degree of independence, took in piecework while at the same time fulfilling her end of the agreement—remaining at home with her cousin's children.

In New York, few women complained about either the work or low wages, perhaps because they failed to view their skills as valuable or perhaps because home work offered compensatory benefits, as previously pointed out. Puerto Rican pieceworkers seldom described themselves as victims of exploitation. One migrant, typical of the pieceworkers of the early settlements, emphasized the degree of independence and other advantages when she declared:

> At that time (1937) I started to hem handkerchiefs in the house while I awaited the birth of my first baby, to earn extra money. My husband worked for the Works Progress Administration, three weeks out of every month earning fifteen dollars a week. A Mexican lady had a small factory on Eighth Avenue and either me or my husband would go there to pick up packages of handkerchiefs once a week. I would work a little in the morning and some more at night. The rest of the time was devoted to housework, cooking and cleaning and that sort of thing. Later on, my spare time went to the baby.[10]

Similarly, several years later, Doña Clara, a newcomer from Cabo Rojo believed her most important function as a young mother was to raise her children, remaining at home with them and being at home when they returned from school. This decision motivated an interest in piecework.

> I had four children to care for so I only worked at home. In that instance, they gave out work to do in the house so I hemmed handkerchiefs or sewed blouse collars. I would get twenty dozen handkerchiefs a day for me and my sister-in-law, who also had young children at that time. They paid little—about thirteen cents a dozen but the cost of living was also less than now. A subway ride to pick up more piecework was only five cents. Later on, when my girls were young, I made blouse collars which was very easy for me to do on my machine at home. The children would all help me by counting the collars or turning them inside out. This type of work paid more—about twenty-five cents a dozen. You'd be surprised how that extra money helped us to buy little extras—or helped to stretch my husband's earnings.[11]

Doña Clara's recollections highlight two significant factors regarding piecework. First, she provides a realistic evaluation of the work in terms of wage earnings; and second, she reaffirms the benefits connected with the venture as viewed by the migrant work-

ers themselves. Throughout the late twenties and during the
Depression period, salaries for unskilled Puerto Rican workers
averaged about twenty-one dollars a week or less.[12] But during the
thirties, most Puerto Ricans fortunate enough to be employed
earned wages below WPA (Work Progress Administration) and
Home Relief Bureau levels. Unskilled WPA workers earned fifty-
five dollars for fifteen days of work each month and a family of
five on relief received between fifty and sixty dollars a month. Families often relied on the earnings of female workers, particularly
during crisis, when many heads of households were unemployed.

During the thirties migrants like Doña Clara or Doña Elisa estimated their earnings from piecework over the period of a week
fluctuated between five and ten dollars depending on how much
time they could devote to sewing. Moreover, increasing restrictions
placed on piecework by the New York State Department of Labor
and the minimum wage laws of the period failed to control the
growing numbers of bootleg illegal business ventures which
abounded in this business fostering a continuation of exploitative
practices. Employers paid little heed to minimum wage requirements, especially since few Puerto Ricans knew about or complained regarding their rights in this area. Thus, Puerto Rican
pieceworkers remained at the economic mercy of their employers.
Although piecework was believed to have declined considerably by
the mid-thirties, it continued well into the sixties and seventies
according to the women interviewed.

Similarly, needlework, which formed the basis of piecework in
the home, played an important role in the lives of migrant women.
Nurtured in a tradition of quality needlecrafts for generations,
Puerto Rican women almost always possessed skills in sewing,
crocheting, and embroidering. In fact, these skills were part of the
Puerto Rican school curriculum, taught as early as the second or
third grades. One migrant proudly explained she learned embroidery and lace working before her tenth birthday. Another described
her experiences in the factories of María Luisa Arcelay, a well-
known factory owner and industrialist in Mayaguez, crediting this
episode in her life as one responsible for learning the trade and
skills she brought with her to the New York garment factories:

> I worked with María Luisa Arcelay for ten years before com-
> ing to New York. I was always a great help to her since I could

work in the factories or in the home, doing piecework. This great and bountiful lady had such confidence in me that I often made bank deposits for her, walked her children to and from school, and would oversee the premises if she was busy somewhere else.

Our family was poor and my father was blind, so financial responsibilities rested on my shoulders, on my mother's, my sisters and brothers. Doña María Luisa Arcelay always had work for me and she understood the importance of it for our family's survival. In the beginning when I was still under age, do you know what she did? She would hide me in the bathroom when the investigators came. My earnings would appear as my mother's.

When I was older, a married woman and a mother myself, I never wanted for work because no sooner was my child born but there was a bundle of piecework for me to do. Do you know sometimes I made as much as forty dollars a week? (This was during the early forties.) That was a lot of money for those times. So everything I learned from this great lady made it easier for me to work when we moved to New York.[13]

Pura Belpré, writer and folklorist, noted the same resiliency among the migrant women of the early settlements, who relied on their needlework, in hard times, selling handicrafts from door to door. Others recalled highly intricate needlework decorations adorned their migrant homes particularly as doilies, tablecloths, and mantlepieces.

In addition to enhancing employment opportunities, needlecrafts, especially in piecework, provided a setting in mainland Puerto Rican homes for social interaction similar to that created by the North American custom of holding quilting bees or sewing circles. Young and old, grandmothers, aunts, mothers, and children all participated in this process, transmitting needlecraft traditions from one generation to the next in an almost exclusively feminine world. Working together in the home stimulated informational exchanges among adults while allowing children a glimpse into the adult work world as well as into a part of their heritage. The practical transmission of skills fortified cultural and community traditions while providing a degree of economic security. These practices, the combination of traditional needlecraft skills in the home and piecework as an income-producing venture, were followed by other enterprises with similar goals.

CHILDCARE PRACTICES

As Puerto Ricans entrenched themselves in the various *colonias* throughout the city, other income-promoting opportunities emerged enabling homebound women to secure supplementary or, in some cases, primary incomes for their dependents while upholding traditional family structures. Minding children and taking in lodgers represented two such opportunities. Although a few women in the city could rely on the ready availability of grandmothers, aunts, or *co-madres* (godmothers) to look after their families while they worked, others were forced to leave their children behind with relatives in Puerto Rico while they sought to secure a livelihood.[14] Many more developed alternative methods for the care of their children. For the most part, childcare responsibilities in the early community remained within the family whenever possible and the care of the young often delegated to unemployed household members. Yet, due to the unique Puerto Rican family composition in the early *colonias,* this was not always possible.

If, as the 1925 census suggested, the bulk of the Puerto Rican residences in South Central Harlem fell into the categories of "simple" or "nuclear family" households, then the "extended family" which had historically allowed women the peace of mind to work outside the home in Puerto Rico was somewhat limited in New York. An analysis of the 1925 census, moreover, indicated that "nuclear" or "simple families" and "simple families with lodgers," outnumbered "extended families," "extended families with lodgers" and "multi-family" dwellings during the decade of the twenties. Of the 7,322 Hispanics residing in the four key Assembly Districts cited, for example, 2,259 individuals or 30.9 percent lived in households classified as "simple families with lodgers"; 1,864 persons or 25.5 percent were designated as residents in "nuclear family" households; 1,079 individuals or 14.7 percent fit into the "extended families with lodgers" category; and 988 persons or 13.5 percent resided in "extended family households." The remaining 1,128 individuals or 15.4 percent were distributed among five other categories (see Table 10).[15]

Thus, 56.4 percent of the Puerto Rican households were headed

TABLE 10

Hispanic Household Types in Assembly Districts 16, 17, 18, 19

TYPE	16		17		18		19	
	#	%	#	%	#	%	#	%
Solitaries	6	1.0	58	1.6	37	1.4	13	1.3
Co-residents	14	2.3	141	3.8	103	5.3	40	3.9
Simple family	270	44.2	648	17.3	810	42.0	140	13.4
Simple family with lodgers	94	15.4	1,310	35.0	441	22.8	414	39.9
Extended family	119	19.5	430	11.5	325	16.8	114	11.0
Extended family with lodgers	65	10.6	807	21.6	143	7.4	64	6.2
Multiple family	39	6.4	150	4.0	48	2.5	15	1.4
Multiple, not related	—		174	4.6	26	1.3	224	21.6
N.A.	4	.7	24	.6	10	.5	14	1.3
TOTALS	611	100.1	3,742	100.0	1,943	100.0	1,038	100.0

Source: The New York State Manuscript Census, 1925.

by two parents (nuclear family) or consisted of married couples
without children (see Table 11).[16] Clearly, with the limitations of
extended family groups or multifamily households, coupled with a
scarcity of bilingual-bicultural daycare facilities, another system
for reliable childcare became essential for working Puerto Ricans.

TABLE 11
Hispanic Household Types

TYPE	#	%
Solitaries	104	1.4
Co-residents	298	4.1
Simple family	1,864	25.5
Simple family with lodgers	2,259	30.9
Extended family	988	13.5
Extended family with lodgers	1,076	14.7
Multiple family	252	3.4
Multiple family, not related	422	5.8
N.A.	56	.7
TOTALS	7,322	100.0

Source: The New York State Manuscript Census, 1925.

Childcare tasks previously undertaken by relatives defaulted to
friends and acquaintances outside the kinship network who provided the services in exchange for a prearranged fee. A grass-roots system of daycare was born from the merger of working mothers who
could ill afford to lose job security or union benefits and women
who remained at home. Working Puerto Rican mothers left their
children in the care of friends or relatives, and the arrangements
basically consisted of bringing child, food, and additional clothing
to the mother-substitute and collecting him after work. Women
who opened their homes to care for children found this a practical
means of increasing family earnings.

Although these arrangements fulfilled neither legal nor licensing
regulations, the system boasted several advantages not found in
established childcare institutions. In the first place, children were

often cared for in familiar neighborhood surroundings which especially benefitted the school-age youngster who could attend class
with his neighborhood companions. Secondly, childcare operated
on mutual trust and agreement between the adults involved. Very
often this situation allowed for more flexibility than could be found
in an institutionalized setting. If, for example, the parent(s) worked
overtime or on the weekends, suitable arrangements beneficial to
both parties were easily negotiated. Finally, and perhaps of most
importance, the youngster was cared for within a natural family
setting surrounded by adults and children of varying ages. This not
only encouraged the child to interact in an atmosphere where his
language, customs, traditions, and parental family values were constantly reinforced, but also fostered learning from one another
among the children.

As late as 1948, a report issued by the Welfare Council of New
York City deplored the situation wherein Puerto Rican children
were being placed in unlicensed homes for care, but neglected to
suggest alternative measures for minding Puerto Rican children of
working mothers aside from requesting more daycare centers with
bilingual personnel. The report posed the thesis that multitudes of
working Puerto Rican mothers meant young children were often
denied adequate care.[17] Furthermore, while many youngsters
received care in nursery schools or settlement houses, these centers,
often viewed as impersonal alien institutions by Puerto Ricans,
could not accommodate all the children in need of such services.
The lack of adequate bilingual, bicultural institutions which could
deliver services without appearing intimidating further motivated
the placement of Spanish-speaking children in neighborhood
homes.

During the early periods of the twenties and thirties, women paid
two or three dollars weekly per child for daycare, but by 1948 the
Welfare Council speculated fees paid in private homes ranged between ten and twelve dollars a week. Almost all of the women interviewed placed their children in the homes of friends or relatives at
some time throughout their working lives, and this system continued to offer more advantages than established centers. Moreover,
women who did use public nurseries for their children found the
institutions offered little flexibility, and they combined these services with home care as well.

Several migrant women shared the experience of being on both
sides of the system. Doña Julia's daughter, for example, was cared
for by her aunt; but after Julia's second child was born, she sometimes took care of other women's children. Another became a foster mother after she decided to remain at home with her three children. Doña Celina came to New York on the eve of the Second
World War with her infant daughter, whom she left in her sister's
care while she worked in a local factory. Five years later, the births
of a son and a daughter curtailed outside employment but permitted Doña Celina the opportunity to mind neighborhood children.
This practice continued for thirty-five years. Without a husband
and on public assistance during hard times, the woman nevertheless
managed to raise her own three children on the unpredictable earnings from piecework, selling her own handicrafts, and caring for
other people's children. Throughout the years the family prospered
moderately, and the income for her various enterprises made possible a long-awaited move to a more stable neighborhood with better
schools. Today, a senior citizen, Doña Celina cares for her grand-
chidren and devotes vast energies to Hispanic religious and community projects, but the familiar sign—*se cuidan niños*—(children
cared for) still adorns her front window from time to time.[18]

Certainly childcare practices as they emerged in the pioneer settlements were strongly influenced by the family customs and institutions of Puerto Rico. Among the cultural institutions brought by
Puerto Ricans to New York were those of ritual kinship—*compadrazgo*—and informal adoption, the rearing of *hijos de crianza*.
The former institution, based on Spanish roots, provided compan-
ion parents for the natural parents who in turn were godparents for
the child. Most often, these sponsored a child at baptism or confir-
mation, but the *compadrazgo* relationship could also form on the
basis of common interests or the intensification of friendships
which led men and women to consider themselves as more than
friends—*compadre* or *comadre*. The *compadres* were sometimes
relatives, but more often they were not. Within this relationship the
parties developed a deep sense of obligation, support, encourage-
ment, commitment, and even financial assistance toward one
another.[19] The institution of informal adoption, on the other hand,
guaranteed that children within an extended family circle were
always assured of a home, food, and basic necessities regardless of

whatever misfortunes might befall the immediate family. Within this structure children were easily and frequently transferred from one family to another, often in attempts to relieve financial burdens.

Within these significant institutions in the family system, members of a nuclear family developed close bonds with non-kin individuals. These customs proved essential to the survival of the infant New York community. First, the attitudes regarding children and childcare customs aided the enlargement of family networks at a time when the numbers of nuclear family households in the city predominated and when these families were struggling to gain a foothold in the new environment. Second, childcare facilitated the formation of intimate friendships, if not ritual kinship. These personal contacts based on common language, heritage, and customs encouraged and maintained a social structure in the early settlements which perpetuated Puerto Rican values and interests. Third, with the enlargement of the family network and the cementing of relationships through ritual kinship, a support system was created for periods of crisis. During times of financial stress, job or housing scarcities, or family illness, there were now people to whom they could turn. The extended family unit which had been so important in Puerto Rico, and which would not appear en masse until the great migration, was being recreated in the New York settlements.

One migrant, Doña Eliza, for example, commented on the close relationships which frequently developed through the practice of minding children, an experience common for many who worked in this area. She arrived in New York in 1930 and spent most of her thirty-year residency caring for the children of others. Genuinely fond of children, her home was almost always equipped with the paraphernalia of her trade, which included extra cribs, high chairs or playpens. As a result of her childcaring, close to twenty youngsters were placed in her home, six of whom became her godchildren.

Doña Elisa remembers her home as a haven for unfortunate children, and in two extreme cases she became the adoptive parent of *hijos de crianza*. She recalls one incident which dramatically sums up the amount of responsibility inherent in the business of childcare as it developed among the New York Puerto Ricans:

José Luis was only two years old when he came to live with us—I remember because my own children were seven and two at the time. We lived in a four room apartment in the South Bronx; my husband had a good job and he never objected to my bringing in extra children to mind during the week. From the beginning Joselito was different. He and my little girl, Titi, made fast friends right away. At first, I took care of him and his brother on a weekly basis from nine until about six in the evening. His mother, María, was forced to work as she was their only support. As the time went by, life became harder for María. She was in and out of jobs and very depressed about her life. I found myself keeping the boys longer and longer without pay. The older boy did not like to be left with me when his mother went to work but the little one, Joselito, thought I was his mother and he soon started to call me Mami just like my two girls did.

Once, on a snowy winter night, my brother-in-law who worked the night shift found the boys scantily dressed hanging around the Jackson Avenue El Station at 2 A.M. He recognized them as the boys I took care of and brought them to my house. That night they stayed with us and the next morning I told María a thing or two for leaving the children alone. She pleaded with me to keep the little one while she and her other son went away for a while — to get herself together — and I consented. I don't know where she went but from time to time I'd get a letter and some money for Joselito. I raised him as my own for more than one year. When she returned for him, my heart broke. Of all the children I've taken care of, he was my first and very favorite but I vowed never to get so attached again.[20]

TAKING IN LODGERS

As childcare provided supplementary incomes and strengthened bonds among New York Puerto Ricans, so did taking in lodgers. Census enumerations often designated Puerto Rican women as heads of households composed primarily of lodgers. Within the lodger group many newly arrived migrants sought accommodations in the homes of friends, relatives, or hometown acquaintances, and married couples or family units also boarded with one another.

Lodgers often came from the same hometown as the head of the household. Through friends and relations, migrants quickly discovered, in many cases before coming to New York, where they could obtain lodgings. The informational network previously described in connection with women's roles, along with the Latin tradition of hospitality expressed in the saying, *mi casa es su casa* (my home is your home) contributed to many migrants' successful quest for housing. In some cases multifamily or extended family dwellings were classified as households with lodgers, since the census takers listed but one household head. In reality, several families shared living space and expenses equally. Doña Julia, for instance, recalls sharing an apartment with her husband, baby, and her brother and his family during the Depression.

Sharing households either as lodgers or as heads of households with lodgers appeared to be a common experience among the women interviewed. Almost without exception, those women who migrated from Puerto Rico lived in New York residences as lodgers while those who were born in New York related tales of woe regarding the not infrequent unannounced arrival of some relative or hometown acquaintance. One woman stated, "We never knew when we left for school in the morning if our bedrooms would still be ours in the evening. Sleeping arrangements were in constant flux depending on how many people lived with us at any given time."[21] Doña Celia evoked a scene of childhood memories worth noting:

I remember as if it were yesterday. We lived on the first floor of a small apartment in the Bronx. We shared five rooms among the four of us—my parents and my younger sister, and myself, because a boarder, who was my father's cousin, Don Antonio, had just moved out after living with us for a number of years. That summer I was ten years old, starting to feel quite the young lady. My mother had recently decorated Don Antonio's old room for me in shades of pale blue. It was the tiniest room in the apartment but it was perfect for me.

I was the first one to answer the buzzer that September afternoon. From our apartment's front door you could see directly into the downstairs vestibule with its double row of bright metal mailboxes on both sides. The sun shone brightly into the area but did not obscure the couple standing there and the baby held in its mother's arms. They were an uncle I had never met, his wife, little more than a child herself, and their infant son. They had arrived without warning from Puerto Rico on the assumption that if there is room for one, there is always room for one more. My heart sank as I remembered my father's favorite value—you never turn away relatives, no matter how little you have for yourself. I knew instinctively they would be well received and my room with the matching blue spread and curtains would be given to them for as long as they needed it.[22]

Many women recalled meeting their future husbands as lodgers. Others became extremely attached to the friends they made in shared households continuing these relationships into the present often through ritual kinship systems. As early as 1925, 1,745 individuals or 23.8 percent out of 7,322 individuals listed in the census were classified as lodgers. Of these, males outnumbered females almost two to one. The majority of this population fell into the fifteen-through-forty-five age bracket as did 55.6 percent of the females and 64.2 percent of the males.[23] The lodger group, therefore, was in its most productive work years, often single, and represented the future household heads of the Puerto Rican communities. One interviewee, Doña Rosa remembered her experiences:

I came to live in my stepsister's house in 1926, when I was about twenty years old. Quite a few of my cousins were already there with wives and children—all living in my stepsister's house on 116th Street and Park Avenue. The household consisted of about fifteen people and each suitable bedroom was assigned to several of us. Most of us worked except for my stepsister who had youngsters and her sister who did all the cooking and cleaning for all of us. I started to work right away but never got used to the dirty winter darkness of the city. I earned about fifteen dollars weekly and paid six or seven dollars for my room out of that even though I hardly ate at the house. (This amount was for room and board.) On my days off, I'd go visit other relatives in the city and usually ate with them. I suppose now that I look back, that was an awful lot of money to pay for just a room but I was young with little responsibility and didn't know the value of money. Seven dollars went a very long way for me.

From this house I moved in with friends on 114th Street. At that time there were few Hispanics in this area. There was only one store which sold Hispanic articles. It was called Sefía and located on 113th Street and Fifth Avenue. As I recall there were few of us but we all lived in shared households until we married and set up our own homes. Then it was our turn to take in lodgers.[24]

It was not unusual for women migrants to make the ocean crossing alone, since they were met, for the most part, by relatives who had either invited them to come or were prepared to assume responsibility for them once they arrived. Doña Clara, a person who arrived almost a decade after Dona Rosa, recalled few changes in the customs and practice of lodgers. Her experience was similar to many others travelling the same road:

> My brother sent for me as he had been in New York several years and we both lived with a cousin on 144th Street. New York didn't really seem too oppressive to me, perhaps because I arrived during the summer months and people socialized outdoors all of the time. Afterwards, I moved into the home of friends from my hometown of Cabo Rojo and when my brother married, I was invited to live with them. I stayed in his home until I was married myself. Then I moved to the West Side.[25]

One individual, Doña Perfecta, added yet another dimension to the functioning of boarders within a household. From her position as the wife of the household head, her New York home became the base for relatives, siblings, and friends who migrated from her hometown. These migrant lodgers, intent on carving a niche for themselves as soon as they were able, contributed financially to Doña Perfecta's household, eventually leaving to form households of their own. But the relationship between household heads and lodgers did not disintegrate with the latter's leaving. These remained within the extended family circle, frequently developing into *compadrazgos*. Both Perfecta and her husband often stood as godparents of the children born to their ex-lodgers. On many occasions the home and family life of the receiving host family served as models for the type of home the lodgers established. One migrant particularly recalled the type of household established by her godparents, the first home her parents lived in as lodgers upon their arrival in the city.

> I still remember growing up surrounded by caring family members. It was our custom to spend holidays and Sundays together usually at my godparents' home. Many of my aunts and uncles began their stay in New York by living with my godparents as boarders. To me their home represented a symbol of what my own should be. I was always impressed with its cleanliness, orderliness and I guess you might say, middle class values. To us, they had "made it." But my earliest memories about their home was that we were always served dessert after dinner—a custom which I in my youthful innocense considered extraordinary![26]

Thus, lodgers added important aspects within the household structures of the pre-World War II *colonias.* Sometimes they were hometown friends or acquaintances; more often they were close or extended family members. The functions of lodgers within these households were crucial not only for the general survival of the *colonias,* but for the individual families as well. Lodgers kept open the networks of communication between the island and mainland enclaves; they contributed to the financial support of the household; and they enabled women especially, who frequently carried the full burden of providing room and board, to supplement the family's income. Moreover, through ritual kinship, lodgers expanded the familial network at a time when the Puerto Rican *colonias* were at their most vulnerable both in size and in keeping traditional values intact.

The practice of taking in boarders based on the purchase of room, board, and domestic services within an established household was not limited to Puerto Rican communities. Lodgers had resided in Jewish and Italian households since the turn of the century. In some instances the desirability of the geographic area in which a family resided determined the abundance of lodgers. One

Jewish family, for example, decided to return to Manhattan "where they could get lodgers more readily and thus eke out their income of four hundred dollars by an addition of one hundred and twenty dollars a year. Out of the earnings of five hundred and twenty dollars, one hundred and eighty-six—that is, fifteen dollars and fifty cents a month—had to be paid for rent."[27]

Similarly, black Harlem settlements disclosed the existence of enlarged households often containing kin and unmarried lodgers in the census records of 1915 and 1925:

> A large number were lodgers. Nearly three in ten women aged fifteen and older, for example, were lodgers or lived alone. . . . In 1925, just one in three West Indian and two in five native black households were nuclear in composition. About half of all black households had one or more lodgers in them and about one in five households had one or more relatives other than members of the immediate families.[28]

Interestingly, the census records for East and South Central Harlem households convey a sense of community and mutual support among the many ethnic groups inhabiting those areas, since Puerto Ricans were found living as lodgers in European or South American homes, while the latter held similar positions in Puerto Rican homes. However, after the thirties when large numbers of Puerto Ricans resided in the city, ethnic mixtures within the households appear to diminish.

WORKING OUTSIDE OF THE HOME

If migrant women faced with the need to provide supplementary or primary incomes attempted to combine familial values with modified income-producing enterprises, many more also maintained regard for the traditional role of the family but integrated themselves into the city's labor force. Close to 25 percent of the female migrant population participated in the labor force as cigar makers and domestics; typists and stenographers; in the needle-trades industries as operators and unskilled workers; in the laundries or restaurants; and in the fields as agricultural workers. The first reports of female factory and field workers appeared in newspapers and government documents around the turn of the twentieth century. Puerto Rican women were part and parcel of the migrant labor force contracted to work in various parts of the Western Hemisphere, in the process establishing communities in which cultural traditions and institutions would flourish.[29]

The twenties witnessed an increase in the numbers of Puerto Rican women working in New York factories. Skilled labor predominated in at least two industries traditionally associated with Puerto Ricans—the needle trades and the tobacco industry. Women were well represented in the cigar-making industry, not only among skilled and unskilled workers, but as readers in many of the New York factories.

During the same period, Spanish language journals and newspapers vigorously advertised in their classified sections for both skilled and unskilled garment workers. Want ads frequently called for sewing machine operators, workers in embroidery, in crocheting and lace, as pieceworkers in the home or in the factory. Advertising attracted the attention of job-seeking women. The following ad, typical for the period, appeared in 1923: "se necesitan mujeres que sepan manejar máquinas de coser; 44 horas a la semana; $20.00; bordaderas, operarias en casa, crochet y abalorios."[30]

By mid-decade more women were employed in the production end of private industry than in any other sector. Of the 3,496 women listed in the four sample districts, 600 or 17.2 percent were involved in factory work of some sort, as operatives, dressmakers, or seamstresses. One hundred and fifty-six or 4.5 percent labored in services including laundries or restaurants while 118 or 3.4 percent worked in jobs requiring an exchange of money such as bookkeeping, sales, or as cashiers. About sixteen, or 0.5 percent, supervised or owned their own businesses, and a mere handful worked in the public sector, in the post office, or in other city agencies.[31]

However, participation in the labor force presented difficulties for many women workers. Among these were the necessity to communicate effectively in the English language and to negotiate the sometimes troublesome intricacies of transportation in the city. While many had been taught English in Puerto Rican schools, they were unprepared for the idiomatic, dialectical, and sometimes accented English encountered in New York. A command of English became essential for the Spanish-speaking working woman and

many hoped to perfect their knowledge of the language by attending night school. One pioneer, Doña Petra, emphasized the importance of language in her early experiences in the city by stating:

> At first, I enrolled in high school to learn English but before
> graduating, I was forced to get a job. School was not difficult
> for me because as you know, in Puerto Rico we had been
> taught in English and Spanish, so I could understand a great
> deal when I came here. The greatest difference was in pro-
> nunciation because Americans usually slur their words. When
> I arrived there were pathetically few Hispanics living in the ci-
> ty. An Italian woman whom I had met in Puerto Rico but
> who was now in New York got me my first job. I became a
> packer in a candy factory and I soon realized I was the only
> Puerto Rican employee there. Can you imagine what a lonely
> feeling; to have people speak to you and not to understand
> and not be able to communicate in everyday situations? From
> that time I purposely set out to get a command of the lan-
> guage (a la brava aprendí el inglés). Within a short time I was
> able to defend myself in English and then it was I who took
> the newcomers all over the city in search of jobs, houses or
> whatever.[32]

Some women minimized language difficulties and emphasized
appearance as the greatest deterrent to gainful employment. Discrimination against Puerto Ricans, especially if they were black,
radically curtailed job opportunities. "If you looked Irish or Ger-
man," explained one respondent, "it didn't matter how limited
your English was. Most jobs were on assembly lines and it didn't
take much talking to learn the procedure." Frequent descriptions
of discrimination on the basis of color and language continued
throughout the period. Almost all of the workers interviewed related tales of this nature.[33]

Transportation problems, on the other hand, presented relatively
fewer problems since jobs were often found through the intercession of friends and relatives. One account, for example, suggested
the typical pattern followed in seeking employment rested on a personal relationship where a fellow lodger or relative took the new

migrant to make the rounds. Some revealed there were jobs await-
ing them when they disembarked at the Brooklyn or Manhattan
piers. Others conceded they waited at least a week before working.

> My first job in 1926 was at a candy factory. Luis, a young
> man who lodged in my stepsister's house, took me to the fac-
> tory. It was located on Eleventh Street and Ninth Avenue. I
> remember I had to ride two trolleys to get there from where I
> lived. This is the kind of work I did. Do you know what
> Seven-Elevens were? Have you ever heard them mentioned
> before? This was a confection made out of peanuts with a
> caramel or sugar center and I would take this piece of candy,
> mold it in my hand, soak it in syrup then roll it in nuts again.
> Then we would weigh the pieces by hand. If it felt right we
> would package it; if not, we'd take a little off the end. I don't
> think that candy exists anymore.
>   After that I went to work in Washington—not D.C. but
> Washington Street in Brooklyn. What I did there was make
> parts for luggage or suitcases. It was difficult in the beginning
> to find jobs you really liked. We worked in that place for the
> money. Forty-four hours a week to earn six, seven or eight
> dollars a week. There were no unions to protect us and no
> taxes. And sometimes, we worked forty-eight hours a week
> for the same pay. After I became more skilled, I earned about
> thirteen dollars a week. Eventually I went to work in *costura*
> (the needle trades) but that was after I married in the thirties.[34]

Some interviewees, however, felt the period of the thirties and
especially the forties offered greater diversity in the kind of work
available to women, although mainly within the blue-collar occupations. In 1936, for example, Doña Mary worked as a seamstress
and later in a drapery factory for ten dollars a week. Within that
decade she also worked the evening shift in a defense plant and
again as a seamstress when the war ended.[35] In 1930 the Department of Labor of Puerto Rico established an employment service in
response to the growing number of migrants living in the city. Over
a six-year period, about six hundred women obtained job place-
ments through this agency.[36] Approximately 42 percent were employed as domestics while needleworkers, hand sewers and factory

workers comprised an almost equal percentage. Of all the Puerto Rican women workers who applied to this agency, roughly 80 percent found work as operatives or in domestic services. Although jobs were at a premium during this decade, the bureau's activities indicate the types of work available to Puerto Ricans, and these continued to be among the blue-collar sector.

Regardless of the type of work in which Puerto Rican women participated, the family remained uppermost in their minds, and work continued to be a necessity in order to maintain family unity. Women persisted in rationalizing their role in the work world as a natural extension of their home and family life. To work was not considered a luxury embarked upon to prove one's equality or to challenge or change in any way, traditional roles within the family. Doña Margarita, for example, best summed up this attitude in describing her experience in New York during the period of the forties. The first year of their New York residency found the family dependent on home relief due to her husband's unforeseen illness. As soon as she could confidently leave the home, after guiding her children into a familiar routine within the home structure, she returned to work. This woman took great pride in eventually repaying all the money the family had received from home relief.

> I accepted a job doing general factory work because I had to help my husband support us all. I folded handkerchiefs; I did everything that needed doing in the shop; I cleaned machines or cleaned the floor if it had to be done. My philosophy was that I would even clean latrines—because I did this in my own home—if I was getting paid. After a few months my husband returned to his job and I quit mine to stay at home with the children. But he wasn't able to make any more than seventy-five dollars to feed and dress six people. When our four children needed clothing, it presented hardships—four at one blow, without any outside help! Our children needed so much that I decided to return to work.
>
> My boys were getting older, more responsible and my girl was a tremendous help—very serious, honest and mature. They took care of one another. During the day when I was in the factory, I trusted them to look after one another. When I returned in the evenings, I took care of household duties. I

had Saturdays to clean house, buy groceries and wash clothes. Then I had Sundays . . . Saturdays and Sundays to do my things and Monday to return to work.[37]

WHITE COLLAR, PROFESSIONALS, AND VOLUNTEERS

While the majority of the female migrant community worked as skilled or unskilled blue-collar laborers, a handful, usually skilled, bilingual, or educated women wrested a foothold in other occupations. Some became known for their dedication to volunteer or creative work necessary for shaping their community. Others worked in clerical positions. The contributions of these few have often been overlooked. Yet as professionals or as white-collar workers, as *colonia* activists, as feminists, or as artists, this handful appeared before the public eye, serving as spokespersons, as role models, or as objects of emulation for the broader, working-class base. These were the women who held jobs which required some degree of academic preparation; who made possible the functioning of community organizations which in turn helped structure the early settlements; who wrote for the magazines read in the *colonia*. Within the latter group, many maintained contacts with their peers in Puerto Rico or Spanish America, essentially linking class interests across the ocean. Thus, in spite of their limited numbers, the group played a part in the formation of perspectives and predelections of the overall community.

Sister Carmelita Bonilla, a case in point, represented Puerto Rican womanhood among the religious, as the first Trinitarian nun from Puerto Rico. She arrived in the city as a teenager enroute to Georgia where she took her vows. As a nun she was assigned to a Brooklyn convent. Her new responsibilities required involvement in social welfare, housing, educational and vocational counseling, public health, and religious education. Her recollections evoke memories of a poor community, where she was frequently called upon as a translator and as an intermediary between the Spanish-speaking settlement and the wider, non-Hispanic society. Youngsters of that period credit Sister Carmelita with directly encouraging their academic growth and aspirations. Her own education included earning a bachelor's and a master's degree. As one of the founders of the early settlement house, Casita María, she continued to direct and influence the social, cultural, and educational welfare of the early migrants.[38]

Doctora Eloísa García Rivera, on the other hand, made her mark in politics and in higher education. A university graduate upon her arrival in the city, Doña Eloísa completed graduate work in Spanish literature and dedicated herself to community services. Firmly adhering to the traditional philosophy that women should be helpmates to their spouses, she contributed time and energy to her husband's bid for the Albany legislature by campaigning and directing voter registration drives on his behalf.[39]

Yet a different perspective appears in the case of Honorina Irizarry who came to live in her brother's comfortable Brooklyn home during the twenties. An accomplished secretary with B.F. Goodrich in Puerto Rico, Doña Honorina had studied and perfected her clerical skills before undertaking the move. Once in the Brooklyn *colonia,* determined to work, use her mind and skills, she sought employment against the wishes of her family who considered working "unladylike." In her own words she recalls:

> One day I saw an ad in the newspaper for a bilingual secretary/ stenographer. I applied for the position but withheld this information from my sister and brother. The office was located across from City Hall. The trolley cars used to pass City Hall from Brooklyn so I had no trouble finding the office building and the company which placed the ad. When I arrived, they gave me an interview and dictation in both Spanish and English and asked me to translate for them. I got the position without any difficulty and that's how I started my work career in New York.[40]

Doña Honorina was an exceptional woman for her time. She studied at Erasmus Hall High School at night while she continued to work days, mastered five languages fluently, and eventually earned a liberal arts degree. Clearly, Doña Honorina's past experiences in Puerto Rico directly molded her subsequent activities in New York, as was the case with many of the women found in this category. In time Doña Honorina participated also in the political organizations of the Brooklyn settlement where her position within the community afforded her a degree of leadership as well.

Finally, one individual who epitomizes the professional, organizational, and well educated woman was Doña Josefina Silva de Cintrón. She began her career as an elementary school teacher in

Puerto Rico. Distinguished as a community leader in the island, Doña Josefina was also credited with establishing the first Post Office in Hato Rey, Puerto Rico, working with the Red Cross and with various other organizations. In the journalistic field, she collaborated with feminist Mercedes Sola in the publication of a journal, *La mujer en el siglo XX,* and contributed to the literary arena as a writer.[41]

Successful enterprises also followed in New York where Doña Josefina pursued similar intellectual inclinations and took part in a variety of social, political, and cultural community organizations. Among the latter were the *Unión de mujeres Americanas* and the League of Spanish-speaking Democrats. But perhaps her foremost contribution was the creation of the monthly journal, cited in previous chapters, *Revista de Artes y Letras.*

Conclusion

The integration of Puerto Rican women into the economic mainstream of the United States and particularly in New York City requires more intensive exploration and interpretation not merely in terms of their relationship to the non-Hispanic world, but also in their relationship to their respective communities. Migration and work did not produce major changes in their roles within Puerto Rican society, for the image of dutiful wives, loving mothers, and respectful sisters and daughters remained paramount to their way of thinking. Neither did changes occur in the work world to which they were committed, since they neither demanded nor were given the opportunity to control strategic resources or educational facilities.

Only a handful became factory foreladies or union representatives, and fewer owned their own establishments. A small group assumed the reins of community leadership, volunteer work, professional, or clerical endeavors. Through group work and involvement, they were frequently in the public eye, their actions reported in the presses of the early *colonias.* In most fields, however, decision making remained male-dominated and organizations male-oriented. Yet subtle messages were filtering down to younger generations. Women worked; women were wives and mothers; women were involved.

Notes

1. Estelle M. Smith, "Network and Migration Resettlement: Cherchez la Femme," *Anthropological Quarterly* vol. 49, no. 1 (January 1979), pp. 20–27. See also Clarence Senior and Donald O. Watkins, "Towards a Balance Sheet of Puerto Rican Migration," in U.S.-P.R. Commission on the Status of Puerto Rico, *Status of Puerto Rico: Selected Background Studies* (Washington, D.C.: Government Printing Office, 1966), p. 706.

2. New York State Manuscript Census, 1925, Assembly Districts 16, 17, 18, 19. New York City Hall of Records, Municipal Building. See also History Task Force, Centro de Estudios Puertorriqueños, *Migration Under Capitalism: The Puerto Rican Experience* (New York: Monthly Review Press, 1979), pp. 147–149.

3. New York State Manuscript Census, 1925.

4. Herbert Gutman, *The Black Family in Slavery and Freedom, 1750–1925* (New York: Pantheon Press, 1979), p. 153.

5. Interview with Margarita Hernández, Mayaguez, Puerto Rico, July 1977.

6. In Puerto Rico women became essential to the labor force particularly as piece workers and in the needle-trades industry as early as 1910. A decade later they constituted close to 25 percent of the island's work force. See Celia Fernández Cintrón and Marcia Rivera Quintero, "Bases de la sociedad sexista en Puerto Rico," *Revista/Review Interamericana* vol. 4, no. 2 (summer 1974), pp. 239–249. See also Marcia Rivera Quintero, "Capitalist Development and the Incorporation of Women to the Labour Force" (paper presented at the Latin American Studies Association Conference on April 6, 1979, Pittsburgh, Pennsylvania). Isabel Picó de Hernández, "Estudio sobre el empleo de la mujer en Puerto Rico," *Revista de Ciencias Sociales* vol. 19, no. 2 (June 1975), pp. 141–144.

7. Rivera Quintero, p. 16. See also Caroline Manning, *The Employment of Women in Puerto Rico* (Washington, D.C.: Government Printing Office, 1934).

8. Lawrence R. Chenault, *The Puerto Rican Migrant in New York City* (New York: Columbia University Press, 1938; reissue, Russell & Russell, 1970), p. 76. See also Rinker Buck, "The New Sweat Shops: A Penny for Your Collar," *New York* vol. 12, no. 5 (January 29, 1979), pp. 40–46.

9. Interview with María Bonilla, New York City, summer 1976.

10. Interview with Julia González, Rio Piedras, Puerto Rico, July 1977.

11. Interview with Clara Rodríguez, Cabo Rojo, Puerto Rico, July 1977.

12. Chenault, *The Puerto Rican Migrant,* pp. 69–88. In 1914 the average "real" weekly wages in the United States was $10.73. This rose to $13.14 in 1926. For unionized trades during the same period, it increased from $8.22 to $23.94; miners, from $11.56 to $15.03; printers, from $19.67 to $21.63.

See Samuel Eliot Morrison, *The Oxford History of the American People,* vol. 3 (New York: New American Library, 1972), pp. 234–237.

13. Margarita Hernández interview.

14. Lourdes Miranda King, "Puertorriqueñas in the United States," Commission of Human Rights, *Civil Rights Digest* (Washington, D.C., spring 1974), p. 23. See also Rosemary Santana Cooney and Alice Colón Warren, "Work and Family: The Recent Struggle of Puerto Rican Females," in Clara E. Rodríguez, Virginia Sánchez Korrol, and José Oscar Alers, eds., *The Puerto Rican Struggle: Essays on Survival in the U.S.* (New York: Puerto Rican Migration Research Consortium, 1980), pp. 58–73.

15. New York State Manuscript Census, 1925.

16. Gutman, *The Black Family,* pp. 455–456. These findings are comparable with black households in central Harlem where the typical Afro-American family consisted of two-parent households. "The two-parent household was not limited to better-advantaged Afro-Americans," wrote Gutman in his study.

17. Welfare Council of New York City, *Puerto Ricans in New York City* (New York, 1948).

18. Interview with Celina Santiago, Brooklyn, New York, summer 1976.

19. Joseph P. Fitzpatrick, *Puerto Rican–Americans* (Englewood Cliffs, N.J.: Prentice-Hall, 1971), pp. 81–82. See also Kal Wagenheim, *Puerto Rico: A Profile* (New York: Praeger Press, 1970), pp. 189–190.

20. Interview with Elisa Baeza, Mayaguez, Puerto Rico, July 1977.

21. Interview with Celia Santiago, Brooklyn, New York, 1977.

22. Celia Santiago interview.

23. New York State Manuscript Census, 1925.

24. Interview with Rosa Roma, Santurce, Puerto Rico, August 1977.

25. Clara Rodríguez interview.

26. Celia Santiago interview.

27. Irving Howe, *The World of Our Fathers* (New York: Harcourt, Brace, Jovanovich, 1976), p. 132.

28. Gutman, *The Black Family,* pp. 453–4.

29. *New York Times,* "The Porto Rican Exodus," April 4, 1901, cited in History Task Force, Centro de Estudios Puertorriqueños, *Documentos de la migración Puertorriqueña, 1879–1901* (New York: Centro de Estudios Puertorriquenos, Research Foundation of the City University of New York, 1977), p. 32.

30. *La Prensa,* vol. 8, July 21, 1919, p. 463.

31. Interviews with Antonio and Raquel Hernández Rivera, Rio Piedras, Puerto Rico, August 1977. Also Julia González interview.

32. Interviews with Petra and Valentín Negrón, Rio Piedras, Puerto Rico, August 1977.

33. Rosa Roma interview.

34. Ibid.

35. Interview with Mary Geraldini, Levittown, Puerto Rico, July 1977.

36. Chenault, *The Puerto Rican Migrant,* pp. 79–84.

37. Margarita Hernández interview. See also Nancie L. González, "Multiple Migratory Experiences of Dominican Women," *Anthropological Quarterly* vol. 49, no. 1 (January 1979), pp. 36–43, for a comparative view toward work and family life in New York City.

38. Interview with Sister Carmelita Bonilla, Puerto Rican Oral History Project, Long Island Historical Society, Brooklyn, New York. See also Anthony Stevens Arroyo, "Puerto Rican Struggles in the Catholic Church," in Clara E. Rodríguez, Virginia Sánchez Korrol, and José Oscar Alers, eds., *The Puerto Rican Struggle.*

39. Interview with Eloísa García Rivera, New York City, 1977.

40. Interview with Honorina Weber Irizarry, Puerto Rican Oral History Project.

41. Interview with Josefina Silva de Cintrón, New York City, 1977. See also Virginia Sánchez Korrol, "Between Two Worlds — Educated Puerto Rican Migrant Women of the Early Settlements" (paper presented at the 14th Annual Conference of Caribbean Historians, San Juan, Puerto Rico, April 1981).

Plates

PLATE 1 Puerto Rican migrant woman,
New York City, circa 1927. Courtesy of Mrs. Helen
Guzman Steffens, Centerreach, New York.

PLATE 2 Formal portrait of
woman migrant, circa 1927.
Author's private collection.

PLATE 3 Woman and children on board the
Borinquen, circa 1930. Courtesy of Mrs. Clara
Rodriguez, Cabo Rojo, Puerto Rico.

PLATE 4 Family group on board ship, late 1930s.
Courtesy of Mrs. Clara Rodriguez, Cabo Rojo,
Puerto Rico.

PLATE 5 Formal portrait of Antonio Sanchez
Feliciano, New York City, circa 1930. Author's
private collection.

PLATE 6 Formal portrait of Elisa Santiago Baeza
in New York City, circa 1930. Author's private
collection.

PLATE 7 Puerto Rican children on Manhattan
rooftop, circa 1930. Courtesy of Mrs. Helen
Guzman Steffens, Centerreach, New York.

PLATE 8 Mother and first-born
child in New York City's Central
Park, circa 1940. Courtesy of
Mrs. Clara Rodriguez, Cabo
Rojo, Puerto Rico.

PLATE 9 Family gathering in Central Park, circa 1940. Also courtesy of Mrs. Clara Rodriguez.

PLATE 10 Musical trio entertaining at a house
party, circa 1945. Courtesy of Mrs. Helen Steffens,
Centerreach, New York.

Organizational Activities Among Puerto Ricans in New York City Settlements

For Puerto Ricans in New York City, the first decades of the twentieth century provided a significant degree of group involvement which reinforced and redefined the community image of the Spanish-speaking neighborhoods. Associations formed which acclimated incoming migrants to their new environments, allowed them to participate in group activities based on common interests, and represented the *colonias* before the host society. Group formation proliferated as the settlements increased in population aiding both the structure and survival of the early communities as identifiable Puerto Rican entities and confronting those issues which most affected them. Some groups concerned themselves with education, culture, or social service needs within a continental context; others functioned as buffers between the wider non-Hispanic society and the Spanish-speaking enclaves, seeking to represent the *colonias* during critical periods or on a city-wide basis.

Yet the issue of the existence of organizational structures among Puerto Ricans has often been debated; the value of such community networks, as well as the potential leadership with they fostered, was a controversial point. Some scholars, such as Elena Padilla or Lawrence Chenault, who wrote about New York Puerto Ricans before and after the Second World War, observed group activity among Puerto Ricans, but failed to explore the subject in depth.[1] While social scientists argue the pros and cons of Puerto Rican

organizational structure, most agree it is a topic about which little
has been written.

A Review of the Literature on Puerto Rican Organizations

Perhaps Moynihan and Glazer best typify those fostering a concept of limited communal development. In their popular work the
authors repeatedly not only call attention to an apparent shortcom-
ing in cultural organizational action on behalf of the migrant community, but allude as well to what they interpret as a lack of leadership. Lacking information for the pre-World War II period,
Moynihan and Glazer begin their discussion with the post-war
period: "In 1948, only six percent of the migrants belonged to
Puerto Rican organizations, somewhat more men than women and
more of the older migrants than recent arrivals." Moreover, the
authors refer to "many social organizations, based on places of
origin," but judge these to be less important and inferior when
compared with the associations of earlier immigrant groups.[2]
Moynihan and Glazer believed the relative weakness of neighborhood organization and community leadership was characteristic of
Puerto Ricans in New York. The working-class composition of the
pre-World War II migration, furthermore, encouraged the alienation of the community's few professionals from their fellow Puerto
Ricans, inhibiting also the creation of associations or emergence of
leadership among the early groups. On these themes Glazer and
Moynihan raised more questions than they answered, and they
failed to grasp the significance of the groups which they did
observe. Among these were the neighborhood or hometown groups
which served as orientation facilitators for incoming migrants.
Their structure was often not unlike that of the hometown societies
in operation among the Jews and Italians of the earlier period.[3]
More important, the authors ignored completely other types of
organizations in existence at that time.

Similarly, Donald Stewart's short history of the Harlem community which appeared in 1972, supported the Glazer and Moynihan
thesis.[4] While acknowledging a rapid intensive concentration of
Puerto Rican migrants in Spanish Harlem, the belief continued to
be that Puerto Ricans had not progressed to the point of effectively
organizing for any purpose. The author reported, "Except for the

Jewish-Italian Socialist movement in the twenties and thirties, the black and Hispanic communities were not represented by organized politically oriented committees until the 1950s."[5]

More recently, historian Adalberto López recognized the existence and potential of early Puerto Rican associations, but admittedly lacked sufficient evidence on their structure and modes of operation to evaluate their roles effectively within the Spanish-speaking settlements. Lopez believed groups emerged to cope with some of the social and economic problems affecting early *colonias,* but these units "rarely drew national attention or funds and ordinarily limited themselves to asking for small and inadequate funds from urban government."[6] López, however, offered one possible suggestion to explain the apparent lack of organizational involvement. "Throughout the 1950s more and more Puerto Rican workers joined labor unions but within these unions they were discriminated against and rarely enjoyed any power or influence."[7] While López skillfully assessed the situation for the period under scrutiny, he makes no mention of union organization among Puerto Ricans before the 1950s. How much experience did Puerto Ricans have with unions or labor movements before coming to New York City and to what degree was this reflected in the early associations?

Significantly, an important source for the early period used by many researchers was Lawrence Chenault's study on the Puerto Rican migrant. His work, considered groundbreaking for the period before the Second World War, offered valuable insight into communal organizational activity. Although he neglected to draw a connection between organizations in Puerto Rico and associations in the migrant settlements, or between Latin and non-Latin groups in the city, his description of Puerto Rican societies is among the first to appear in print. Referring to the hometown or neighborhood clubs, Chenault observed numerous social organizations were in operation for a variety of reasons ranging from groups favoring independence for Puerto Rico to others operating as social outlets for small groups of people from particular cities or towns on the island. Many of these sponsored dances in a number of halls suitable for this purpose. Of the smaller groups, few appeared to be permanent and many were constantly broken up to be formed again into new units.[8] The fact that associations were constantly being broken up suggests either that the groups were rather immature in the ways of maintaining an organization; that members were not committed enough; or that the group's membership needs were not satisfied.[9] While we may speculate on the motivation behind Chenault's observation, it remains clear that new associations *were* constantly being formed. Did the new groups rely on new leadership as well or were they composed of the same membership under a new name? What degree of organizational experience existed among the early migrants and what connection, if any, was kept with island counterparts? While Chenault viewed organizational activity as either socially or politically oriented, he failed to investigate the wide range of purposes for which groups formed and he was unable to provide insights into community leadership within an organizational structure.

However, Rosa Estades, a sociologist, does address the issue of leadership within the *colonias* throughout the decade of the thirties.[10] Examining group structure, she describes socially, culturally, and politically active settlements, particularly in the East Harlem section of Manhattan. Here groups formed based on common interests and/or experiences. Financing came from membership dues. Most of the organizers met in members' living rooms, with the exception of a few who met in hotel suites. Estades lists thirty-three organizations composed predominantly of Puerto Rican membership, even though other Spanish-speaking individuals finding familiarity and communalism based on language and culture were also welcomed.[11] Estades does draw a connection between club leaders and local non-Hispanic political groups, stating that the Spanish-speaking leaders were often sought out as contacts with the early *colonias*. With regard to the connections between island and mainland Puerto Rican groups, Estades believed a connection indeed existed based on issues, styles, and experiences, but that the New York groups did not depend on Puerto Rico either in terms of finances nor in bargaining for their political situation with the New York political leaders.[12] Was this the case with all types of New York Puerto Rican associations? Estades focused mainly on political participation and her descriptions of social, cultural, or civic groups offered limited historical reconstruction and analysis.

One report which not only recognized the significance of social and cultural associations confirming also their existence in the New York area over several decades was *A Study of Poverty Conditions in the New York Puerto Rican Community.*[13] Although references are made to group activity during the mid-sixties, the report's descriptions of hometown associations provided excellent examples of Puerto Rican social units and are not unlike descriptions found for the pre-World War II period. For example:

> On Sunday in New York one can wander into hundreds of "Hometown Club" meetings, where members gather from every part of the city to spend their leisure day together, eating, playing cards, making plans for future activities, or talking over old—and new—times. These and other similar groups have helped the family in its role to cushion the individual in the face of adversity. There are many church clubs that have various extra-religious functions, a small number of private social agencies and federated citizen's groups.[14]

Here, the role of the organization as broker between Hispanic resident and the wider society becomes obvious. With few exceptions, the groups in operation during the late fifties and early sixties were extensions of similar associations of an earlier period.

Models of Puerto Rican Organizations

An examination of group formation between the turn of the century and the decade of the forties revealed many organizations emerged based on common interests or relevant issues. Within this period at least three types of associations predominated. The first, the mutual aid societies of the early decades, patterned themselves on island counterparts, addressing migrant needs in New York as enthusiastically as they had previously served the community in Puerto Rico. In time, these attempted to organize the working-class *colonia* into trade unions affiliated with those on the island and on the mainland.

By the mid-twenties another type of organization emerged representing migrant settlements before the non-Hispanic community. These groups, exemplified by the Porto Rican Brotherhood of America, embodied some of the characteristics of the earlier mutual aid groups, but equally emphasized cultural values and traditions and responded to more immediate issues and concerns affecting Puerto Ricans in New York or in Puerto Rico. Yet another type of association characterized the decades of the thirties and forties. These were societies appealing to common interests of subgroups within the *colonias* and often lacked a cultural or community vision. Based on professional or occupational needs, these emerged as special-interest or single-issue associations. An example of this third model was the Post Office Workers' Organization. What were the issues which concerned the different types of organizations in operation over a period of several decades and how did they respond? As important, why did these groups come into being and how did they operate? A survey of several representative organizations provides some answers.

The earliest groups to function in New York Puerto Rican settlements were the mutual aid societies established by pioneer migrant tobacco workers in Manhattan's Lower East Side and Chelsea district. Based on similar groups operating among the urban artisans of Puerto Rico, the concept of self-help organizations came into New York harbor along with the first working-class representatives. When the *Federación Libre de Trabajadores,* tacitly recognized as the island's first central craft union, came into being in 1899, artisan group organizations based on common needs and interests had already been in existence on the island for several decades.[15] *Gremios,* patterned on the Spanish guild system, limited competition, regulated artisan markets, controlled conditions of employment, and provided fairs for the exchange of merchandise. *Cofradías* and *Hermandades* provided medical and hospital aid, raised dowries or ransoms, supplied burial, social, or religious services for its members. It was the *Hermandades,* for example, which supplied the monies to emancipate the slaves during the last third of the century. Based on occupational common interests, the groups dealt with the material needs of their members. In tragedy, death, or illness, the *Cofradías* and *Hermandades* both pledged support for the stricken family. Vying with one another in the grandiosity of the celebrations honoring their patron saints, the groups combined religious purposes with social services.[16]

The experience of skilled workers on the island, particularly in fostering labor movements, promoting strikes, and forming guild-like associations would stand to benefit the early workers' organizations in the New York *colonias.* Included in their collective history were the initiation of militant labor movements begun well before 1898, the strike and syndicalist ideology. Strikes, the most effective working-class weapon, became an integral part of labor movements in Puerto Rico well before the Spanish-American War. About the same time, urban artisans including printers, tinsmiths, carpenters, cigar makers, painters, typesetters, and shoemakers became influenced by European radical, anarcho-syndicalist ideas. Within this climate, study circles formed to analyze and propagate the new ideology based on working-class solidarity. Radical newspapers appeared and regional federations of the workers' international movement motivated the conversion of guild-like organizations into trade unions in the island's three or four principal urban centers.[17] These then incorporated within the larger *Federación Libre de Trabajadores* and subsequently affiliated with the American Federation of Labor.

The labor-related activities of the Puerto Rican workers were further enriched by familiarity with and knowledge of North American and international labor movements. It was precisely in the arena of labor organization and participation as well as in the commitment to socialist ideas that Puerto Ricans most resembled European and South American workers. Affiliation with the American Federation of Labor brought Puerto Ricans into contact with North American labor issues while information shared through the practice of *la lectura,* the traditional reading period in the island's tobacco factories, highlighted international workers' struggles within an organizational context. Concern for the problems of all of the working people as a class, regardless of national origin, would foster a degree of camaraderie between the various workers' groups in New York City. Thus when the Puerto Rican workers became the migrants of the early *colonias,* they were adequately prepared to continue working-class struggles in New York City. As skilled workers, especially cigar makers, were well represented among the city's earliest migrants, it was not unusual that groups such as mutual aid societies and trade unions associated with this segment of the working population in Puerto Rico would also flourish in the New York settlements.

The trade unions most patronized by the early Puerto Rican migrants in New York City were *La Internacional,* affiliated with the American Federation of Labor, and *La Resistencia.* Most of the

Spanish-speaking tobacco workers belonged to the latter. *La Internacional's* membership closely followed the basic guidelines set forth by North American trade unionism including collective bargaining, better working conditions, and wages, but excluded support for social revolution or the formation of a worker's party. *La Resistencia,* on the other hand, considered itself more revolutionary, favoring principles of Latin American anarcho-syndicalist organization. In a pre-welfare environment, these unions became instrumental in fostering benefits for the Spanish-speaking working class. They also succeeded in nurturing the formation of mutual aid societies and cultural units similar in operation and purpose to those which coexisted alongside or within trade unions on the island.[18]

Based in New York City and responding to pioneer migrants' material and supportive needs, *La Aurora, La Razón,* and *El Ejemplo* were three such organizations. Cigar maker Bernardo Vega asserted that these groups along with the trade unions were the only active Hispanic associations in New York City following the decline of Antillean immigration at the conclusion of the Spanish-American War. He based his assertion on personal community involvement, observation, and on conversations held with senior workers in the industry. One interview taken with a fellow tobacco worker who had resided in New York since 1913 yielded the following information:

> There did not exist exclusively Puerto Rican societies but the tobacco workers had mutual aid organizations such as *La Aurora, La Razón, El Ejemplo.* . . . The educative circles were always of anarchist ideology with the exception of the *Círculo de trabajadores* in Brooklyn which admitted workers of diverse ideologies. The trade unions were the *Internacional* of Tobacco Workers and the *Resistencia.* . . . In my neighborhood there was a club called *El Tropical* which sponsored dances and celebrated conferences from time to time. . . . On the West Side, I remember that Dr. Henna presided over the Club *Ibero-americano.*[19]

The *Círculo de Trabajadores* mentioned in the interview suggests that some socialist-oriented Puerto Rican affiliation may have existed between tobacco workers and others of related ideologies. This organization, originating in the nineteenth century, was supposed to be the exception "which admitted workers of diverse ideologies." It is not known whether this group was founded by Spanish-speaking cigar makers, along the lines of the mutual aid societies, or patterned after the popular Jewish Workmen's Circle, supported by working-class socialists, as the name implies. If it was indeed modeled after the Jewish Workmen's Circle, did this mean a degree of reciprocity existed between Puerto Ricans and non-Hispanics? While answers are merely speculative, one cigar maker who frequented the *Círculo* described it as an Hispanic association patronized predominantly by tobacco workers of that period, regardless of ethnic background, who shared common interests as the working class of the trade (see chapter 6 for discussion of political groups of that period).[20]

Another group frequented by Puerto Rican tobacco workers and functioning similarly to the Workmen's Circle was the *Círculo de Tabaqueros*. Originating in Brooklyn around the turn of the century, the *Círculo* along with the Francisco Ferrar y Guardia School located at 107th Street near Park Avenue, provided a meeting center for tobacco workers and their families. It operated like a European casino, a mixture of social organizations and philosophical forum. Many who frequented that organization favored progressive or radical ideas, openly identifying themselves as anarchists, socialists, or leftist republicans. A typical gathering at the headquarters of this association found individuals participating in recreational group activities, playing chess, dominoes, or conversing in small groups. Topics of interest ranged from discussions of current events to the planning of forthcoming projects. On a typical Sunday afternoon, visitors might be treated to a series of formal presentations, for example, Spanish language interpretations of Russian playwrights such as Chekov and Gorky, or informal presentations including lectures and workshops. Refreshments and light snacks were also available. One afternoon in particular, the following series of lectures were presented, a testimony to the great variety of an afternoon's entertainment:

> The particular day which I am remembering, Carlos Tresca, director of the newspaper *Il Martele,* spoke in Italian on

"Anarchism and Darwinian Theory"; Elizabeth Gurley Flynn spoke in English on "Utopian Communities and Free Will"; Pedro Esteves spoke in Spanish on "War and Peace and the Role of the Proletariat"; and Frank Kelly, a Catholic anarchist, spoke also in Spanish on "Jesus Christ, the First Communist." Discussions were followed by a question and answer period.[21]

In presenting lecture series and discussions on a variety of social issues, the *Círculo de Tabaqueros* was following an international pattern long established among Puerto Rico's skilled workers, as well as among other immigrant groups in New York. First, the study circles connected with the birth of the island's labor movement and the subsequent foundation of the trade union, *Federación Libre de Trabajadores,* used the lecture and discussion model in much the same way as the presentations of the *Círculo.* Second, the Latin practice of employing a reader in the tobacco factories of Puerto Rico and New York similarly engaged the lecture and discussion method. Here readers devoted the morning's session to the dissemination of factual material, news of the day, and cablegraphic information. The afternoon's reading session included literary or philosophical studies followed by a lively period of discussions. Third, passion for lectures similarly infused the earlier immigrant residents of the Lower East Side, setting a precedent in ethnic settlements for this type and method of communication. In New York City scores of lectures were advertised in the local presses, in many languages, and on a variety of topics. Historical or literary themes often followed lectures on trade unionism or religion. Many were scheduled for weekends in consideration for the working-class composition of the audience. Sometimes a fee of ten or fifteen cents was charged for the evening. That this method of sharing ideas and communication was not unique to any one ethnic group or Puerto Ricans in particular is exemplified by the recollections of a Jewish worker recalling his experiences just after the turn of the century.

> I began to buy newspapers and watch for the notices. There were scores of lectures every week. . . . One night it was Darwin and the next it might be the principle of air pressure. On a

Saturday night there were sometimes two meetings so arranged that both could be attended by the same audiences. I remember once going to a meeting at Cooper Union to protest against the use of the militia in breaking a strike somewhere in the West, and then retiring with a crowd of others to the anarchist reading room on Eldridge Street to hear an informal discussion on "Hamlet Versus Don Quixote."[22]

It was no accident that tobacco workers' associations, mutual aid groups, and trade unions should be among the first to emerge in the Puerto Rican *colonia*. For the first decades of the century, tobacco workers and their families predominated among the Puerto Rican working class. Small in numbers, these workers recreated the organizations which they had known in Puerto Rico and which were most beneficial to their trade and welfare. Since they were based on island counterparts articulating familiar ideologies and modes of operation, they helped to ease the migrant's adjustment to the mainland settlements. Groups like *La Aurora, El Ejemplo,* or *La Razón* provided essential supportive services for their membership while *La Resistencia* and the *Internacional* brought contact with other ethnic groups through their affiliation with anarcho-syndicalist or socialist associations.

By the mid-twenties the Puerto Rican settlements experienced significant changes producing limitations in the effectiveness of these pioneer organizations. Precipitated by a numerical growth of the Spanish-speaking settlements, now estimated to number around one hundred thousand individuals, the *colonia* expanded beyond the original nucleus of tobacco workers. At the same time, their influence was further reduced by critical changes in the tobacco industry. Throughout this period, the effects of mechanization in cigar manufacturing coupled with an increase in cigarette consumption resulted in a reduction in the employment of skilled cigar makers. Since the nineteenth century, these individuals had manufactured cigars using their hands and simple tools, but the newly mechanized industry of the twentieth century could now stimulate the employment of less skilled and less experienced persons.[23] This factor contributed to a geographic dispersal of Puerto Rican cigar makers and drew them into competition with other ethnic groups for unskilled jobs in other sectors. A reduction of tobacco workers meant also a reduction in the membership of those associations previously connected with the office. Therefore, declining membership and failure to recruit new dedicated individuals combined to diminish the popularity of the mutual aid societies. By mid-decade other groups emerged which incorporated some of the elements of the mutual aid groups but expanded their scope to become more representative of the entire community.

ORGANIZATIONS DURING THE TWENTIES

The very growth of the Spanish-speaking settlements in New York City and the recognition of the existence of a community with urgent needs and varying interests prompted the appearance of other types of organizations. These included more social units such as the hometown or regional clubs; groups pledged to support island or continental political persuasions; Latin cultural societies or civically oriented associations. By the mid-1920s at least forty-three three Hispanic organizations operated in the heart of the Latin *colonias* in Brooklyn and Manhattan. Group formation and the effective use of organizations became topics of frequent discussion. These commentaries often appeared in print. One group, considered a key organization during the period of the twenties, expressed its position on that issue (see Figure 3 and Maps 5, 6, and 7).

> In the city of New York the Puerto Rican community is today undoubtedly the largest among the Spanish-speaking. Its organization into a strong and powerful nucleus would produce incalculable results, not only for the residents of the continental communities but for the island as well. We speak English and are citizens of the United States, valuable attributes for the defense of our individual and collective interests. Organization is mandatory. It is an urgent imperative and truly patriotic necessity. If the task is a task of heroes— difficult and crude—it is not impossible. Let us begin at least by joining existing societies. Perhaps it will be easier later on to accomplish the complete consolidation of the community.[24]

If the organizations and their leadership, aware of their potential impact, sought to consolidate and mobilize the community behind an associational network, the *colonias* also looked to the organizations for leadership. Newspapers and journals which frequently

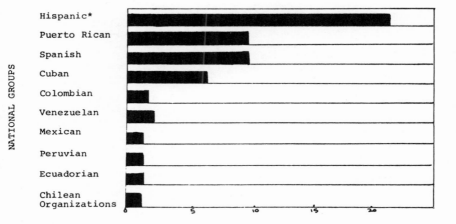

*Note: Hispanic organizations were those groups which were composed of Spanish-speaking membership but whose name did not imply orientation to a specific national group.

Source: Based on information provided by the Souvenir Program of The Porto Rican Brotherhood of America, June, 1926 and 1927.

Figure 3 Distribution and Ethnicity of Organizations in Operation in 1926

Club Estrella de Borinquen	134 West 112th Street
Centro de Amigos	100 West 113th Street
Peruvian Social & Sporting Club	197 Lenox Avenue
South American Sporting Club	33 West 113th Street
Rialto Social & Sporting Club	197 Lenox Avenue
Centro Equatoriano	101 West 87th Street
Club Patriótico Social Cubano	144 West 132nd Street
Asociación de Maestros de Español	419 West 117th Street
Alianza Obrera Puertorriqueña	38 West 117th Street
Ateneo Obrero Hispano	62 East 106th Street
Casa de las Espanas	247 Park Avenue
Fraternidad Hispano-Americano	2059 Eighth Avenue
Asociación Cubana	2061 Broadway
Porto Rican Brotherhood	36 West 120th Street
Club Esperanza	624 West 156th Street
Beneficiencia Cubana	50 West 122nd Street
La Razón, Inc.	233 East 75th Street

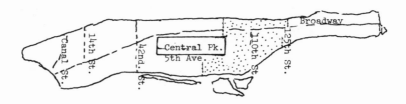

Source: Based on the Souvenir Program of the Porto Rican
          Brotherhood of America, 1926-1927

MAP 5 Hispanic Organizations in Operation in Upper Manhattan,
1926-1927

Centro Hispano-Americano	353 West 17th Street
Galicia Sporting Club	108 West 14th Street
Casa Galicia	108 West 14th Street
Comité Pro-Cuba	Hotel Waldorf Astoria
Centro Vasco-Americano	77 Catherine Street
Sociedad Mutualista Americana	City Hall Station
Sada y Sus Contornos	311 Water Street
Logia Teosófica "Mayflower"	255 West 14th Street
Sociedad Naturista Hispana	255 West 14th Street
Instituto de las Espanas	2 West 45th Street
Club Excelsior	218 E. 19th Street
Chilean Social & Sporting Club	420 West 23rd Street
Club Colombia	17 Battery Street
La Cosmopolita	239 West 14th Street

Source: Based on the Souvenir Program of the Porto
Rican Brotherhood of America, 1926-1927

MAP 6 Hispanic Organizations in Operation in Mid and Lower
Manhattan, 1926-1927

145

Club Reflejo Antillano	310 Adams Street
Centro Andaluz	59-61 Henry Street
Centro Montañes	166 Pacific Street
Centro Asturiano de New York	50 Willow Street
Centro Social Venezolano	140 Adams Street
La Nacional	1153 Fulton Street
Unión Obrera Venezolana	4 Willow Street
Centro Asturiano de la Habana	50 Willow Street
Segura Football Club	27 State Street

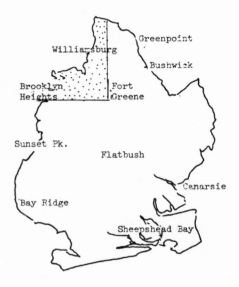

Source: Based on the Souvenir Program of the Porto
Rican Brotherhood of America, 1926-1927

MAP 7 Hispanic Organizations in Operation in Brooklyn, 1926-1927

advertised the activities of the settlements' organizations were quick to criticize them for failing the community in this direction from time to time. In 1928 an editorial in *Gráfico* openly chided the associations currently in operation for failing to unite, enlighten, or prepare the migrants "so our living conditions would improve."[25] This was followed by a series of editorials postulating plans for converting "our fraternities and social groups into useful instruments to achieve our economic goals and political betterment." Organizations of the twenties and thirties were expected to act not only in the interests of their membership or a particular interest group, but also on behalf of the community at large. Such a group was The Porto Rican Brotherhood of America *(Hermandad Puertorriquena);* another was *La Liga Puertorriqueña e Hispana.*

Founded in 1923, The Porto Rican Brotherhood emerged as one of the most significant organizations of the period. The purposes for incorporation, as stated in its charter several years later, offered only a partial indication of what the group's actual functions were:

> The promotion of sociability and friendship among its members, their social and intellectual advancement, and with this end in view, to provide a club house, or club rooms by lease or purchase or otherwise for the use and benefit of its members. The above objects are voluntary and the club is not organized for profit.[26]

Between the time of its appearance in 1923 and its incorporation in 1927, the Brotherhood covered a wide range of activities. It labored toward promoting unity, brotherhood and mutual aid among Puerto Ricans according to the consent of its members. While it strove to achieve the maturity necessary to properly describe itself as a true brotherhood, the group purposely deleted politics from its agenda. A letter which appeared in San Juan's *El Imparcial* described the Brotherhood in positive and realistic terms for the island's readers.[27] It also suggested a degree of interest in the affairs of the migrant community on the part of Puerto Ricans in Puerto Rico:

> The Brotherhood founded two years ago has had its ups and downs: situations in which enthusiasm has been feverish and others where its frigidity has placed it in danger of extinction.

Actually, it is a Puerto Rican organization with a large following—in the month of February it listed fifty members. To
unite the Puerto Rican *colonia* here is a Herculean task. It
must first attack the indifference with which we greet everything Puerto Rican and the feverishness with which we follow
all the exotic. Within this limitation, the Brotherhood has
developed a plausible organization, not only because of its
ideology but also for the harvest of its results.

What was its ideology? While it was not stated as part of its purposes for incorporation, the Brotherhood's platform certainly
demonstrated an expanded sense of commitment which did not lim-
it itself to one segment of the Spanish speaking *colonias* as the
mutual aid groups had done in the past. Included among their principles were:

1. An awareness concerning the working-class base of the
   organization's membership.
2. An awareness of the importance of mutual assistance and
   defense of the Puerto Rican *colonias* within the framework of the city's political structure.
3. Involvement in island political issues and a commitment to
   the advancement in the United States of the cause of Puerto
   Rico.
4. An awareness of issues concerning United States politics
   abroad, particularly in Latin America and most of all, the
   Caribbean.
5. A belief that Puerto Ricans themselves will define their
   problems and needs and devise their own remedies.[28]

The Brotherhood sought to be the type of group which could
defend the Puerto Ricans within the political structure of New
York City while maintaining links with Puerto Rico and acting as
watchdog in issues involving the United States and Spanish America. While these commitments appeared to be overambitious for a
young and relatively small group, an analysis of their activities over
a period of several months documents the association's integral
role in the community and dedication to its principles.[29]

One example of the Brotherhood's involvement took place when the group was called upon as advocate for four Puerto Ricans erroneously detained at Ellis Island as aliens, unable to prove their American citizenship. With the aid of the Puerto Rican resident commissioner in Washington, D.C., the Brotherhood acted in defense of Puerto Rican civil rights, successfully clearing the individuals.[30] On other occasions the Brotherhood set aside funds for needy Puerto Rican families, assisting them during critical periods in much the same way the earlier mutual aid societies had done. The annual report of 1926 to 1927 mentioned two instances in which the organization extended itself to cover the burial expenses of indigent Puerto Ricans, not necessarily members of the organization.

Throughout that year, the Brotherhood organized various social and cultural activities. These included *jaranas,* social gatherings, dances, and several youth-oriented celebrations supervised by the women's auxiliary. The work of the women's auxiliary was vital for the general survival of the organization. Their committee, patterned on the constitution and bylaws of the larger Brotherhood, provided for the election of officers and a board of directors. It was the women's auxiliary, for example, which generated publicity and propaganda for the Brotherhood, supervised fund raisers and bake sales, directed youth groups, and performed charitable works. Fund raisers secured monies to cover the year's activities and functions, but a small amount was also set aside for miscellaneous social services.

Another important activity sponsored by the Brotherhood during that period took place in conjunction with the Romance Language Department of Columbia University, the *Centro de Estudios Históricos de Madrid* and the *Instituto de las Españas.* This was a conference honoring illustrious Puerto Rican patriots. Among those honored were Luis Muñoz Rivera and Dr. José Celso Barbosa, both connected with the island's political development, and the historical playwright and essayist Alejandro Tapia y Rivera.[31] Muñoz Rivera led the island's autonomist movement in the nineteenth century and was instrumental in securing the Charter of Autonomy from Spain in 1897. Celso Barbosa, on the other hand, was a physician who served in the cabinet of the autonomous government and later formed the island's Statehood Republican Party.

For the most part the Brotherhood's activities fulfilled specific social service, cultural, or political community needs. But the increasing numerical growth and geographical expansion of the migrant population produced changes even beyond the scope of the Brotherhood's control. The everyday adjustment problems faced by *colonia* residents still undergoing the psychological effects inherent in the migration experience included such difficulties as providing a livelihood, securing adequate housing, or enduring frequent bouts of discrimination, hostilities, or suspicions on the part of the more established immigrant groups. These worries far outdistanced the efforts of the best community organizations. While the Brotherhood continued to act as caretaker for the Puerto Rican settlements, incidents based on migrant adjustment problems arose which provoked *colonia* residents to take matters into their own hands.

Such a situation took place in July 1926 when migrants engaged in a series of confrontations with other non-Hispanic area dwellers. Following a heat wave of several weeks' duration, the residents of Spanish Harlem had begun to literally live in the streets, hoping to gain relief from the torridness of their tenement dwellings. People slept on rooftops, fire escapes, and in Central Park where light breezes blew across the lake with the onset of evenings. The Puerto Rican *piragueros,* peddlers of cupfuls of scraped ice drenched in sweet syrups *(piraguas)* were much in demand by thirsty customers.

The conflicts were described as "Harlem Riots" by the *New York Times* and supposedly stemmed from "ill feeling of recent weeks between young Porto Ricans and others of Spanish blood who have been moving into Harlem in large numbers recently and the older residents of the district."[32] Sporadic street fights, arguments, and bottle throwing from the rooftops had characterized the relations between the "old settlers and the new residents" for over a week. These encounters culminated in the arrests of three Puerto Rican youths, all under the age of sixteen, charged with disorderly conduct. In retaliation, groups of Puerto Ricans descended upon 115th Street and Lenox Avenue armed with "staves wrapped in paper," but these were scattered by the reserves of four police precincts who then proceeded to disperse crowds of onlookers estimated to number in the thousands.

According to the reports of several migrants who lived through the episode as well as spokespersons of several Puerto Rican organizations, the riots were caused primarily by irritations over the steady encroachment of Spanish-speaking merchants in commercial areas predominantly controlled in the past by Jewish merchants. The situation was further complicated by repeated harassment against Puerto Rican men and women residing in the area, finally ending in violence, destruction, and the overthrowing of peddlers' pushcarts as well as a general boycott of both Jewish and Spanish-owned stores in the vicinity. Added to the fear of losing business, the old residents' distrust of Puerto Ricans and other West Indians was compounded by the fact that Puerto Ricans were racially mixed, perhaps provoking fantasies of future alliances with nonwhites, along racial lines.

One narrative described this particular incident as a surprise attack by hordes of individuals armed with sticks. Several Puerto Rican-owned stores were vandalized. Broken glass, mixed with rice, beans, plantains, and *yautias* (Puerto Rican root vegetable) littered the sidewalks and gutters in front of neighborhood *bodegas*. All of this was viewed by the observer as purposely directed against the *Barrio Latino.*[33] "It was not until much later that we found out with certainty what had happened. The first attacks resulted in over fifty wounded, some seriously. Upon learning what had transpired, Puerto Ricans reacted taking to the streets to avenge the wrong. It was then that the police arrived."[34]

In accordance with this version, the *Times* subsequently reported, "the bad feeling is said to have been caused by the rapid influx of Latin and West Indian negroes who describe themselves as Porto Ricans. The newcomers have opened their own stores and patronize no others. The old residents of the district have resented the invasion."[35]

> The ill-feeling between the Spanish-speaking people and the old residents of the section it was declared by one speaker, was due to rivalry between the Jewish and Spanish residents. Speaking on behalf of the Jewish people, Joseph N. Schultz, a former President of the Liberty Republican Club, declared there were no real grounds for ill-feeling and called upon the factions to forget their differences and remember that they were all residents of the United States.[36]

If the Harlem riots were any indication, the problems and issues confronting the *colonias* of the mid-twenties were indeed a far cry from those facing the tobacco workers of the past decade.

Faced with an expanding and visible Puerto Rican population, the surrounding ethnic groups resented their presence on the competitive job market and in the Spanish Harlem tenements. The fact that Puerto Ricans were also citizens of the United States, allowed to travel without restrictions at a time when European immigration was legally curtailed, did little to eradicate feelings of cultural and racial discrimination on the part of the older immigrants. The Porto Rican Brotherhood set forth to deal with the more complex situation on both a communal and a national level. The Harlem conflict, for example, was handled on several fronts. First, the Brotherhood selected and sent a representative committee to the local police precincts to request protection for the innocent citizens and punishment for the guilty, regardless of ethnic origin. Second, the Brotherhood secured *La Prensa's* cooperation in unleashing a vigorous campaign calling for a return to normalcy in the *colonias*. *La Prensa* by this time enjoyed a certain degree of prestige as it was considered a major newspaper for the Spanish-speaking population throughout the city. Third, the Brotherhood telegraphed Mayor Walker, Governor Smith, the resident commissioner, and other federal authorities, demanding the reestablishment of order and protection in general for the entire community.

Although the Brotherhood was somewhat successful in coping with this particular incident, the need for a comprehensive group composed of representatives from all of the active organizations became apparent. Instigated primarily by the Brotherhood the development and planning of such a group was soon undertaken and an organization created to act on behalf of the community emerged before the end of the year.

Thus, throughout this period the Porto Rican Brotherhood succeeded in its caretaker role by confronting the large non-Hispanic society; by representing the individual members of the *colonia;* by carrying out charitable works; promoting cultural and social activities designed to strengthen the Puerto Rican identity; and by assuming a position of leadership. Was the Brotherhood a unique organization, or was it characteristic of other groups of the period? How was the Brotherhood able to achieve so many of its goals in so short a period? Certainly one reason for its success was that few groups fulfilled the many needs and functions which the Brotherhood did. Indeed, the Brotherhood was among the earliest organizations to recognize the fact that the *colonia* needed groups to represent them before the host society, to handle particular problems, such as discrimination, affecting all Puerto Ricans and to categorically articulate the *colonia*'s position on the many issues which concerned them. The recurrence of situations which disadvantaged the migrant community and affected its expansion in general prompted the creation of a group specifically structured to assume these responsibilities and to share in its composition the input of most of the Hispanic community through the representation of different groups. Recognizing the importance of such a move and secure in the endorsement of other *colonia* organizations, the Brotherhood took the lead in the establishment of *La Liga Puertorriqueña e Hispana* for this purpose.

The idea of a federation of organizations had surfaced four years before when community leaders first attempted to form *La Liga Puertorriqueña* in 1923.[37] These individuals issued a call for a nonpartisan, diverse membership to represent the settlements at large. *La Prensa* reported the new association's goals as: "to widen the bands of confraternity among the city's Puerto Rican residents and to sustain the integrity of the Puerto Rican community; its moral and intellectual prestige, to foster its economic interests and protect its progress and welfare."

This organization appears to have disintegrated over a political issue, but its principles reemerged in *La Liga Puertorriqueña e Hispana,* a group deeply traumatized by the Hispanic-Jewish confrontations of the recent past. Taking credit for the group's formation, the Porto Rican Brotherhood dutifully reported the undertaking in its annual report explaining the functions and bylaws of the new unit.

The *Liga Puertorriqueña e Hispana* intended to serve the interwar settlements as an association whose constituency came from other groups already in existence. As such, it benefited from the past community organization experience of its leadership. The new leadership and their affiliations were: president—Blas Oliveras, president of the Porto Rican Brotherhood of America; vice-presidents—Joseph V. Alonso, president of the Caribe Democratic

Club, and Pedro San Miguel, president of *Alianza Obrera Puerto-rriqueña*.[38] The remaining officers were all voting members of other organizations as well. In short, the first set of *La Liga*'s directors were remarkably well equipped to represent the Puerto Rican community.

The announcement of the group's formation at the Harlem Casino declared the general purposes for organizing were "obtaining civic defense and promoting the general welfare of United States citizens of Porto Rican and Spanish birth."[39] Included among its specific goals were:

1. To unite all Hispanics without national distinctions

2. To represent the community before the authorities

3. To be a benevolent society

4. To provide an education center

5. To provide an information (referral) center

6. To propagate the vote among Puerto Ricans

7. To work toward the economic, political and social betterment of Puerto Ricans and Puerto Rico

8. To refrain from partisan politics[40]

As with the Brotherhood before it, *La Liga Puertorriqueña e Hispana* worded its purposes for incorporation almost a year after its actual creation. These appeared in the certificate of incorporation as:

> The promotion of sociability and friendship among its members, their social and intellectual advancement, and with this end in view, to provide a club house or club rooms by lease or purchase or otherwise for the use and benefit of its members. The above objects are voluntary and the club is not organized for profit.[41]

While there is little conflict between the purposes as stated in the incorporation document and the goals of the group as expressed in the press, it is clear from the issues which the group confronted that the association accepted very seriously its militant mandate to act on behalf of the community. Within a relatively short period they were indeed representing the *colonia* before the non-Hispanic society as they sought to better the social and political situation of the migrants.

Outstanding among the first incidents attracting *La Liga*'s attention as an organization which stood for Puerto Rican interests was the situation immediately following a highly publicized visit to Puerto Rico by the nation's first lady, Eleanor Roosevelt.[42] In an attempt to stimulate national concern toward granting federal aid for the people of Puerto Rico after a series of natural disasters, Mrs. Roosevelt called attention to the island's poor health and living standards. Stressing as inexcusable the high incidence of tuberculosis among the people, Mrs. Roosevelt innocently cautioned Americans against contracting the disease through contacts with Puerto Ricans in the United States. The inference that most Puerto Ricans therefore carried the contagious disease placed the migrant community in a precarious and prejudicial situation, according to *La Liga,* especially as large numbers of the New York migrants were employed as waiters or countermen in the hotels and restaurants of the city. In a vigorous campaign, *La Liga* pointed out the dangerous repercussions of Mrs. Roosevelt's statement focusing on the unintentional damage it would create. Launching a defense of the migrant working class, *La Liga* presented its position in the community's newspapers, and while it appeared the issue was forgotten after a while, it reappeared in a matter involving the children of the migrant communities.[43]

The Federation of Protestant Welfare Agencies had customarily sponsored a series of nondenominational summer camping programs for the city's underprivileged children. Until the summer of 1934, close to six thousand Puerto Rican children had participated among the campers, but that year the funding foundation failed to provide for the inclusion of Puerto Rican children and advised the Federation of its action. *La Liga* responded rapidly, interpreting this action on the part of the Foundation and the Federation as discriminatory, a direct result of the tuberculosis episode.[44] In their role as community representatives and to publicize their position on the issue, *La Liga* called for a mass meeting in which the matter was debated. A council of twenty-three representatives of Hispanic workers and religious organizations denounced the actions of the

Federation and called for retraction of the questionable policy. An intensive publicity campaign within the *colonia* brought the issue before the non-Hispanic public as well, and through the intercession of various religious groups, the situation was resolved in favor of the *colonias,* allowing the reinstatement of camping privileges.

Yet another incident in which *La Liga* marched at the forefront of community organizations took place the following year. It was in 1935 that the New York City Chamber of Commerce administered and interpreted the results of an experiment in which 240 Puerto Rican children were given an intelligence test. Numerous organizations, newspapers, and community newsletters indignantly greeted the Chamber's report that scores of Puerto Rican children were mentally deficient and intellectually immature. Following *La Liga*'s lead, community journals, newspapers, and group associations viewed the Chamber's findings as blatantly irresponsible and inflammatory. Associations and area leaders fanned communal wrath by addressing the incident as an important community issue. This particular episode, for example, became one of the East Harlem politician Vito Marcantonio's battle cries on behalf of his Puerto Rican constituency. The congressman from the Twentieth District advocated in support of Puerto Rican children whom he viewed as victims of subtle discrimination resulting from adverse classifications based on IQ tests. In administering these tests, Marcantonio contended, Puerto Rican children were placed in unfavorable positions because of inadequate allowances for social, economic, linguistic, and environmental factors.[45]

One journal, *Revista de Artes y Letras,* added its voice to the furor against the Chamber's actions. Josefina Silva de Cintrón's editorial called for community unity on this issue, Hispanic community representation among the examining committee, and the administration of the questionable examinations to a control group of non-Puerto Rican children living under similar socio-economic conditions.[46] Unequivocably believing the Chamber of Commerce's mode of operation was unfair and the results of interpretations inconclusive, *La Liga* agreed with the recommendations set forth in *Artes y Letras.* Adding yet another recommendation to the *Revista's, La Liga* suggested the creation of a Spanish-speaking teachers' committee and offered a list of suitable candidates for that purpose. These recommendations were apparently ignored by the non-Hispanic community.

In addition to the more publicized activities in which *La Liga* participated, the association sponsored numerous cultural acts and festivities. Determined to serve the Spanish-speaking *colonias* as a resource center, the group took the lead in matters affecting the future of Puerto Rican children, established courses for them and for the education of adults in Spanish on political and sociological topics, and sponsored the celebration of literary and artistic endeavors through conferences or *veladas*.

If groups like the *Liga Puertorriqueña e Hispana* and the Porto Rican Brotherhood personified sentinel associations, concerned with the representation, protection, and perpetuation of the city's Spanish-speaking, other groups also formed based on subgroup or individual interests. Responding to different needs, defining other issues, these groups drew a varied constituency. The *Club Ibero-Americano* and *La Asociación Latino Americana,* for example, appealed to the small group of well-educated elites and emphasized cultural heritage, language, Hispanic traditions, and professionalism.[47] Others, like the *Ateneo Obrero* and the *Alianza Obrera,* drew their membership primarily from the working class. The first proposed the expansion of Hispanic literary and artistic expression focusing on the educational development of the new Puerto Rican generation, most of whom had been born in New York. The second group promoted class awareness and related to the workers' syndicalist movements in the city. Similarly, groups such as *Puerto Rico Literario* catered to the special interest of Puerto Rican writers. Finally, the hometown or regional clubs responded to more basic needs, providing both social and recreational activities for the incoming migrant.

Among the earliest hometown clubs, the *Club Caborrojeño* was founded during the early twenties especially for migrants from the town of Cabo Rojo. Its purposes included providing social, civic, cultural, and recreational activities for its membership. The club depended on dues whenever possible and on fund raising for its budget. Originally envisioned as a nostalgic endeavor where migrants from the same geographic location could interact within a familial setting, the hometown clubs grew in membership and in importance until they became integral units of the Spanish-speaking neighborhoods.[48] Within a short period, clubs like *Mayaguezanos Ausente, Hijos de Penuelas* or *Hijos de Camuy* dominated the social organizational network.

These groups progressed from social clubs to more sophisticated units when they began to provide social services along with their informal activities. Tasks designed to alleviate the migrant's feelings of alienation covered a wide range depending on the specific association. It was not unusual among the older clubs to offer job-related information; to visit the sick, aiding with monetary contributions; composing and typing letters or other correspondence in English; resolving problems with written contracts; organizing demonstrations for protesting the myriad incidents which made up the migrant's condition; and other similar tasks. The club's rent and other utilities, stationery, and miscellaneous needs were paid from activities conducted among the members, and collections were often taken to meet emergency expenditures.[49]

The neighborhood clubs or hometown groups of the twenties and thirties evolved at a time when the survival of the individual and the community was at its most tenuous. The hometown club provided migrants with an oasis in an otherwise hostile territory, served to link the New York environment with the village or island town they had left behind, and in general cushioned the inevitable adjustment. Already composed of a membership which knew one another either directly or by word of mouth, the clubs also served as a substitution for the extended family and friends left in Puerto Rico. In years to come, these would mark the highlight of grass-roots involvement among Puerto Ricans and, united under the Federation of *El Congreso de los Pueblos,* constitute the backbone of the Puerto Rican Day Parade in New York City.

SPECIAL INTEREST GROUPS

By the last half of the decade of the thirties, other groups emerged to rival the veteran associations of the twenties. Some continued to form in the patterns of federation. *La Confederación de Sociedades Puertorriqueñas,* for example, founded under the directorship of José Camprubi, editor of *La Prensa,* attempted to function as an umbrella agency representing several community groups, but this type of organization would not be as effective as those which came before.[50] At least three factors mitigated against the success of federations during this period. First, *La Liga Puertorriqueña* was still in operation and other federated groups would serve to splinter and duplicate its functions; second, social service agencies which became more intensive in their response to the Depression communities duplicated many of the services provided by the older Hispanic units; third, many of the groups which bridged the period of the thirties and early forties appeared to be more professionally or occupationally oriented, not expanding their concerns to the community at large, but rather limiting their purposes to their own interests, issues, and survival. One exception was the community settlement house, Casita María, which provided social services for over twenty-five thousand Puerto Ricans since its establishment by the Trinitarian nun Sister Carmelita in 1934.[51]

Similarly, groups like the Club Eugenio María de Hostos, part of whose membership came from *La Liga Puertorriqueña* and the Puerto Rico Civic Club, exemplified societies which focused on internal issues. The Club de Hostos termed itself a cultural or educational association, and its purposes for coming together included stressing Hispanic culture, offering classes in Spanish, and sponsoring literary conferences and *veladas*. The Puerto Rico Civic Club, on the other hand, sought to: "further, promote and foster the sociability and friendship between the members of its association; to volunteer aid and assist the said members in times of sickness and distress; and in general, to do all the things a social civic group would do."[52]

Perhaps the best example of a successful organization oriented around special needs and specific interests was the Spanish Grocer's Association. Cited by Fitzpatrick as one of the oldest groups to operate in the Spanish-speaking community, the association began in 1937 as the Spanish Merchants' Association and continues to function to the present.[53] Founded at a time when the growth of the small businesses within the community paralleled the physical growth of the early settlements, its purposes for incorporation testified to its concern with the welfare of the merchants. Covering several areas of importance for the merchant membership, the group formed to:

1. Unite all Hispanic merchants in the City of New York, socially, fraternally, and commercially

2. Better their living conditions through better social and business ethics

3. Assess and assist effectively the problems facing the Hispanic merchant

4. Protect the close union of all Hispanic merchants established in the State of New York

5. Organize and maintain a center for information and advice[54]

This interest group succeeded in bringing together the owners of numerous small *bodegas* or *colmados* which dotted many Puerto Rican neighborhoods in the *colonias*. The Merchants' Association became a significant group in aiding the advancement of Puerto Ricans into small private businesses.[55] They published a newsletter which became a sophisticated enterprise entitled *FUERZA: Órgano Informativo de los Comerciantes y la Comunidad*. Here the *colonias'* merchants publicized and photographically illustrated their many activities, advertised their products, and kept the merchants informed of events in Puerto Rico and in the United States. Furthermore, the association served to police its own ranks, operating as an internal better businessmen's bureau and also guiding its membership in dealing with the business and banking institutions of the city.[56]

While the Merchants' Association functioned as an orientation point for the businessmen of the Spanish-speaking settlements, the civil service workers forged their own groups to provide social and civic direction. The Puerto Rican Veteran's Welfare Postal Workers' Association became incorporated in 1951, but the connection between the Puerto Rican worker and civil service dated to the twenties. Post office employees, schoolteachers, and social workers included Puerto Ricans among their ranks. By 1926 the Brotherhood's report charged, "400 (four hundred), more or less Porto Ricans are holding different ranking positions with the Postal Service and about six are with custom house service in the city of New York."[57] Within a decade, *Revista de Artes y Letras* listed an organization named *Asociación de Empleados Civiles de Correo* whose purpose for joining together was both civic and social in nature.[58]

With the onset of the Second World War, Puerto Ricans were hired as postal workers in greater numbers. Many filled essential positions as censors in that agency's departments. Bernardo Vega, who worked as a censor during the war years, affirmed that over one thousand Puerto Ricans were employed in that division, many of whom held university or advanced degrees, were college professors, distinguished writers, and artists. All were required to pass a civil service examination which demonstrated their proficiency in at least two languages as well as other subjects.[59]

Another migrant employed by the censorship department at that time was Raquel Rivera Hernández. A recent college graduate, Doña Raquel's first job consisted of intercepting civilian mail en route to Spain, Latin America, and the Spanish Caribbean. Rivera Hernández believed her work with the Post Office was essential to the war effort. Her goals were to perform her responsibilities as efficiently as possible and to support the workers' group which coalesced around the Spanish-speaking employees. This group sponsored recreational activities, fund raisers for important causes or for the group's own projects, cultural events, and extravaganzas in which the talents of the employees themselves were the main attraction. Doña Raquel often marveled at the numbers of talented and well-educated Puerto Ricans who, through unforeseen circumstances, found themselves working together in the city's Post Office. Had the Puerto Rican community harnessed the potential leadership and ability displayed within this setting, it would have made a tremendous impact at a crucial period in the development of Puerto Rican settlements, according to Doña Raquel.[60] But this group alienated itself from political or leadership situations and failed to assert itself as a community representative. Their reasons for uniting were probably not unlike those expressed in the certificate of incorporation of 1951. These were:

To promote friendship and encourage social and intellectual intercourse among veterans born in Puerto Rico employed in the service of the United States of America; to disseminate among its members and families knowledge and practices for health advancement in civic spheres, and in their call; to sponsor social activities among them, all to the exclusion of political subjects, said corporation being non-sectarian and non-political, and in general, to promote the general and social well-being of its members in a social and civic manner.[61]

Conclusion

Thus the Puerto Rican community of the period before the Second World War was defined in yet another perspective—its organizational structure. Groups evolved to meet the needs of the pioneer settlements based on common interests and in response to changes within the migrant situation. The first groups, mutual aid societies and trade unions, served the needs of a relatively small community of skilled workers who lived close to the tobacco factories of Chelsea and the Lower East Side. These continued to follow the patterns of counterpart active groups on the island, identified with the workers' struggles on an international level, but formed for the specific benefit of their New York members. With the numerical growth of the *colonia* and its eventual concentration in East Harlem and Brooklyn, two other types of groups predominated: the fraternal, which represented the community on a city-wide basis; and the hometown group which began simply as a place where migrants from the same hometown, feeling lost in the unfamiliar city, came together. Thus, where one group concentrated on the external issues affecting the early settlements, the other focused on the internal needs of the migrants in an alien environment.

By the mid-thirties and into the war years, many groups appeared to turn inward, once again satisfying the special needs of their specialized membership. Here again we can see a return to the organizational patterns of the earlier decades, this time decidedly motivated by the creation of city government agencies designed to smooth the adjustment of the newcomers. One prime example was the Migration Division of the Labor Department of Puerto Rico, established in New York in 1948 to clear migrants for jobs, provide them with proper identification, and refer those needing help to appropriate public agencies.[62] Another was the Mayor's Committee on Puerto Rican Affairs established by William O'Dwyer in 1949. These groups proposed to investigate problems associated with the migration and provide leadership and supervision in solving them. These agencies thus aided in duplication and eventual eradication of many grass-roots groups which had previously provided social services.

Clearly the issue is not whether or not a communal organizational network existed within the pioneer settlements, but rather how such a network managed to survive at all. The predominantly working-class nature of the *colonias* prohibited many migrants from becoming active members of any group. We can only speculate then on how many individuals could actually afford to spend their time supervising or planning activities, fund raising, publicizing group events, attending meetings, and recruiting membership after an eight-hour day[63] at the factory. That groups functioned as they did and received the support from the community which they did is a tribute to the Puerto Rican community structure and to the individual's own sense of commitment. As social and civic associations grouped around occupations or special interests and non-Puerto Rican city-wide agencies became more dominant, other groups would emerge to deal with the host society. To an extent the political units which had been in operation since the turn of the century would help provide models in this direction.

Notes

1. Elena Padilla, *Up from Puerto Rico* (New York: Columbia University Press, 1958). See also Lawrence R. Chenault, *The Puerto Rican Migrant in New York* (New York: Columbia University Press, 1938; reissue, Russell & Russell, 1970).

2. Nathan Glazer and Daniel Patrick Moynihan, *Beyond the Melting Pot* (Cambridge: MIT Press, 1968), pp. 101–107.

3. Irving Howe, *World of Our Fathers* (New York: Simon and Schuster, 1976), pp. 183–184. See also Puerto Rican Forum, *A Study of Poverty Conditions in the New York Puerto Rican Community* (New York: Puerto Rican Forum, Inc., 1964); Carlota Suárez, "Don Ralph Rosas, Puerto Rico en Nueva York: Visión y Práctica" (unpublished manuscript, Department of Educational Services, Brooklyn College).

4. Donald Stewart, *A Short History of East Harlem* (New York: Museum of the City of New York, 1972), pp. 49–50.

5. Ibid., p. 52.

6. Adalberto López and James Petras, *Puerto Rico and the Puerto Ricans: Studies in History and Society* (New York: Schenkman Publishing Co., 1974), pp. 328–329.

7. Ibid. See also Clara E. Rodríguez, "Puerto Ricans in the Melting Pot," *The Journal for Ethnic Studies,* vol. 1, no. 4 (winter 1974), pp. 89–97; Herbert Hill, "Guardian of the Sweatshops," in Lopez and Petras, pp. 384–416.

8. Chenault, *The Puerto Rican Migrant,* p. 149.

9. The phenomenon of constant reformation of organizations was not

limited to the Puerto Rican community. Roy V. Peel comments on it among non-Hispanic groups as well. See Roy V. Peel, *The Political Clubs of New York City* (New York: G.P. Putnam & Sons, 1935), pp. 138–147.

10. Rosa Estades, "Patterns of Political Participation Among Puerto Ricans in New York City" (New School for Social Research, Ph.D. Dissertation, 1974), chapter 3.

11. Ibid., p. 71.

12. Ibid., p. 72.

13. Puerto Rican Forum, *Study of Poverty Conditions,* p. 12.

14. Ibid., p. 12.

15. Miles Galvin, "The Early Development of the Organized Labor Movement in Puerto Rico," *Latin American Perspectives,* vol. 111, no. 3 (summer 1976), pp. 17–33. See also Angel Quintero Rivera, "La clase obrera y el proceso político en Puerto Rico," *Revista de Ciencias Sociales,* nos. 1–4, 1974; Juan Carreras, "Bandera Roja," in Jose Ferrer y Ferrer, *Los ideales del siglo XX,* pp. 125–134.

16. Galvin, "Early Development," pp. 17–33.

17. Ibid., p. 24. Luisa Capetillo, "Recuerdos a la Federación Libre de Trabajadores," in Angel Quintero Rivera, *Lucha Obrera en Puerto Rico* (Rio Piedras: CEREP, 1971).

18. César Andreu Iglesias, ed., *Memorias de Bernardo Vega* (Rio Piedras: Ediciones Huracan, Inc., 1977), p. 123.

19. Ibid., p. 147.

20. Howe, p. 184 and p. 311 for reference to functions and growth of the Workmen's Circle during the early decades of this century. Also interview with Homero Rosado, Brooklyn, New York, October 1980. This individual was active in socialist organizations and affirms there was ethnic integration within this group.

21. Iglesias, *Memorias,* pp. 144–147.

22. Howe, *The World,* p. 239.

23. W. D. Evans, "Effects of Mechanization on Cigar Manufacturing," *Works Progress Administration Report No. B-4* (Washington, D.C.: Government Printing Office, 1934).

24. The Porto Rican Brotherhood of America, "Puerto Rico in New York," Brotherhood Newsletter, 1926.

25. *Gráfico,* September 2, 1928 and August 12, 1928.

26. Porto Rican Brotherhood of America, Certificate of Incorporation, File No. 05660-27C, March 23, 1927, New York City County Clerk's Office, Municipal Building, New York City. See also Peel, *The Political Clubs,* p. 141.

27. *El Imparcial,* cited in the Porto Rican Brotherhood of America Souvenir Program, June 1926. It is not clear if the reference to fifty members

meant additional new members for the month or for the organization's entire membership roster.

28. Taller de Migración, Centro de Estudios Puertorriqueños, *Cuaderno de la migración* (New York: Centro de Estudios Puertorriqueños, Graduate Center, CUNY), April 1974.

29. Porto Rican Brotherhood of America, Annual Report, June 1926. See also Iglesias, *Memorias,* p. 178.

30. Porto Rican Brotherhood of America, Annual Report, June 1926. The Resident Commissioner was the nonvoting, nonspeaking observer in the U.S. Congress who represented the interests of Puerto Rico.

31. See Antonio S. Pedreira, *Un hombre del pueblo: José Celso Barbosa* (San Juan: Instituto de Cultura, 1965); Philip Sterling and María Brau, *The Quiet Rebels* (New York: Doubleday, 1968).

32. *New York Times,* July 27, 1926, p. 21.

33. Iglesias, *Memorias,* p. 188.

34. Ibid.

35. *New York Times,* July 30, 1926, p. 29.

36. Ibid., August 9, 1926, p. 5.

37. *La Prensa,* January 15, 1923, p. 1.

38. *New York Times,* August 9, 1926, p. 5.

39. Ibid.

40. *Gráfico,* April 3, 1927, p. 13.

41. La Liga Puertorriqueña e Hispana, Certificate of Incorporation, File No. 056-59-27c, March, 1928, County Clerk's Office, Municipal Building, New York City.

42. Iglesias, *Memorias,* pp. 223–225.

43. Ibid.

44. Ibid., p. 224.

45. *Revista de Artes y Letras,* March 1936. See also The Marcantonio Collection, New York Public Library, Archival Division, Boxes 2, 3, 4; Salvatore La Gumina, *The People's Politician* (Iowa: Kendall Hunt Publishing Co., 1969), p. 48.

46. *Revista de Artes y Letras.*

47. *New York Times,* February 3, 1924, p. 23. See also Iglesias, *Memorias,* pp. 137, 147.

48. Rosa Estades, "Symbolic Unity: The Puerto Rican Day Parade," in Clara E. Rodríguez, Virginia Sánchez Korrol, and José Oscar Alers, eds., *The Puerto Rican Struggle: Essays on Survival in the U.S.* (New York: Puerto Rican Migration Research Consortium, 1980), pp. 82–89. See also Carlota Suárez, "Don Ralph Rosas."

49. Puerto Rican Forum, *Study of Poverty Conditions,* p. 60.

50. Iglesias, *Memorias,* p. 242.

51. *New York Times,* November 19, 1961. Interview with Sister Carmelita Bonilla, Puerto Rican Oral History Project, 1973–1974, Long Island Historical Society, Brooklyn, New York. See also Anthony Stevens Arroyo, "Puerto Rican Struggles in the Catholic Church," in Rodríguez, Sánchez Korrol, and Alers, pp. 129–139.

52. The Puerto Rico Civic Club, Certificate of Incorporation, File No. 10884-33c, September 15, 1933, County Clerk's Office, Municipal Building, New York City.

53. Interview with Antonio Moreau, secretary, Hispanic Merchants' Association, Bronx, New York, July 1976.

54. *Fuerza,* August-September 1975.

55. Joseph P. Fitzpatrick, *Puerto Rican-Americans* (Englewood Cliffs, N.J.: Prentice-Hall, 1971), pp. 62–63.

56. Antonio Moreau interview.

57. Porto Rican Brotherhood of America, Souvenir Program.

58. *Revista de Artes y Letras,* cited in Estades, *Patterns,* p. 72.

59. Interviews with Antonio and Raquel Rivera Hernández, Rio Piedras, Puerto Rico, August 1977. See also Carlota Suárez, "Don Ralph Rosas," p. 2; Iglesias, *Memorias,* pp. 255–256.

60. Raquel Rivera Hernández interview.

61. Puerto Rican Employees Association, Certificate of Incorporation, File No. 68070-36c, 1936, County Clerk's Office; Puerto Rican Veteran's Welfare Postal Workers' Association, File No. 5440-70-3, 1951, County Clerk's Office.

62. Carlota Suárez, "Don Ralph Rosas," pp. 7–12.

63. Homero Rosado interview. It is estimated that although the actual active membership of an average organization might not number more than one hundred individuals, the functions given by organizations, dances, conferences, etc. might draw additional membership and guests numbering well over two hundred. Based on oral interviews with persons active in early settlement organizations, this appears to be the case for most of the groups.

Politics, Issues, and Participation in Puerto Rican Colonias

If the movement toward sociocultural, social service, and fraternal organizations structured the internal dynamics of the Puerto Rican communities, their political associations went one step further. These provided the rubric for interacting with the host society, for solidifying their identity as a community, and for addressing the relevant political issues of the period. Bostered by a long tradition of political activity in Puerto Rico, political units were among the earliest to emerge in the New York *colonias*. But while the island-related groups formed in the late nineteenth century focused on the colonial relationship between Spain and Puerto Rico, those appearing in New York after 1898 provided communal leadership and facilitated interaction between the settlements and the dominant political system.

Before the Spanish-American War in 1898, Puerto Rican political organizations in New York represented an extension of island politics for the handful of migrants living in the city. The first Puerto Rican political units formed in New York were composed of exiles fighting for independence from Spain. In 1895 they created the Puerto Rican branch of the Cuban Revolutionary Party. Highly organized and working along with the respected Cuban leader José Martí were Puerto Rican patriots such as Sótero Figueroa or Julio J. Henna. Other survivors of the ill-fated Lares insurrection like Juan de Mata Terraforte and Antonio Vélez Alvarado attracted

Latin American supporters, also forced exiles from their countries, to the cause of Antillean freedom. This type of revolutionary fervor and activity, basically unconnected with New York non-Hispanic political patterns, was instrumental in the formation of other Latin supportive associations. One of these was the *Club Borinquen* led by Sótero Figueroa, aimed at propagating the cause of Cuban and Puerto Rican liberation through community newsletters and organs like *El Porvenir* and *La Revolución*. Another was *La Liga Artesanos* and its sister organization, *La Liga Antillana*.

Founded initially as a cultural and civic association, *La Liga Artesanos* disseminated propaganda and raised funds for independence. Among the names of its founding members were active, organizationally minded individuals who were repeatedly represented on the rosters of numerous early associations. *La Liga Aresanos,* for example, listed the aforementioned Sótero Figueroa along with Flor Braega and Felipe Rodríguez as members. *La Liga Antillana,* on the other hand, held the distinction of being a racially integrated women's group, composed predominantly of working-class women. It was considered among the first of its kind within the Hispanic settlements, and besides supporting Spanish and Caribbean independence, focused much of its attention on fund raising and cultural presentations. Because of the group's interracial composition, however, the association was often denied access to many meeting places in the city, thus they held their reunions in the Masonic Temple, Hardman Hall, or the meeting rooms of the Socialist Party. Here distinguished guests gathered including José Martí, Figueroa, and Pachín Marín. Active revolutionaries, both Marín and Martí gained recognition as poets and essayists as well.[1] Others, including Lola Rodríguez de Tío, poetess and author of the island's revolutionary anthem, and Arturo Schomberg, specialist in black Caribbean and Spanish-American history, also took part in the group's activities. Both *Ligas* were believed to have been frequented predominantly by tobacco workers, skilled laborers, and their families, who were among the earliest Puerto Rican settlers in Brooklyn and Manhattan.[2]

Besides the groups already cited, other organizations, political, social and civic in orientation, fleshed out the communal structure of the turn-of-the-century Puerto Rican settlements in both boroughs (see Map 8 and Table 12). Many of these turned toward events hap-

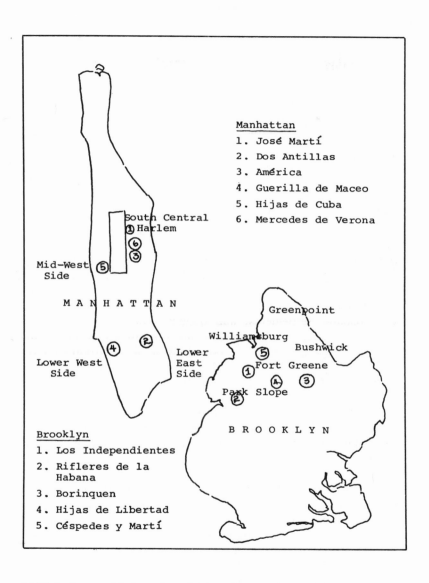

Manhattan

1. José Martí
2. Dos Antillas
3. América
4. Guerilla de Maceo
5. Hijas de Cuba
6. Mercedes de Verona

Brooklyn

1. Los Independientes
2. Rifleres de la Habana
3. Borinquen
4. Hijas de Libertad
5. Céspedes y Martí

MAP 8 Geographic Location of Hispanic Organizations in Brooklyn and Manhattan

TABLE 12
Geographic Location and Officers of Active Hispanic Associations in Brooklyn and Manhattan, circa 1895

NAME	LOCATION	OFFICERS
Manhattan		
1. José Martí	1642 Park Avenue Manhattan	B. H. Portuondo Sotero Figueroa Felipe Rodríguez
2. Dos Antillas	1758 Third Avenue Manhattan	Roseando Rodríguez Arturo A. Schomberg
3. América	231 E. 61st Street Manhattan	J. R. Álvarez E. M. Amoros
4. Guerilla de Maceo	146 W. 24th Street Manhattan	Juan B. Beato Juan Fernández
5. Hijas de Cuba	116 W. 64th Street Manhattan	Angela R. de Quesada Carmen Matillas

6. Mercedes de Verona	235 E. 75th Street Manhattan	Inocencia M. de Figueroa Emma Betancourt
Brooklyn		
1. Los Independientes	839 Fulton Street Brooklyn	Juan Frago Genero Baez
2. Rifleres de la Habana	2141 Pacific Street Brooklyn	Antonio Camero Adelaido Marín
3. Borinquen	129 McDougal Street Brooklyn	J. M. Torreforte Domingo Collazo
4. Hijas de Libertad	1115 Herkimer Street Brooklyn	Natividad R. de Gallo Gertrudis Casano
5. Céspedes y Martí	2012 Fulton Street Brooklyn	Petrona Calderón Juana Rosario

Source: Based on César Andreu Iglesias (ed.), *Memorias de Bernardo Vega.*

pening in Puerto Rico, and while they served to unite the exiled population of the small *colonias,* it was understood that their concerns were for the homeland and not for the future of the pioneer settlements in New York. In fact, the existence of a permanent community outside of Puerto Rico was not within their frame of reference. With the culmination of the Spanish-American War, these groups became inactive, but the example set by the associations and their leadership was not easily forgotten by the early migrant settlers. Inasmuch as some community leaders like Dr. Henna and the Figueroa brothers continued to exert direction in the New York settlements after 1898, they were instrumental in the foundation of new groups now concerned with the stabilization of Puerto Rican migrant status within a North American orbit.[3]

Thus the influences of the pre-twentieth-century political organizations on the infant Puerto Rican settlements were significant. First, groups composed of a Spanish-speaking membership existed and operated as politically oriented units in New York City, setting a precedent for this type of activity. Second, many of the original leaders of these units exerted similar dynamics in the new post-1898 associations, bringing together a small but effective cadre of experienced organizers within the pioneer settlements.

Political Groups After the Spanish-American War

The new units to appear after 1900 responded to the political and economic pressures faced by the migrants in New York as well as the political issues affecting the island. Responding also to the internal insecurities inherent in the massive relocation of a people struggling to survive in alien surroundings, the new political associations provided supportive units which reaffirmed migrant values and interests. It was not unusual for such groups to set aside funds for needy Hispanic families, offer advice on housing and job inquiries, perform charitable deeds, and provide social and recreational outlets. Migrant interviews attest to the direct involvement of organization members in the everyday problems of the migrant community. This involvement ranged from playing on baseball and other sport teams to removing the furniture of evicted tenants from city sidewalks back into their apartments. The latter activity reinitiated lengthy eviction proceedings which allowed the migrants to accumulate the necessary rents in the interim. Thus the relationship between the groups and the *colonia* rested firmly on personal considerations from the very start.

Utilizing a paternalistic approach, the clubs assumed a familiar role in settlement structure, not unlike the *hacendado-agregado* relationship still in effect within the island's predominantly agrarian society. The *hacendado,* or landowner, by virtue of his social and economic status, traditionally protected and provided for the welfare of his workers. The *agredados,* landless peasants or sharecroppers, sought the favors and protection of the *hacendado,* usually through their good work and loyalty. Based on a rigid class structure, deference, and personalism, Puerto Rican workers were conditioned to respond best to those relationships rooted in personal contact.

As early as 1918, the first Puerto Rican political clubs patterned on a paternalism-patronage model and connected with the New York City political party system took shape. These were the *Club Demócrata Puertorriqueño* in Brooklyn headed by Joaquin Colón and J. V. Alonso; the Harlem Branch of the Manhattan Democratic Party whose leaders J. C. Caballero and Domingo Collazo had participated in the organizations of the turn of the century; and the Puerto Rican Committee of the Socialist Party which included among its founders the community activists Bernardo Vega, Jesus Colón, and Homero Rosado.[4] Following the examples set by other immigrant groups and Hispanic associations before them, the Brooklyn clubs offered a wide range of activities and sponsored dances, sports programs, and social services. The clubs made provision for health referrals, legal aid, and advice on housing and employment as well as counseling on other working-class problems. Credited with spearheading political organization in that borough, Carlos Tapia and Luis F. Weber became the power brokers between the Brooklyn Democratic Party and the Puerto Rican *colonia.* As such, they commanded respect as informal intercommunity leaders while at the same time receiving a degree of acknowledgment as intermediaries from the borough's wider Democratic organization leaders, Frank V. Kelly and John H. McCoy.[5]

During the twenties and early thirties, political activity continued to increase as did the migrant population. One individual outlined the borough's Puerto Rican political history in the following manner:

> It is to be noted that up to the year 1927 when the Liberty Republican Club was organized in "El Barrio" (then part of Harlem's 14th Assembly District, Manhattan) by Puerto Ricans all the Puerto Rican political organizations in the city of New York originated in Brooklyn. The Puerto Rican Democratic Club, Inc.—1923—operated in the 1st Assembly District, as did the later—1928–1932—De Hostos and Guaybana Democratic Clubs. The Betances Democratic Club, Inc., founded by Carolos Tapia and other Puerto Ricans in 1918, operated in the 3rd Assembly District. The Baldorioty Democratic Club, Inc.—1932—operated in the Navy Yard area in those days in part of the 4th Assembly District and the Tompkins and Marcy Avenues, then part of the 6th Assembly District. The Guarionex Democratic Club, Inc.—1929—operated in the Greenpoint area then part of the 15th Assembly District and densely populated by Puerto Ricans.[6]

Almost all the clubs listed incorporated under the names of past Puerto Rican political figures, honoring the memory of patriots like Betances, de Hostos, or Baldorioty or indigenous persons like Guarionex or Guaybana. In this way the club originators appealed to the migrants' dual sense of pride and patriotism. In actuality, these were subsidiary political clubs some of which were but loosely connected with the Brooklyn Democratic Party machinery. It was also significant that the major part of political action among Puerto Ricans centered in Brooklyn rather than Manhattan.

As the first seat of Puerto Rican settlement, the Brooklyn *colonia* developed along the same lines as did the Manhattan settlement, but more of the Brooklyn Puerto Rican clubs outrightly admitted their political orientation than did the other. Incorporated into the city of New York in 1898, Brooklyn along with the Bronx and Staten Island maintained less rigid patterns of political participation. Conversely, political growth in Manhattan dominated by Tammany Hall, was stunted along racial, ethnic, and geographic lines. The Harlem area in which the Spanish-speaking population predominated had been divided into four Assembly Districts to discourage the political ascendency of Jewish or black District leaders.[7] While a proliferation of Hispanic political clubs was not evident in Manhattan, there did exist a concentration of socio-cultural and fraternal associations, many of which appeared frequently in political affairs or expressed their positions on political issues.

While funding for the functioning of political organizations often depended on the meager dues of their working-class membership, dances, pageants, contests, and other fund raisers added to the club treasury. Significantly, much of the outside funding for the Brooklyn clubs during the first decades of the century came from the *colonias' boliteros,* or numbers-game operators. As an assistant secretary to the Puerto Rican Democratic Club and later as president of the Baldorioty Democratic Club, Ramon Colón recalled raising money in the offices of the local Puerto Rican *bolitero.* These individuals were in no way regarded as lawbreakers within the *colonias,* and several migrants testified that the people involved in the numbers rackets were often thought of as modern-day Robin Hoods. Alluding to the outside funding, Colón remarked:

> The principal donors were the numbers game *bolita* operators at that time. Their response was always prompt and generous. It seemed that the financial help given by them to the Puerto Rican Democratic organizations paid off in the form of political "protection" for their numbers game operation.[8]

Luis Felipe Weber, a Puerto Rican migrant recognized by both the Spanish-speaking community and the non-Hispanic society as a leader among Puerto Ricans in Brooklyn, was involved in the numbers rackets as well as in the political organizations of the twenties and thirties. Weber's sister, Doña Honorina, admittedly scorned the rackets in which he was linked, but conceded that community attitudes toward Weber's role as a *bolitero* were seldom negative or condemning. Her recollections of her brother's role in the Brooklyn settlement emphasize instead his contributions rather than his involvement in the numbers game. More important, Doña Honorina's remembrances present a picture of the operation of both clubs and leaders which solidly fit the Puerto Rican clubs into a paternalistic mold:

Luis was the one who took care of the unfortunate Puerto
Ricans. In fact, he was called the father of the Puerto Ricans.
He made a little fortune and whenever anybody needed help
either because of illness or lack of employment he was ready
to give his help or to get it through politics. He had three
political clubs. None of the members paid any dues. Luis
funded the clubs himself. One on Adams Street—Agueybana;
Betances on Sackett Street and Hostos on Jefferson Street.
These were all Democratic Clubs. I remember that during the
holidays they donated over two hundred baskets of groceries,
toys and confections to needy families.[9]

Clearly Weber's role as a bolitero in Brooklyn partly laid the
financial groundwork for working-class migrant political activities.
As a prominent *colonia* leader and patron, Weber was credited with
building playgrounds for neighborhood recreation, donating food
baskets, and extending a helping hand when needed. In many ways
this justified his internal community leadership role. Weber, moreover, represented the Puerto Rican community outside of the
Brooklyn settlement, acting as an intermediary or power broker
between the migrants and the dominant political party structure.
Yet his involvement in *la bolita* raised more questions than accept-
ance. How legitimate was Weber in his role as community leader,
under these circumstances, and to what extent were the Brooklyn
neighborhoods gaining from the arrangement?

For the most part, Puerto Ricans viewed the numbers game as a
harmless pastime not connecting nickel and dime bets with illegal
racketeering. Betting on numbers or combinations of numbers significant to the bettor, perhaps based on dreams or premonitions,
the migrants sought to realize their fantasies. A winning bet yielding perhaps $150 to $200 meant a return trip to Puerto Rico, or new
furnishings and clothing, or monetary gifts for family members
and a tip for the *bolitero,* who made it all possible in the first place.
The *bolitero,* on the other hand, symbolized someone who had succeeded, to a degree, in conquering the new environment, who beat
the system, but remained true to his people in the community. He
was also, on occasion, the neighborhood connection, visiting a
series of homes or stores on his collection rounds. Commanding

respect based on his economic and social status in the *colonia*, the *bolitero* also lived comfortably, able to afford such luxuries as cars or telephones.

Nevertheless, by the mid-1930s the Puerto Rican Democratic clubs made a conscious effort to sever the association with the numbers game. At a meeting of all the Brooklyn Hispanic branch officers it was decided to rely solely on membership dues and other more acceptable means of fund raising. In a speech delivered by community leader Carlos Tapia to this assembly, he praised the unique working relationship in the past between the clubs and the boliteros recognizing that the alliance had been a necessary evil for both parties:

> Without it, these clubs, perhaps would not have been possible, but we cannot continue this way, because there is a feeling among our people that neither the regular party leaders nor the community would have any respect for our organizations as long as these situations continue. Luis and I (referring to Luis Felipe Weber) have talked about the problem and he agrees with me that it is about time we get due political recognition and respect from the regular party leaders.[10]

If "due political recognition and respect from the regular party leaders" concerned Carlos Tapia, just what was the relationship between the New York City political party system and the Puerto Rican clubs? Some researchers believe Puerto Ricans were not at all considered politically by the dominant Democratic or Republican party organizations. Others insisted Puerto Ricans failed to integrate themselves into city politics because they were not organizationally mature enough to do so.[11] But some felt a limited relationship did exist and that it was decidedly more beneficial for the dominant parties than for the Puerto Rican clubs. Based on this premise, the Puerto Rican community was given a semblance of political representation through the intercession of two non-Puerto Rican bosses, Jimmy Kelly and George McCure. Throughout the early thirties, these two individuals saw to it that any contact between Puerto Ricans and dominant party politics existed through them and because of this, Puerto Ricans were kept aloof from politics.[12]

Dominant Party Politics and the Puerto Rican Organizations

Along with minority party participation, especially the Socialist and Communist parties, Puerto Rican political club activity was indeed connected to dominant party politics. The concern for migrant welfare on the part of *colonia* organizations required a working relationship between the Puerto Rican associations and the political units of the larger non-Hispanic society. The Democratic party organization, traditionally the party of immigrants and the working class, functioned on paternalism and patronage patterns remarkably similar to the Puerto Rican clubs and familiar to the migrants themselves. Moreover, while Puerto Ricans would not be directly drawn into the city's political arena until the late forties and early fifties, the group as a potential voting bloc did not escape the notice of the New York politicians, particularly Democrats whose clubs outnumbered Republicans throughout the earlier decades.[13]

An association between European immigration and New York politicians can be traced to the mid-nineteenth century when Irish contractors connected with Tammany Hall brought over thousands of their countrymen on indenture, renting them out to canal builders in return for passage money.[14] Toward the last decades of the century when the Society of Tammany gained control of the Democratic Party in New York City and State, the immigration of Southern Italians and East European Jews was at its peak. These immigrants would participate in an association with Tammany Hall based on patronage and paternalism, the latter symbolized by the boss system. The boss or leader of the party organization on the borough or county level managed party affairs, often with an eye to his own private advantage. It was this individual, the party boss, along with the Assembly District leaders and the party faithful of the districts or neighborhood clubs throughout the city, who established the first contacts between the immigrant and American society. Meeting the boats at Ellis Island, the boss and his supporters assumed paternal responsibility for guiding the newcomer from alien status to citizenship, providing legal, housing and/or health aid, jobs, and even entertainment, for which the immigrant paid by loyal party support, party funding, and more important, the votes which kept the party in power. In exchange for their votes, the immigrants could turn to the local political machine when in need; party politicians and district clubs responded with holiday food baskets, annual picnics and clambakes.[15]

In the absence of a competitive civil service the boss system provided patronage on another level—jobs on the public payroll. The borough boss could reward a follower with a job as an office clerk, night watchman, garbage collector, street inspector, or policeman. For a price, saloons and gambling house owners in the city's ghettoes were protected from penalties on law violations; traffic tickets and jury notices were fixed; reduced tax assessments were procured; and building and sanitary code violations were overlooked. Theoretically, the party boss dealt with political matters only, but practically he was the economic overlord, social arbiter, unofficial government agent, and community patron.[16] All services rendered to the community by the district party were credited directly to him. Moreover, it was the party machine so closely connected with immigrant support and bossism which fostered political careers and influenced legislation through elected officials.

The unofficial union of party members into a cohesive self-governing society composed the city's "regular" Democratic or Republican clubs. These groups served as intermediaries between their constituency—the man on the street—and the city or state elected office holders. While the party's continued political entrenchment depended on votes, its objectives were to:

1. maintain political and financial control of the city and state.
2. advance the political fortunes of leaders, organizers of the group who exercised leadership functions.
3. improve political opportunities of the party membership.
4. develop loyalty to the party and as a result to serve the political interests of its membership.[17] With this end in mind, the clubs promoted social, civic, political, and welfare activities financed by private donations, fund raisers, and membership dues.

Leadership at the national level formed the apex of the party structure followed by leadership at the state, sectional, and regional levels. Among these were the County or Borough leaders. Their functions included the administration of party affairs through state and city-wide fund raising, collaboration, and consensus among themselves on political issues and supervising the election activities of their representatives on the local or district level, the Assembly District leaders. In the mid-thirties, seventy-six Assembly District leaders fulfilled their obligations as heads of the dominant clubs in sixty-two Assembly Districts. (Some districts had more than one leader.[18]) These individuals concerned themselves with "getting out the vote" and were charged with selecting captains and co-captains for each election district. These numbered from thirty to two hundred and fifty depending on the size of the Assembly District. Finally, the captains and co-captains supervised block captains, apartment house captains, and members of the election district committee (see Figure 4). Thus, when Tapia, Weber, and Ramón Colón became the power brokers between their clubs and county or district leaders, they were fulfilling roles in this capacity.

The political steps taken by Puerto Ricans in New York City during the late twenties and early thirties were intended to further the stability and ensure the permanence of the pioneer settlements. Puerto Rican political club leaders sought to trade welfare and social benefits for the migrant vote, and in turn aspired to deliver the votes to non-Hispanic politicians in exchange for patronage and protection. In this respect, the functions and objectives of these local units were similar to other political groups throughout the city; but while most of the latter constituted regular clubs within the dominant party structure, the Puerto Rican organizations fell into the category of subsidiary or "nationality" clubs.[19]

The clubs which occupied an undetermined or subsidiary status were categorized as: ordinary; nationality; racial or religious; or antisocial. These formed independently of the regular Assembly District leader, but often sought and received the recognition of the county, borough, or Assembly District leader. Recognition symbolized the acknowledgment by those above the local level, of the claims made by the clubs upon the rewards and resources of the party. A few groups existed without recognition, completely independently, and only the club name itself identified them with a particular party:

> The so-called "national" clubs are technically not part of the regular organization at all but they and other aristocratic

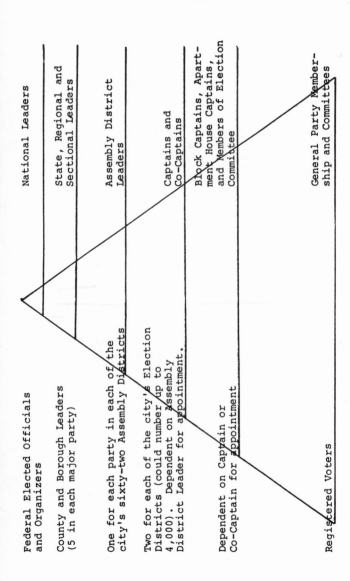

National Leaders

State, Regional and
Sectional Leaders

Assembly District
Leaders

Captains and
Co-Captains

Block Captains, Apart-
ment House Captains,
and Members of Election
Committee

General Party Member-
ship and Committees

Federal Elected Officials
and Organizers

County and Borough Leaders
(5 in each major party)

One for each party in each of the
city's sixty-two Assembly Districts

Two for each of the city's Election
Districts (could number up to
4,000). Dependent on Assembly
District Leader for appointment.

Dependent on Captain or
Co-Captain for appointment

Registered Voters

Figure 4 Party Structure and Function of Party Officials in New York, 1936

clubs may participate very frequently and significantly in normal political club activities. Another class comprises the
nationality clubs whose local units may, or may not be integral parts of the Assembly District organization, but are affiliated with each other on a county-wide, city-wide, state-wide
or national basis.[20]

Of the three categories, it was the nationality type to which the
Puerto Rican clubs belonged. Nationality clubs embodied contradictory purposes. While they performed useful services in uniting
heterogeneous groups into municipal, state, or national party politics, the organization also served as a disruptive force by upholding
the particular traditions, language, and leadership of the ethnic
group. The Puerto Rican locals did just that. Utilizing Spanish as
the principal language of communication, the clubs were, after all,
named for Puerto Rican historical and patriotic figures and perpetuated island heritage through the celebration of traditional holidays. Nevertheless, the necessity to support a city-wide political
system through the electoral process, for the rewards garnered in
terms of patronage, brought the group into contact with mainland
politics. On the other hand, regular party leaders had no fixed purpose in stimulating the organization of nationality clubs for any
reason other than the immediate one of harnessing votes. In fact,
one of the financial obligations which the district leader agreeably
accepted was the provision of payment of a few dollars for Puerto
Rican poll watchers on election day.[21] One observer commented:

> The Czech, Armenian, Greek, French, Syrian, *Porto Rican,*
> Jewish, Ukranian and Hungarian clubs are generally affiliat-
> ed with the Democratic Party but, since they are usually
> *starved for patronage,* their loyalty is uncertain. Most of
> them are "recognized" by the Tammany leaders only during
> campaigns.[22]

Subsidiary clubs including the nationality groups formed in several different ways. Some were organized on the initiative of the
Assembly District Leader himself, who would invite members of a
particular ethnic group to join him in the creation of such a club.
Here, the leader would aid in securing club headquarters and would

recognize his cofounders as captains or marshals in the city-wide party structure. Others came about on the initiative of the nationals themselves. These might have begun as social or civic groups which achieved political status when singled out by the regular party leaders for political purposes. A third method depended on the local club leaders assembling their compatriots as outright Democrats or Republicans. This was the case when Ramón Colón formed the Puerto Rican Republican Party Club in Brooklyn in 1935. After its formation, the club then seeks the support and affiliation of the regular party leaders. Finally, there were quasi-political units, such as social, fraternal, civic, or recreational groups, which in time acquired political interests and attitudes, reinforcing common heritage and traditions among their members and taking stands on relevant political issues.

The Puerto Rican Vote

If the recognition of Puerto Rican subsidiary groups rested on the potential voting bloc pledged to the regular party county or district leader, just how important was the Puerto Rican vote and how frequently did they, citizens since 1917, exercise this franchise? The answers to these questions are merely preliminary, since research on the political attitudes and the degree of participation in the *colonias* of the twenties, thirties, and forties is still scanty. Many Puerto Ricans obviously did not vote, for they were kept directly and indirectly from joining regular political clubs dominated by old-line Irish and Italians, and from participating in voter-connected activity.[23] Discouraged also by the unnerving experience of registration and submission to an English literacy test, a significant number of Puerto Ricans felt they had nothing to gain from electoral participation. As one migrant political activist who participated in community organizations during the period remarked:

> Many Puerto Ricans did not exercise their right to vote. In addition, it was not an easy matter to vote at that time. The officials submitted the aspirant to an interrogation with the purpose of frightening them and making them abandon their original political persuasions. This only served to keep Puerto Ricans away from the polls. But they [Puerto Ricans] also believed that they had nothing to look for in American politics.[24]

Yet as early as 1927, Fiorello La Guardia, congressman from East Harlem from 1923 to 1933 and subsequent Mayor of New York City, had courted the potential Puerto Rican vote. "Could you send me a list of Puerto Rican organizations located in my Congressional District?," he petitioned an aspiring Puerto Rican organization leader. "I would like to hear your plans as to the best way of getting Puerto Ricans interested. Do you know if they are interested in any particular legislation in Congress?"[25] However, it was always assumed by researchers like Chenault or Moynihan and Glazer that few Puerto Ricans responded to these overtures and that it was not until the mid-thirties that Hispanic and non-Hispanic politicians emerged who captured the imagination of the migrant voter.

Interestingly, the available evidence suggests the Puerto Ricans of the interwar years were far more politicized than previously assumed. One estimate is that over seven thousand registered Puerto Rican voters participated in the 1918 election of New York State Governor Alfred E. Smith. Most of these voters aligned themselves with the Democratic clubs of Brooklyn and Manhattan. A decade later, during the mid-twenties, the organizational report of the Porto Rican Brotherhood of America stated: "In the last general election of 1926, two thousand Porto Rican voters were credited to the 19th Congressional District while the entire registration for the city was over five thousand."

The next period in which a surge of electoral participation would occur among Puerto Rican voters was in the forties. Over 30,000 voters registered in Hispanic districts. Of these, 80 percent supported Franklin D. Roosevelt for the presidency and Vito Marcantonio for the East Harlem congressional seat.[26]

More personal indications of political activity appear in the migrants' own recollections of their experiences. Residents of the early Brooklyn community reported tremendous interest among the migrants in political organization and participation. One in particular, Guillerma Echevarria, devoted a good part of her time to political activities. Arriving in Brooklyn as a child in the early twenties from her native Vieques, most of Doña Guille's concerns were for the growth and integration of Puerto Ricans into the American political system. With an excellent command of both English and Spanish, she acted as an interpreter whenever Spanish-speaking individuals faced legal or bureaucratic entanglements. As a poll watcher, she was knowledgeable of the electoral processes, lecturing her neighbors on the power of the ballot and admonishing them not to abuse the privilege of casting their vote.[27]

In addition to electoral participation, at least two other factors guaranteed dominant party interest in cultivating Puerto Rican support. First, the decline in European immigration necessitated party support from other bases; second, the Seabury investigations' exposure of graft and corruption within the Democratic ranks reduced the power of the party in New York City.

Beginning with the twenties, European immigration began to decline at a time when the Puerto Rican settlements were both numerically and geographically expanding. While early-twentieth-century Jewish and Italian immigrants had found *Landsmanschaften* or regional associations already in existence upon their arrival, it had been the Democratic Party machinery which offered itself as political broker between the new immigrants and their new environment. Tammany Hall had traditionally given daily attention and assistance to the immigrant community through the boss system. But the First World War coupled with the first immigration restriction laws placed unfavorable quotas on Southern and Eastern European immigration, radically reducing the numbers of aliens coming to New York City.[28] The district political clubs, conditioned to transforming immigrants into ardent supporters and voting citizens, needed a new immigration to replace second and third generations of Europeans whose ties to the political machine were based more on convenience than necessity.

The Seabury investigations consisted of three separate probes running consecutively from 1930 to 1932, which included a full-scale exposure of corruption within the entire city government and resulted in virtually shattering the strength and credibility of the Democratic Party in New York. Moreover, by mid-decade President Franklin D. Roosevelt's New Deal program generated job-creating agencies such as the Works Progress Administration, Public Works Administration, Civil Conservation Corps, as well as social security and unemployment insurance programs on a nationwide scale, radically undermining the traditional paternalistic role of the city's party machine.[29]

Thus it was in the interest of the dominant party to court Puerto

Rican support. The Puerto Rican voter of the mid-twenties and thirties represented a replacement for the declining numbers of Italian and Jewish immigrants so important for the continued entrenchment of the party. Similarly, the Puerto Rican migrant leaders, dependent on patronage and protection for their community, sought due political recognition and respect from the regular party leaders and projected concerns which suggested the overriding importance of remaining within the Democratic party orbit. It was this organization, after all, which would provide the benefits, patronage, and protection for the Puerto Ricans as it had for immigrant groups before, forming bonds between city politics and the pioneer settlements not easily broken.

In the opinion of Puerto Rican community leaders, the relationship between the borough-wide Democratic party and the Puerto Rican local clubs was crucial for the survival of the Hispanic settlements. For example, in a perceptive dialogue with his colleagues, Carlos Tapia revealed practical and far-reaching ideas not only on the future of Puerto Ricans in New York's political affairs, but also on their own political future as a people. To achieve these aims, the working relationship between the city's politicians and the *colonias* remained top priority. Tapia explained the underlying basis for keeping an intact connection when he stated:

> So that when some unfortunate Puerto Rican is arrested by the police I can ask some politicians to talk to the judge on his behalf. So that I can ask the same politician to help some poor Puerto Rican who needs medical attention in some municipal hospital. . . . I am looking ahead for my people in Puerto Rico also and that is what every one of us should have in mind. The only way for our island to get political recognition is through the Puerto Ricans here in New York and in other states of the Union. Someday the Puerto Ricans in New York and in many other states of the United States, will by their political power get what our brothers on the island will never get, congressmen who in exchange for our help to elect them will have to help our beloved Puerto Rico. Someday our island will be a state like New York, or a republic like Cuba. Besides very soon we should be able to elect right here in New York, to begin with, some "Puerto Ricans" as aldermen.

Once we start doing that, the rest like electing Puerto Rican
district leaders and Puerto Rican assemblymen, etc., would
come as a matter of course.[30]

Tapia knew the importance of making personal contacts to
ensure the continuation of political favors which repaid loyal party
support. Among these were the eventual election of Puerto Rican
aldermen, district leaders, and assemblymen. More important, in
Tapia's opinion, these officials represented the vehicles through
which the political status of the island would be resolved. In this
way, the paternalistic relationship which had formerly existed
between the party politicians and other ethnic groups continued to
operate in the Puerto Rican settlement. Able to deal with district or
county politicians on a personal basis, a trait highly prized among
Puerto Ricans who functioned best within a network of personal
relationships, Tapia fostered associations designed to produce
immediate benefits for his people in the community.

Throughout the thirties and forties, political paternalism, personalism and concern for the Puerto Rican community in New
York and on the island continued to be integral factors in the political actions of *colonia* migrants. While the decade before was characterized by the domination of Democratic Party politics and its
conditioning on the Puerto Rican local clubs, succeeding decades
brought increased activity from rival political party contenders.
Moreover, both Hispanic and non-Hispanic political figures
emerged as representatives of the pre-World War II settlements and
these continued to base their performance on traditional paternalistic patterns.

Political Leadership

Few non-Hispanic politicians captured the imagination and the
vote of Puerto Ricans as did Vito Marcantonio, congressional representative from Manhattan's Twentieth Assembly District. Born
and raised in a Harlem tenement, Marcantonio was educated in
New York schools, receiving his law degree from New York University in 1926. A protégé of Fiorello La Guardia, Marcantonio
became a charismatic politician whose public speaking, knowledge,
and familiarity with East Harlem and highly developed ability at

organization merged to form the necessary leadership qualities to which people were drawn. After almost a decade of political experience as a lawyer, and as La Guardia's campaign manager in the district, Marcantonio ran for Congress in 1934, opposing the Democratic incumbent, J. J. Lanzetta. Marcantonio gained the endorsement of the Fusion and Republican parties, the Knicker-bocker Democrats and the Liberal party.

Marcantonio relied on the patterns of paternalism and personal contact, *personalismo,* so vital to the Puerto Rican migrant. In tune with the Depression needs of his district, the congressman staffed his Harlem office with Spanish-speaking personnel, law-yers, and secretaries who advised on legal and bureaucratic affairs or relief rolls. Bernardo Vega's position as a community activist afforded an opportunity to assess Marcantonio's rapport with the Puerto Rican settlement, and he wrote:

> His office and campaign headquarters located at 247 East 116th Street were practically full of people at all hours of the day or night. People spoke in no less than six languages: Italian, Spanish, Polish, Yiddish, Hungarian and English. They were men and women, young and old with citizenship, health or relief problems, accidents, housing, immigration and the hundred and one preoccupations of the poor.

The relationship between the migrant community and the con-gressman centered on bread-and-butter issues, and the support given Marcantonio would in time supersede that given to any other non-Hispanic politician. It was solidly based on the personal atten-tion paid to community situations as well as his firsthand experi-ence and knowledge in attacking *colonia* problems. Personal migrant accounts repeatedly described the individual care given their problems. One woman, wrongly accused of not paying her rent, sought Marcantonio's help. Another denounced the local butcher for overcharging. No problem was too insignificant. The fact that Marcantonio and his representatives concerned themselves in this manner on basic daily issues assured him community sup-port in times to come and in a very real sense filled the void left by the old-style Democratic party connections.[31]

One migrant and long-time resident of the Spanish-speaking

community conveyed the sentiments of other working-class Puerto Ricans with regard to Marcantonio. As a representative of neighborhood clubs and a confirmed supporter of the congressman, his description expressed a devotion rooted in the fatherly leadership which Marcantonio personified:

> Marcantonio was the best. People said he was a communist, may the Lord rest his soul, but he was the best New York ever had. At that time he was a congressman but he aspired to become mayor of New York but because people thought he was a communist, well, he couldn't accomplish his goal. Marcantonio would say to us when we would get together, always, he would say, "we will struggle so that New York would not become a disaster." I would always remember those words. He would say, "do you see you are paying five cents in the subway today. If New York doesn't look to where it's going it will soon be sixty cents a fare" and we are already seeing that. And there is very little that Marcantonio said which did not come true.[32]

A spokesperson for the working class, Marcantonio sat on the committees on Territories, Civil Service, and Labor, instrumental vehicles for passing legislation affecting his Puerto Rican constituency both in New York City and on the island. At mid-decade, he was the undisputed political leader of the area. He gained fame for defending the Puerto Rican nationalist leader, Don Pedro Albizu Campos, who was convicted and incarcerated for political acts against colonialism in Puerto Rico. He commanded respect for opposing a proposed change in the Fair Labor Standards Act which would exempt the island from minimum wage provisions. These and many more stands endeared him to the Puerto Rican community. Moreover, in city politics, he was equally concerned with the plight of the Puerto Ricans in his district, denouncing as discriminatory the New York City Board of Education's classification of Hispanic students based on biased testing.[33]

Marcantonio's presence within the Puerto Rican political orbit signaled the start of a new era for the political aspirations of the pre-World War II settlements. Understandably, the community offered him their unlimited support, particularly through clubs and

organizations. *La Mutualista Obrera Puertorriqueña,* the Communist Party, *Centro Obrero Español, Unión Industrial de Tabaqueros* and the Committee Against Facism and the War, all endorsed
Marcantonio. In addition, small churches, some leftist intellectu-
als, and the working class also came out in his favor. But some
Puerto Rican community leaders, loyal Democratic Party endors-
ers, opposed Marcantonio's candidacy, preferring instead his
opponent the Democratic incumbent. These were clearly influenced
by the widespread belief that Marcantonio used the Puerto Rican
community for his own advantage, gaining support from the group
by declaring his sympathy for Puerto Rican independence, condemning the treatment of the island by the United States, and
vigorously pressing for concessions for the distressed people living
in the Harlem area.[34] Certainly, the ties between the Puerto Rican
community and the Democratic party were not yet severed.

Perhaps the best example of a Puerto Rican political leader during the same period was Oscar García Rivera. He was the first
Puerto Rican to run for the New York State Legislature in the elections of 1937. A lawyer by training and at first a Republican,
García Rivera later ran on the American Labor Party ticket in
1938, but was defeated the following year during a Roosevelt
Democratic landslide. At that time it was not unusual for a Puerto
Rican candidate running on a Republican ticket to gain the
endorsement of Puerto Rican Democrats. First, as in the case of
García Rivera, Puerto Ricans readily crossed party lines to support
a candidate or an issue which directly affected them.[35] Second, the
Republican party appeared in a remarkably favorable light after
the Seabury investigations succeeded in crippling Democratic control. Although a Republican, García Rivera preached a social
reform program more akin to socialist ideology than to a conservative stance. Third, the Republicans had also courted the Puerto
Rican vote, aligning themselves early in the century with sympa-
thizers for Puerto Rican independence. The Liberty Republican
Club had operated in Manhattan since the end of the twenties with
migrant representation. Moreover, in 1935, the first Puerto Rican
Republican party local had been founded in Brooklyn by Ramón
Colón in an attempt to offer the Puerto Rican voter a two party
system.[36]

García Rivera's candidacy was heartily endorsed by Puerto Rican voters for yet another reason. In a personal interview, his widow, Dr. Eloísa García Rivera, confirmed the Spanish-speaking community turned out en masse, relentlessly campaigning in his behalf as a result of the super organization of his party headquarters. Campaigners knocked on doors, distributed propaganda, personally escorted potential voters to the polls, arranged for babysitting, and launched intensive voter registration drives in the neighborhoods of Spanish Harlem.

Aware of the special needs of the Harlem migrants, and particularly of the intimidation of facing a voter registration board, Doña Eloísa herself designed a program to prepare potential voters for registration. Along with a trained cadre of political supporters which included bilingual-bicultural high school and college students, Doña Eloísa commandeered a small office adjacent to campaign headquarters where she tutored residents in the intricacies of the literacy test and registrational procedure. In her opinion, this task force did more to secure García Rivera's seat in the State Legislature than any other maneuver.[37]

While in office, García Rivera spoke often in support of his Harlem tenement constituency, proposing reforms and endorsing legislation sometimes in conflict with Republican party priorities. Maintaining his law offices on 116th Street, García Rivera also concerned himself with the immediate problems affecting Puerto Ricans in the metropolitan area. One example in particular centered on a series of investigations and subsequent reports issued on the exploitation and crude work experiences of Puerto Rican seasonal migrant agricultural laborers in the states of New York and New Jersey. Legal representative for local businesses and private residents of the *colonia,* Oscar García Rivera also represented many of the Puerto Rican associations of the period.

Yet, in spite of the show of support exhibited in the elections of 1937 and 1938, Puerto Ricans for the most part apparently continued to identify with the Democratic party. "Between the two major political parties, the Puerto Rican is almost without exception Democrat," declared one researcher on the topic.[38] Throughout the thirties and forties, the Democratic party and related associations continued to court Puerto Rican favor. After close to two decades of participation, the Puerto Rican political clubs appeared to have become increasingly dominated by a handful of professionals within the *colonia*. Instead of grass-roots politicians like Tapia or Weber, the new leaders were doctors, lawyers, or other professionals. Rosters of prominent community leaders appeared on club stationery along with secretarial and public relations personnel. In 1932, for example, a letter written on letterhead stationery of The League of Spanish Speaking Democrats demonstrated the growing tendency among professionals to engage in politics. Written in Spanish, the communication alludes to a void in the directorship of the public relations committee offering the post to one Dr. Gabriel E. Álvarez, a chiropractor based in New York City. The offer, made in recognition of Dr. Álvarez's continued and enthusiastic service in association activities, carried the authorization of the publicity committee members.[39] This particular organization numbered among its board of directors six doctors, one lawyer, a clergyman, a professor, and four women, all recognized for their dedication and support of the Hispanic community.

An example of a professional who distinguished himself as a political leader within the Puerto Rican *colonias* as well as with the host society was Dr. José Negrón Cesteros. A native of Bayamón, Puerto Rico, Cesteros came to the United States in 1913 at the age of nineteen, where he studied at the University of Iowa, graduating also from Howard University Medical School. After coming to New York, he received staff privileges at Manhattan General Hospital. Dr. Cesteros lived and practiced medicine in that borough, was vice chairman of the Mayor's Committee on Puerto Rican Affairs, and a member of the Hispanic Medical Association.[40]

Dr. José N. Cesteros became one of the political representatives of the Harlem community during the late thirties and forties. Assuming leadership during the difficult period of the Depression, he quickly rose through the political ranks, serving on such committees as the Emergency Unemployment Relief Committee and the South Harlem Committee Headquarters. These committees represented a cross-section of the Puerto Rican and Hispanic leadership. Through civic participation, Dr. Cesteros promoted Democratic party goals. Appointed chairperson of the Puerto Rican Division of the Democratic National Committee by 1936, Cesteros formed a coalition which included Robert F. Wagner, United States senator from New York, Dennis Chavez, senator from New Mexico, and Representative Adolph J. Sabath from Illinois as honorary members. Moreover, thirteen coordinators from New York City, a 150-member advisory committee, and twenty-seven members of a ladies' committee, the majority of whom were Puerto Rican, also sat on this body. Cesteros continued participating in the political arena until his death in 1958 at the age of sixty-three.

Thus, on the one hand, Cesteros fulfilled one of the major goals articulated by Tapia decades before as part of the underlying reasons for Puerto Rican involvement in party politics—that of key placement of Puerto Rican political figures. On the other hand, as a professional, Cesteros was not quite typical of those Puerto Rican major party supporters of the late thirties and forties, who were overwhelmingly working class. Who spoke for the migrants? Those too preoccupied with job and family responsibilities, with survival in a Depression era, to dedicate themselves to party politics? Who spoke for the issues most relevant to the Spanish-speaking *colonias*? At least two alternative developments during the interwar years partially answer these questions. One was, of course, the emergence of populist politicians like García Rivera or Vito Marcantonio, already discussed, who continued the paternalistic pattern of party politics evident before the thirties; the other was the creation of numerous politically oriented community groups which spoke in the name of the *colonias* (see Appendix II).

Politically oriented associations or quasi-political groups demonstrated political involvement in several different ways. One was through the sponsorship of particular candidates whom they permitted to address their groups. Another was through the support given to certain political issues. Yet another was through the creation of or participation in organizations which aligned themselves to specific political stands. The latter often endorsed minority party politics such as socialist, communist, or liberal. Because of the unique migratory patterns between Puerto Rico and the settlements in the United States, those issues which most affected the island either of a political, social, or work-related nature affected the New York settlements as well.

The nature of the migration was such that ties between the island and the continental communities were never severed and constantly reinforced by the circular migration. Puerto Ricans traveled freely between both points, keeping abreast not only of domestic interests but of organizational and political issues as well. It was not surprising then that the relationship between Puerto Rican politics in Puerto Rico and electoral behavior among the migrants of the New York settlements had more in common than just methods of electioneering, campaigning, or voter registration drives. Frequently, island politicians and elected officials appeared before migrant organizations soliciting their support and goodwill on behalf of continental office-seekers.[41]

In the 1930s, for example, the Puerto Rican politician Antonio Barceló came to *El Barrio* to speak in support of Vito Marcantonio. Similarly, during the 1940s Gilberto Concepción de Gracia, founder of the island's Independence party did the same. One migrant's personal account affirmed that between 200 and 250 individuals would turn out to hear Concepción de Gracia. Similarly, Santiago Iglesias Pantín, active in Puerto Rican union organizing and one of the founders of the *Federación Libre de Trabajadores* commanded a large audience. He actively campaigned against Marcantonio. Muñoz Marín, founder of the *Partido Popular Democrata* and the first elected governor of the island, did the same. In the 1940s the incumbent mayor of New York City, William O'Dwyer, reaped the benefits of endorsement from the Mayoress of San Juan, Doña Felisa Rincón de Gautier. A familiar figure in the political scenario on both sides of the ocean, Doña Felisa continued to influence the political behavior of the migrant community well into the fifties. So too did New York-based politicians look toward the Puerto Rican social and political organizations as the vehicles through which they could win Hispanic support. The fact that this type of electioneering and campaigning was almost always carried out within the confines of *colonia* organizations points out once again the importance of the network within the Spanish-speaking communities.

Minority Party Politics and Puerto Rican Organizations

The Puerto Rican political clubs or quasi-political organizations which aligned themselves along minority party politics were almost always socialist or communist in outlook. Many were distinctly European or Latin American in their interpretations of and dedication to respective political ideologies. However, neither the Socialist nor Communist parties in New York City benefited from the thorough organization—from local neighborhood to district to county level—that characterized the major or dominant parties. In 1929, for example, there were only forty-three regular organizations operating within the city's sixty-two Assembly Districts and an additional eighteen special organizations catering specifically to the various ethnic groups.[42] Nevertheless, the minority parties functioned to check the secondary (Republican) party, provided more forums for open discussion, and encouraged the participation of the city's ethnic or national groups on a larger scale than did the majority parties. Those attracted to minority parties worked collectively for a more systematic reorganization of government and society rather than for the tangible individual rewards based on the patronage of dominant party structure. Moreover, among the priorities of the Puerto Rican minority-oriented locals, there existed an unconditional concern for the welfare of the working class in Puerto Rico as well as in New York City.

The Puerto Rican *Alianza Obrera* exemplified a quasi-political unit because it supported the political parties which best represented the interests of its membership. Founded in 1922, the group operated as a class-conscious community organization which forged links with the Socialist party. Through its newspaper, *The Socialist Call,* the city's Spanish-speaking population was kept informed of the group's activities. *Alianza Obrera* not only lent its backing to socialist causes; it provided a forum in which candidates and party members could present their ideas. Furthermore, among the membership of the *Alianza* were individuals who belonged to the Socialist party. One of these, Jesus Colón, was a founding member of the first New York committee of the Puerto Rican Socialist party in 1918, and secretary of the *Alianza Obrera Puertorriqueña* in 1922.[43] As one of the *colonia*'s leading writers, Colón bridged the gap between the island and the continent, helping to popularize socialist causes and *Alianza* activities. As a correspondent, he wrote for the socialist press, *La Justicia.* Along with his brother Joaquin and his cousin Ramón, Jesus Colón figured in the founding of several newspapers in Brooklyn with the purpose of informing readers on both sides of the ocean about their respective community issues and events. Of these, *Curioso* was intended to relay political propaganda.

During the 1920s another group, *La Liga Puertorriqueña,* shifted its objectives from its foundation as an apolitical federation of community associations to an affiliation with the regular Democratic party. At that time, Gonzalo O'Neill, the *Liga*'s president, justified this action in the following manner:

> If we are to live within the North American orbit, if we are to form part of the Great Republic, we do not wish, given our aspirations, to vegetate within this atmosphere, like automatons, but instead act like conscientious beings—demonstrating that we possess qualities worthy of valuable workers.[44]

While the *Liga* was not founded specifically with political objectives in mind, other groups combined both social and political goals in their charters of incorporation. The Porto Rican Political and Social League, incorporated on March 31, 1936, vowed to promote political participation among its members in spite of its nonpartisan stand:

> This is a non-partisan political and social organization for the following purposes: to create, promote and develop social and civic activities among its members; to develop a better understanding and political unity among Puerto Ricans and Spanish-American individuals who are eligible to vote within the confines of the city of New York; to hold gatherings at different periods of the year for the recreation of members and their guests; to provide opportunities and places for the expression of social acts and to hold social affairs; nothing in this constitution shall be construed as a limitation on the part of the membership to adhere to any political party who will give recognition to our association and will assist in benefitting its members and will accept our candidates for election, or of the powers of this organization, which shall exercise all those implied and necessary prerogatives to carry on and conduct them within enumerated powers.[45]

In the same year the Puerto Rican Democratic and Social Union stated similar objectives in its certificate of incorporation:

> To maintain an organization for the social and mental uplift of all its members; to take an active and civic interest in gov-

ernmental affairs and to have helpful recreation. These activities shall be carried out without pecuniary profit to the corporation or to any of its members. This organization shall be financed from the collections of dues and voluntary contributions.[46]

The issues which most concerned the quasi-political organizations were: a combination of internal community problems; issues beyond the geographic confines of the *colonias* such as the Spanish Civil War; concerns over Puerto Rico's political status; emergency relief funds, and identification with social and political developments throughout Spanish-America.

One case in point, nationalism and support for the island's independence movement, commanded substantial interest in the New York settlements. Nationalist campaigns for independence, including the formation of groups for this purpose and fund raising, were evident in the settlements during the mid-thirties.[47] A hotly debated issue, the cause for independence was firmly supported in New York with the eruption of the Ponce Massacre in Puerto Rico.

The Ponce Massacre took place on Easter Sunday in 1937 in the Puerto Rican city of the same name. Following a series of sporadic confrontations between Nationalist and anti-Nationalist forces over a period of several years, the former had requested and been given permission to assemble peacefully in Ponce on March 21. At the final hour, the permit to march was revoked, too late for the Nationalists to cancel their procession. Ignorant of the last-minute changes, those who marched were greeted by armed resistence as the police fired into the marchers, wounding and killing hundreds of Nationalists and innocent bystanders.

Thousands of Puerto Ricans in New York City demonstrated against the situation in Ponce. Over ten thousand Puerto Rican members of scores of political and social clubs assembled in Central Park and then paraded through the streets of Spanish Harlem in protest, as they had done the year before over the arrests, trial, and conviction of the island's Nationalist leaders. Their intention, clearly illustrated by the speeches made and placards on exhibition, was to denounce the attitudes and actions of "Imperialist America" in Puerto Rico. Critical issues such as this one united Puerto Ricans of all political persuasions.

Certainly the politics of the island continued to interest early set-

tlement migrants. As groups turned out in support of the Nationalist movement, so did they uphold other avenues of political
thought. As early as the 1920s, for example, Antonio R. Barceló
had articulated a preference for a type of autonomy called the
Estado Libre Asociado (Associated Free State) modeled after the
Irish Free State, as the solution to Puerto Rico's legal status. Aware
of the island's strategic importance to the United States, and
accepting the relationship between the two, Barceló suggested the
formation of a government equally beneficial to both interests. As
Barceló was a frequent visitor to the New York settlements, his
ideas found favor as one viable alternative for the island's political
future.[48]

Finally, groups like the Porto Rican Political and Social League
and the Puerto Rican Democratic and Social Union encouraged the
practice of good American citizenship indirectly condoning the
reality of the Puerto Rican existence within the North American
political orbit. These units would have articulated conformity with
the status quo, conditioning migrants in this direction.

Of equal interest and importance, particularly for those who had
relatives in Latin American countries or in Spain, were the political
and social affairs of those countries. Puerto Rican groups took
political stands opposing the Machado and the Gómez dictator-
ships in Cuba and Venezuela and against the rise of Fascism in
Spain. They supported the Sandinistas in Nicaragua and continued
to closely observe political developments in the Dominican Republic. "We defend the aspirations of Puerto Rico and combat the
tyranny of Juan Vicente Gómez in Venezuela and Gerardo Machado in Cuba," wrote Bernardo Vega in the pages of *Gráfico* during
the thirties.[49]

Commitment was not merely in words, but included practical
action as well. The pioneer settlements demonstrated their support
through relief units and emergency committees, all formed in connection with the existing *colonia* organizations. The Nicaraguan
Sandinistas, for example, received aid from the associations, which
included clothing, food, and medical supplies. In this particular
incident, Sandino's brother, a long-time resident of the New York
Spanish-speaking *colonia,* was able to muster additional support by
personally appealing to neighborhood groups and inviting them to
send a representative, fact-finding committee to Nicaragua, to

observe conditions firsthand. A central committee, *Manos Fuera de Nicaragua,* was formed, medical supplies sent, and communication firmly established between Nicaraguan Sandinistas and the New York settlements.[50]

Similarly, the Spanish Civil War effort generated volunteer services, providing medical aid and ammunition from New York. Puerto Ricans were almost always in support of the Loyalists, but the issues surrounding the war were nevertheless endlessly debated. Many Puerto Ricans had relatives in Spain, and with the bombardment of Madrid in the summer of 1936, thousands of men, women, and children paraded through the streets of New York in protest.

Finally, national issues also garnered attention among Puerto Rican political units. The emigration of Puerto Rican agricultural workers proposed by private corporations in Arizona was soundly denounced by *colonia* groups and presses. One such group, the Workers Alliance, or *Alianza Obrera,* frequently raised human rights issues for both action and discussion. These ranged from the plight of the Oakies in the West, the Chicago riots, and city and national politics, to the importance of activating student unions.[51]

Conclusion

Surely, political awareness and participation among Puerto Ricans in New York was far greater than previously assumed. We have traced political consciousness and action beginning with those foundations laid before the turn of the century to the period just before the Second World War. The earliest groups nurtured leadership as well as a preoccupation with the island's status within the context of Puerto Rican political development. Against the background of the United States occupation, the migration accelerated, taking root in New York *colonias* where political activity also underwent changes commensurate with the growth and predilections of the pioneer settlements. By the twenties, an awareness of the importance of functioning within a North American political orbit intensified causing political or quasi-political clubs to give priority to the problems of the migrants and their community. Aligned with dominant and minority party politics, Puerto Rican groups attempted to exchange the vote for social welfare benefits, as many others had done before them. Based on patronage, paternalism,

and personalism, a new cadre of political figures commanded the
loyalties of the Puerto Rican voter.

Without doubt, the political organizations served as roadways
toward the larger surrounding society, Spanish America and Spain,
and Puerto Rico. Through political associations, Puerto Ricans
kept abreast of the issues and events affecting their Spanish-
speaking compatriots on a global scale. Absent from the homeland,
they expressed their sentiments on numerous topics impacting on
Puerto Rico, but especially the political status of the island. As
migrants they used political groups as buffers between non-
Hispanics and the *colonias*. Moreover, politics embodied a recognition among the migrants of their true situation in America, as settlers in an unfamiliar territory, as an identifiable ethnic group, and
as members of the working class.

Notes

1. Ricardo Campos and Juan Flores, "National Culture and Migration:
Perspective from the Puerto Rican Working Class," *Centro Working
Papers,* Centro de Estudios Puertorriquenos (New York: CUNY, 1978),
pp. 8–9. See also César Andreu Iglesias, ed., *Memorias de Bernardo Vega*
(Rio Piedras: Ediciones Huracan, Inc., 1977), pp. 77–85.

2. Iglesias, *Memorias,* pp. 106–107.

3. Julio José Henna continued his work in community organizations
participating in Groups like the Club Latinoamericano and the Democratic
Party associations in the city. Figueroa similarly appeared on the rosters of
several groups. See Appendices I and II.

4. Iglesias, *Memorias,* pp. 155–156. Also interview with Homero Rosado, Brooklyn College, Brooklyn, New York, November 1980. Interview
with Ramón Colón, Puerto Rican Oral History Project, 1973–1974, Long
Island Historical Society, Brooklyn, New York.

5. Ramón Colón, *Carlos Tapia, A Puerto Rican Hero in New York*
(New York: Vantage Press, 1976), p. 44. Also Ramón Colón interview;
James Jennings, *Puerto Rican Politics in New York City* (Washington,
D.C.: University Press of America, 1977), p. 24. *Note:* Jennings refers to
the Democratic politicians as Jimmy Kelly and George McCure.

6. Colón, *Carlos Tapia,* p. 44; Jennings, *Puerto Rican Politics,* pp.
24–25.

7. Wallace S. Sayre and Herbert Kaufman, *Governing New York City*
(New York: W.W. Norton & Co., 1965), pp. 11–18. See also Warren Moscow, *The Last of the Big-Time Bosses* (New York: Stein & Day, 1971).

8. Colón, *Carlos Tapia,* p. 45.

9. Interview with Honorina Weber Irizarry, Puerto Rican Oral History Project.

10. Colón, *Carlos Tapia,* p. 45.

11. Among the researchers who share this point of view are: Patricia Cayo Sexton, *Harlem Español* (Mexico: Editorial Diana, 1966), p. 133; Nathan Glazer and Daniel P. Moynihan, *Beyond the Melting Pot* (Cambridge, Mass.: MIT Press, 1963), p. 107.

12. Jennings, *Puerto Rican Politics,* pp. 24, 85, 138.

13. *Brooklyn Daily Eagle Almanac,* Brooklyn Eagle Press, 1924 through 1937. Throughout this period the *Almanac* consistently listed a predominance of Democratic Party organizations. See also Wallace S. Sayre, *Governing New York City,* p. 463; Roy V. Peel, *The Political Clubs of New York City* (New York: G.P. Putnam & Sons, 1935), pp. 22–45; Hugh A. Bone, "Political Parties in New York City," *American Political Science Review,* vol. 40 (April 1946), pp. 272–282.

14. Page Smith, *The Shaping of America,* vol. III (New York: McGraw-Hill Book Co., 1980), p. 748. See also Peel, *The Political Clubs,* pp. 56–57.

15. Peel, *The Political Clubs,* pp. 64–68. See also Jack Alexander, "District Leader: Profile of James J. Hines," *The New Yorker,* vol. 12, July 25, 1936, pp. 21–26, August 1, 1936, pp. 18–23.

16. Peel, *The Political Clubs.*

17. Sayre and Kaufman, *Governing New York City,* pp. 70–73. See also Citizens Union, "Party Organization in New York City," *The Searchlight,* vol. 41, May 1951; Marilyn Gittell, "Administration and Organization of Political Parties in New York City" (New York University, Masters Thesis, 1953).

18. Peel, *The Political Clubs,* p. 65.

19. Ibid., pp. 251–267.

20. Ibid., p. 65.

21. Interview with Homero Rosado; Ramón Colón interview.

22. Peel, *The Political Clubs,* p. 258. Emphasis added.

23. Clara E. Rodríguez, "Puerto Ricans in the Melting Pot," *The Journal for Ethnic Studies,* vol. 1, no. 4 (winter 1974), pp. 89–97.

24. Homero Rosado interview.

25. Arthur Mann, *La Guardia—A Fighter Against His Times: Vol 1, 1881–1933* (New York: J.B. Lippincott, 1959), p. 246.

26. Iglesias, *Memorias,* p. 155.

27. References to Guillerma Echevarria recur in the interviews found in the Puerto Rican Oral History Project.

28. Samuel Eliot Morrison, *The Oxford History of the American People, Vol. III* (New York: New American Library, 1972), p. 234. See also

Terry L. McCoy, "A Primer for U.S. Policy on Caribbean Emigration," *Caribbean Review,* vol. 8, no. 1 (January-March 1979), pp. 10-15. The Johnson Act of 1921 limited the numbers of aliens admitted annually to 3 percent of the number of foreign born of that nationality already in the United States according to the census of 1910. The total allowed was 358,000 of which 200,000 were allotted to Northern European countries and 155,000 to those of Southern and Eastern Europe.

29. Rosa Estades, "Patterns of Political Participation of Puerto Ricans in New York City" (New York, New School for Social Research, Ph.D. Dissertation, 1974), p. 65. See also Moscow, *The Last of Big-Time Bosses,* pp. 24-29; Sayre and Kaufman, *Governing New York City,* pp. 535-581.

30. Ramón Colón interview.

31. Numerous interviews discuss the devotion felt for Marcantonio among Puerto Ricans, and many commented favorably on the way he related to the community. Among them were Ramón Colón, Bernardo Vega, Homero Rosado, Antonio Rivera Hernández, Eloísa García Rivera, and Margarita Soto Alers.

32. Interview with Pedro Ruiz and Margarita Soto Alers, Aguada, Puerto Rico, July 1977.

33. The Vito Marcantonio Collection, New York Public Library, Archival Division, Boxes 2, 3, 4, 17. See also Annette T. Rubenstein and Associates, *I Vote My Conscience—Debates, Speeches and Writings of Vito Marcantonio, 1935-1950* (New York: The Vito Marcantonio Memorial, 1956).

34. Lawrence R. Chenault, *The Puerto Rican Migrant in New York* (New York: Columbia University Press, 1938; reissued, Russell & Russell, 1970), p. 155.

35. Interview with Dr. Eloísa García Rivera, New York City, May 1976; Margarita Soto Alers interview; Ramón Colón interview.

36. Iglesias, *Memorias,* pp. 194-195; Ramón Colón interview.

37. Eloísa García Rivera interview. Moreover, in the mid-fifties Ralph Rosas, former director of the Community Organization Division of the Office of the Commonwealth of Puerto Rico, instituted a program of voter registration similar in operation to Dr. García Rivera's, in conjunction with the Council of Hispanic Organizations. See Carlota Suárez, "Don Ralph Rosas, Puerto Rico en Nueva York: Visión y Práctica" (Brooklyn College, 1980, unpublished manuscript).

38. Chenault, *The Puerto Rican Migrant,* p. 155; Iglesias, *Memorias,* p. 187.

39. Correspondence of the League for Spanish-speaking Democrats, October 24, 1932.

40. *New York Times,* February 9, 1958, p. 88.

41. Iglesias, *Memorias,* pp. 183-184. See also Adalberto López, "An

Italian-American's Defense of Puerto Rico and Puerto Ricans," *Caribbean Review,* vol. 8, no. 1 (January-March 1979), pp. 16–21.

42. Peel, *The Political Clubs,* pp. 299–300.

43. Campos and Flores, "National Culture," pp. 40–41; Iglesias, *Memorias,* p. 156; Ramón Colón Interview.

44. *La Prensa,* January 15, 1923, p. 1. See also Iglesias, *Memorias,* pp. 174–175.

45. The Porto Rican Political and Social League, Certificate of Incorporation, File No. 3091-360, March 13, 1936, New York City County Clerk's Office, Municipal Building, New York City.

46. Puerto Rican Democratic and Social Union, Inc., Certificate of Incorporation, File No. 00923-35C, January 17, 1935.

47. Chenault, *The Puerto Rican Migrant,* pp. 153–154.

48. López, "An Italian-American's Defense," pp. 16–21. See also Kal Wagenheim, *Puerto Rico: A Profile* (New York: Praeger Press, 1974), p. 71.

49. Iglesias, *Memorias,* p. 196; interview with Lillian López, New York City, May 1976.

50. *Gráfico,* July 8, 1928.

51. Interview with Evelina Antonetty, Columbia Oral History Project, Columbia University, New York City.

Plates

PLATE 11 Outing of La Liga Puertorriqueña, Inc. Section No. 1, Brooklyn, New York, at Heckscher Park, August 26, 1934. The Jesús Colón Papers. Courtesy of the Center for Puerto Rican Studies, Hunter College, CUNY.

PLATE 12 Borinquen Democratic Club, Brooklyn, 1961. The Justo A. Martí Photographic Collection. Courtesy of the Center for Puerto Rican Studies, Hunter College, CUNY.

PLATE 13 Voter registration committee of the
Hispanic Citizens of New York, Lower Manhattan,
September 1956. The Justo A. Martí Photographic
Collection. Courtesy of the Center for Puerto Rican
Studies, Hunter College, CUNY.

PLATE 14 Jacob Javitz visiting the Spanish
American Civic Organization of Brooklyn, circa
1968. The Justo A. Martí Photographic Collection.
Courtesy of the Center for Puerto Rican Studies,
Hunter College, CUNY.

PLATE 15 Puerto Rican Merchants Association's
new office, 1960. The Justo A. Martí Photographic
Collection. Courtesy of the Center for Puerto Rican
Studies, Hunter College, CUNY.

PLATE 16 Hometown Club, Hijos de Jayuya, Inc.,
May 20, 1962. The Justo A. Martí Photographic
Collection. Courtesy of the Center for Puerto
Rican Studies, Hunter College, CUNY.

PLATE 17 The United Bronx Parents, Inc., and its
founder and executive director, Evelina López
Antonetty, 1970s. The Records of the United Bronx
Parents. Courtesy of the Center for Puerto Rican
Studies, Hunter College, CUNY.

PLATE 18 Student demonstration at Brooklyn
College in support of Puerto Rican Studies, early
1970s. Courtesy of the Center for Latino Studies,
Brooklyn College, CUNY.

From the Great Migration to the Present

As the United States moved toward a peacetime economy follow-ing the Second World War, the Puerto Rican *colonias* in New York City yielded the contours of a distinctive community. Historically situated between the two world wars, the process of building a community had been both arduous and multifaceted. Nourished by a steady migratory stream from island to mainland, and nurtured against the interplay of a continuing colonial relationship, the dis-persal of thousands of Puerto Ricans was influenced by a series of individual and structural factors. Pawns between colonial politics and economic realities, Puerto Ricans rationalized migration for a variety of purposes: better living conditions, employment oppor-tunities, and sometimes even for adventure. Once in New York City, they set about reconstructing neighborhoods solidly modeled on familiar institutions, similar to those they knew in Puerto Rico. In the process, they transplanted distinct attitudes, ideas, values, practices, language, and other cultural traditions that shaped and distinguished their Puerto Rican *colonias* from all other ethnic en-claves. From mid-century through the 1980s the expansion of the community assumed regional and national significance as Puerto Ricans became the second largest group among the nation's Latino population.[1]

The Great Migration: Post-World War II

The nature of the postwar migration was such that movement between Puerto Rico and the United States was continuous. Invigorating and reinforcing communal development, this circular movement of people significantly affected the migrant community's adjustment and assimilation on U.S. terms, so evident in the experience of earlier ethnic immigrations. Leaving the island for the mainland did not entail severing the bonds of Puerto Rican cultural citizenship. Indeed, once their economic situation was secure, most Puerto Ricans expected to return to the island, though others would commit to stateside family connections and never leave, and still others formed part of the ongoing circular migration that intensified with each passing decade. But if the twin torches of language and cultural identity played a dominant role in early settlement considerations, total assimilation was far from the migrants' frame of reference. "I think we have to recognize in this long-standing rejection of a quick transfer of identity a profoundly political act that is decidedly life-affirming and non-suicidal," wrote one second-generation stateside Puerto Rican, reflecting sentiments often articulated by many migrants.[2]

The 1950s witnessed a pivotal point in Puerto Rican migration and mobility. Unprecedented increases in the U.S. Puerto Rican population, a result of relocation to the continent as well as births to those already present, signaled massive transformations of urban enclaves. At mid-century, Puerto Ricans figured in the census of every state of the union. Although at that time 80 percent of the migrants continued to make New York City and its metropolitan environs their point of disembarkation, that percentage dwindled within the decade. Traditional neighborhoods that traced their genesis to earlier migrant *colonias* bore the brunt of modernization projects like urban renewal and found themselves hard-pressed to accommodate the recent arrivals.

The first generation of airborne migrants responded to the fluctuations in the U.S. economy in three discernible waves. The first wave, characterized by a massive out-migration of working-class Puerto Rican men and women, occurred from the late 1940s to the 1960s. This contingent concentrated in the industrial north, where they found low-paid employment in blue-collar trades and the manufacturing industries. Between 1940 and 1960 the number of Puerto Rican residents in the continental United States rose from 69,967 to 887,662, and the Puerto Rican population of New York City is estimated to have increased from 61,463 to 612,574 (see Tables 13 and 14).[3] Three out of every ten Puerto Ricans were born in the United States. By 1960 almost half of Puerto Rican males (47 percent) and females (45 percent) were under twenty years of age.

TABLE 13
Puerto Ricans in the Continental United States, New York State, and New York City, 1930–1950

	CONTINENTAL U.S.	NYS	NYC
1930	52,774	45,973	n.a.
1940	69,967	63,281	61,463
1950	301,375	264,800	254,880

Note: Figures include Puerto Ricans born on the mainland and migrants from the island.

Source: 1950 *U.S. Census of Population. Puerto Ricans in the Continental U.S.* Department of Commerce. Bureau of the Census.

TABLE 14
Puerto Ricans in the United States and New York City, 1960–1980

	U.S.	NYC
1960	887,661	612,574
1970	1,391,463	860,584
1980	2,013,945	860,552

Source: Joseph P. Fitzpatrick, *Puerto Rican Americans: The Meaning of Migration to the Mainland* (Englewood Cliffs, N.J.: Prentice-Hall, 1987) p. 15.

New York City's Puerto Rican community was exceptionally young: Although Puerto Ricans comprised a mere 7.9 percent of the city's population in 1960, they accounted for "11 percent of all youth aged 15 through 19, 11 percent of the boys and girls 10–14 years old, 12 percent of those 5–9, and 14 percent of all children under 5.[4] A census of the city's public schools taken in 1966 showed that students from the island along with second-generation Puerto Ricans comprised 12.5 percent of the school-age population and were represented in every school district in Manhattan and in a majority of districts in the boroughs of the Bronx and Brooklyn.[5] Although Spanish Harlem continued to be regarded as the core of the Puerto Rican community, formidable concentrations continued to form in the South Bronx and in Brooklyn throughout the postwar period.

An additional 20,000 contract farm laborers complemented the migrant flow throughout the fifties and sixties.[6] Regulated by the Puerto Rican Department of Labor's legislation of 1947–48, the recruitment of contract laborers was closely monitored. Contracts guaranteed workers a set number of working hours, housing, worker's compensation, health insurance, transportation, and food. Although evidence suggests that infractions of the contracts were frequent, the program was said to have illustrated "how legislation and social planning . . . combined to help one group attain its dream."[7] It is estimated that, at best, 10 percent of the seasonal workers—who came to plant and harvest the agricultural fields of New Jersey, Massachusetts, New York, Connecticut, Delaware, and Michigan—remained stateside.

The second migratory wave, from the 1960s through the 1970s, was marked by even greater dispersal. Annual net migration rates rose and fell in response to signs of stagnation in the U.S. economy. By 1970 some 1,391,463 Puerto Ricans resided in the United States; 860,584 of them lived in New York City (see Table 14).[8] Economic factors, along with inadequate schooling, lack of job training, and discrimination, relegated the bulk of the Puerto Rican workforce to low-pay, low-status occupations. Despite some evidence of movement toward white-collar and municipal civil service employment, the impact of these jobs on the socioeconomic progress of the community overall was negligible.

The third phase, from 1970 to the present, has been marked by higher levels of return migration, with a gradual equalization of out and return migration during the eighties, when the stateside Puerto Rican population reached 2,013,945.[9] This period, which coincides with depressed economies in both the United States and Puerto Rico, is distinguished by wage declines, a rise in unemployment, and a rise in the number of households headed by women. Manufacturing and blue-collar jobs have disappeared as U.S. production shifted from labor- to capital-intensive operations, and as U.S. corporations have relocated to regions where labor is cheap. Between 1970 and 1980, over half a million jobs in the unskilled and semi-skilled sector were lost in New York City. Although white-collar employment in the city continued to increase, many Puerto Ricans lacked the requisite occupational or educational skills to apply for such positions.[10]

Throughout the seventies, a selective migration, which included both retirees and adults eager to enter Puerto Rico's workforce, returned to the island in greater numbers than ever before. Whereas net out-migration approximated 40,000 to 50,000 a year during the fifties, it declined to 10,000 to 20,000 a year during the sixties, and to even lower levels during the early seventies. In some years, returnees outnumbered out-migrants.[11]

In times of stateside economic stress, it had been traditional for migrants to return to Puerto Rico. During the sixties and seventies, when the island was moving toward a technological and service-based economy, returnees were attracted by new economic opportunities. During the eighties, economic stagnation in both Puerto Rico and the U.S. Northeast, where most of the migrants continued to concentrate (see Table 15), contributed to a significant out-migration; by 1982–1988, out-migration once again exceeded return migration.[12]

The surge in the post-World War II exodus, like that during the period between the world wars, was directly related to the island's economic development. Operation Bootstrap, the plan to industrialize Puerto Rico, originated with the populist governor Muñoz Marín and other Popular Democratic politicians of the commonwealth government. Its viability rested on two inducements: industrialization by invitation or the relocation of U.S. corporate and

TABLE 15
Puerto Ricans in the United States, 1990
(States with at least 45,000 Puerto Rican residents)

	NUMBER OF PUERTO RICAN RESIDENTS	PUERTO RICANS AS A % OF STATE'S TOTAL HISPANIC POPULATION
California	131,998	1.7
Connecticut	140,143	68.9
Florida	240,673	15.5
Illinois	147,201	16.8
Massachusetts	146,015	52.9
New Jersey	304,179	42.2
New York	1,046,896	48.7
Ohio	45,911	34.8
Pennsylvania	143,872	65.3
Texas	45,794	1.1
Continental United States	2,651,815	12.1

Source: 1990 U.S. Census Bureau Estimates, based on sample census tabulations.

manufacturing interests to the island in exchange for lucrative tax incentives, and a cheap Puerto Rican labor pool that was educated and Americanized.[13] Corporations that established subsidiaries in Puerto Rico also received free land and factory buildings. Under the terms of Operation Bootstrap, companies were eligible for tax exemptions for a period of fifteen to seventeen years.[14]

The success of Operation Bootstrap, industrialization and modernization, attracted worldwide attention and was applauded as a model for democratic and capitalist development. During the first decades of its existence, Bootstrap indeed appeared to have inspired miracles. Improvements abounded at all social and economic levels. Indicators for 1954–1964 illustrate the enormity of the transformations: life expectancy rose by ten years; the birth rate declined by 5 percent; per capita annual income doubled, from $423 to $830; the labor force shifted from agriculture to technology; and school enrollments dramatically increased throughout the island.[15] Not quite coincidentally, at a time when Castro's Cuba was undergoing its own Marxist-Leninist transformations, Puerto Rico became the showcase for democracy in the Caribbean—the demonstration project that the United States could proudly point to in its efforts to discourage Latin America and the Caribbean from experimenting with the Soviet model.

But in the early seventies it became clear that the Bootstrap industrialization plan also had its darker side: It never fully incorporated the island's growing population into the workforce; it displaced thousands from agrarian production and reinforced the island's dependency on the United States; and the radical decline of the island's agrarian sector had caused higher unemployment and an escalation in the importation of basic food staples. In 1978, when the U.S. Food Stamp program was extended to Puerto Rico, two-thirds of all families qualified for aid, out of an island population of close to three million.[16] Net U.S. disbursements, which included federal government assistance programs, rose from $608 million in 1970 to $2.38 billion in 1977.[17]

Moreover, the Bootstrap blueprint for industrialization was based on policies that actively promoted emigration as a "safety valve" to alleviate the structural pressures of production. Much of the unprecedented emigration that followed on the heels of Operation Bootstrap was composed of individuals displaced from declining production sectors and those newly unemployed as a consequence of industrial technology.

Finally, a lack of corporate commitment to the island's development had the unfortunate result that profits rarely remained in Puerto Rico for reinvestment. As the tax-exemption period came to an end, some corporations closed their doors and relocated to regions boasting cheaper labor and lower operating costs. Other businesses simply terminated their corporate charters and established new entities eligible for yet another fifteen years of tax exemption.

In an effort to bolster industrialization and the economy, Puerto Rico permitted the introduction of heavy industries and pharmaceutical corporations. But because this phase of production required a small, highly skilled workforce, unemployment markedly increased. In time, corporations also destroyed or damaged portions of the island's ecosystem, which was unprotected under Puerto Rican law and uncontrolled under the island's political structure. A perfect example of growth without development, Puerto Rico was reduced to producing what it could not consume, consuming what it did not produce, and exporting its people.

While many who left the island were victims of displacement from traditional labor sectors, others were not. In 1948, only 5 percent of out-migrants had worked in agricultural production. Most of the migrants had some experience with urban living, manufacturing, and other service industries, and could be classified as skilled or semi-skilled laborers. According to the ramp surveys conducted by the Planning Board of Puerto Rico and other independent studies, between 1957 and 1962 migrants demonstrated a higher proficiency in the English language and higher literacy levels than the island's non-migrant population.[18]

Islandwide surveys taken between 1962 and 1964 produced similar findings and continued to show higher levels in literacy rates, occupational skills, and educational attainment among out-migrants. Two decades later, in 1986, the Planning Board's survey reported that 10.4 percent of out-migrants were college graduates, compared to 9.4 percent of the non-migrating island population.[19]

U.S. Labor Force Participation

Despite the rapid incorporation of Puerto Rican laborers into the continental U.S. economy at the start of the Great Migration, their permanency in the labor force proved to be precarious. Although they were American citizens, Puerto Ricans differed in race, language, culture, and colonial origins from mainstream Americans. The occupational sectors they came to fill were often at the precipice of marginalization and decline.

As early as the 1960s, Puerto Ricans and other ethnic and racial minorities experienced increasing unemployment and declining earning power brought about, for the most part, by structural changes in the U.S. economy. Although industry in the Northeastern states had adequately incorporated Puerto Ricans into the workforce in the decades immediately following the Second World

War, the economic outlook for the seventies and eighties was less encouraging. As a group historically vulnerable to fluctuations in the U.S. economy, Puerto Ricans suffered downward mobility and high rates of unemployment.

The causes were multiple and subject to regional variations. As the United States shifted from industry to service and technology, the sectors in which Puerto Rican labor was concentrated suffered contraction.[20] Clara E. Rodríguez has identified four fundamental changes that undermined the Puerto Rican workforce in New York City:

1. sectoral shifts with significant declines in manufacturing,

2. technological changes in the forces of production (computerization, automation, etc.),

3. relocation of productive firms to the sunbelt and regions with cheap labor,

4. blue-collar structural unemployment.[21]

Although Puerto Ricans, particularly second and third generation, increasingly entered white-collar positions and the professions during this period, the majority of the unemployed were uprooted factory workers, generally unprepared to assume posts in the service sectors. Clustered in highly vulnerable production sectors, jobs calling for unskilled or blue-collar expertise disappeared as employers installed more sophisticated technology. In search of a cheaper labor force, factories relocated, while lucrative employment in skilled trades remained protected by the unions.[22] Trade unions, which had formed an important political component in developing the working-class consciousness of the pre-World War II community while also serving as a vehicle for upward mobility, became an obstacle in the path of labor force participation. Restrictive membership clauses, limited apprenticeship opportunities, unadvertised job recruitment, ethno-racial discrimination, and seniority regulations all contributed to the exclusion of Puerto Ricans from union membership.[23] Growing unemployment, half-time work, and the rise of female-headed households attested to the poor economic circumstances in

which Puerto Ricans found themselves. Of Puerto Rican families
with children, half (49.8 percent) were headed by a woman. And
among these Puerto Rican female-headed households, 75 percent
generated incomes below the poverty level, according to the 1980
census.[24]

The dramatic erosion in labor force participation by Puerto
Rican women in the Northeast, at a time when job opportunities
generally rose for Latinas in other regions of the nation, illustrates
the declining conditions for Puerto Ricans in the workforce. In the
1950s, a booming decade for the garment industry, two out of three
Puerto Rican women were employed. Two decades later, however,
labor force participation rates dropped to below one in three;
among women between the ages of twenty-five to forty-four, full-
time employment fell to one half the rate for African-American
women and one third below the rate for the total population.[25]
Though some blamed the group's low educational achievements
and the tendency toward having large families, New York City's
loss of over 200,000 garment jobs, coupled with the move toward
section work in those that remained, played an even greater role.
Section work, the division of garment sewing into segments, translated into increases in production but also in the hiring of low-paid,
unskilled section workers and the firing of highly skilled operators
who had been the best paid in the industry.[26] Similar restructuring
took place in other industrial sectors as well.

Ironically, although more Puerto Rican women were "making
it," so to speak, because of their entry into office and clerical work,
these new opportunities were insufficient to incorporate the bulk
of displaced workers.[27] For most Puerto Rican women, the prospects were for low wages, an inadequate daycare system, and the
expansion of poverty-level female-headed households. To make
matters worse, the 1980s brought severe cuts in government spending, social programs, job training, and affirmative action programs.

Yet, Puerto Rican men and women were essential to the functioning of New York City's economy, although their contributions
have seldom been taken into account. They dominated the hotel
and restaurant trades and maintained a "threshold level of low-
wage labor" regardless of the circumstances to which they were
relegated. As Rodríguez writes: "Without this source of cheap

labor many more firms would have left the city, and those who stayed would have been confronted with more difficult economic conditions."[28]

Since mid-century all socioeconomic indicators point to a highly depressed Puerto Rican community, but more second- and third-generation Puerto Ricans are moving into the middle class, in management and the professions.[29] Forty-five percent of the Puerto Ricans now living in New York City were born on the mainland. Their economic mobility and that of their children are virtually lost to statistical indicators as this group creates its own status, blending mainstream lifestyles often without relinquishing the world of their parents.

The Community and the Schools

As the Great Migration brought more Puerto Ricans to New York, sharp increases in the number of Spanish-speaking school-age children rapidly overwhelmed the resources of the city's public schools. One teacher noted, "a flight from San Juan on Sunday invariably meant Spanish-speaking youngsters would be registered in the public schools on Monday."[30] As American citizens, these children were entitled to a quality public education. New York City, however, had not seen such a massive infusion of non-English-speaking schoolchildren since the turn-of-the-century immigrations from Europe, and principals and teachers were totally unprepared. Typically, Puerto Rican children were placed in "slow" classes, paired with an English-speaking buddy, or relegated to remediation. At the secondary level, the handful who had not dropped out were often placed in nonacademic, vocational, or general programs. Puerto Rican community leaders, and especially teachers, feared that barrio youth in New York were being tracked toward the lowest rungs of the socioeconomic ladder.

In 1949 the Committee of the Association of Assistant Superintendents conducted a systematic survey of Puerto Rican children in the United States. The committee studied migration, acculturation, assimilation, and education, and concluded that many of the Puerto Rican students enrolled in New York City schools needed at least a year's preparation in English before they could be effectively engaged in primary instruction. For some 13,914 students, many of whom were identified in the report as needing English language instruction, the New York City Board of Education appointed ten Puerto Rican teachers as Substitute Auxiliary Teachers (SATs) and assigned them to schools with the greatest concentrations of Spanish-speaking students.[31] The mission of the SATs was "to assist in the orientation of these children [and to] serve as liaison between the school and the community."[32]

In 1953 the Mayor's Committee on Puerto Rican Affairs issued a second report that essentially endorsed the superintendent's recommendations. The committee also called for the recruitment of Spanish-speaking teachers, the expediting of licensing procedures and examination schedules, the dissemination of information about Puerto Ricans, and the creation of new curricular resources for instruction.[33] In recognition of the importance of a student's being able to "communicate with others in Spanish until he is able to express himself somewhat adequately in English," the committee abandoned the traditional emphasis on English immersion and urged schools to adopt a more comprehensive pluralistic, multilingual, and multicultural paradigm.[34]

Concurrently, the Board of Education initiated a monumental four-year inquiry into the education and adjustment of Puerto Rican students. *The Puerto Rican Study,* the most comprehensive report of its time, advocated a pedagogical focus on educating the whole child, with emphasis on sensitivity to the home, community, language, culture, and the experiences children bring into the classroom. *The Puerto Rican Study* called for a continuation of the employment of Substitute Auxiliary Teachers, Puerto Rican coordinators, school-community coordinators, teachers of English as a Second Language, Spanish-speaking counselors, and Other Teaching Positions (OTPs).[35]

That few Puerto Rican teachers triumphed over the speech-evaluation hurdles of the Board of Examiners was due more to their Spanish accents than to their academic preparation. The 155 educators who applied for employment through the Office of the Commonwealth between 1950 and 1957 provide an excellent profile of Puerto Rican teachers in New York. Their qualifications, age, gender, marital status, English language proficiency, academic preparation, experience and length of residency appear on their employment forms. The majority were between ages 30 and 35; three-fourths were women; 58 described their English language proficiency as moderate, and 88 said they were fluent in the language. Only 3 had not graduated from college; 132 had earned baccalaureates, and the remainder held degrees at the master's level; 29 had earned their degrees at U.S. institutions. With the exception of 11, all had classroom experience; 138 were licensed teachers in Puerto Rico, and 3 held licenses in the United States.[36]

Among Puerto Rican educators, the SAT classification provided entry into the school system. From 1949, when the SAT position was instituted by the Board, until 1971, when the title of Auxiliary Teacher (AT) was changed to "Bilingual Teacher in School and Community Relations," some 234 Spanish-speaking elementary school teachers, most of them Puerto Rican, had been hired.[37]

The ATs anchored the schools to the community by fostering rapport, compatible working relations, and a communication network. As cultural resources throughout the school system, Puerto Rican teachers planned sensitivity training seminars for English-speaking faculty and staff, and implemented programs that enhanced the "cultural heritage and self-concept of the children."[38] Trailblazers in a newly developed intellectual discourse, bilingual teachers created curriculums and the materials necessary for classroom implementation; they formed study groups and academic retreats for their own professional growth; wrote pamphlets, booklets, and workbooks; published material on the history and geography of Puerto Rico; and created filmstrips, with accompanying teacher guides, including *Puerto Rico Today, Children of Puerto Rico,* and *The Bilingual Teacher in School and Community Relations.*[39] At the community level, bilingual teachers generated extensive parental involvement, not only to orient parents to school policies but also to groom them for leadership roles in parent-teacher associations. Bilingual teachers encouraged parents to learn English and offered afterschool language courses for them; the teachers developed support and informational networks that, in turn, fostered survival and occupational skills, and they generally empowered the community by increasing the parents' understanding of stateside society. Bilingual teachers also helped parents hone their advocacy skills through participation at board meetings, political rallies, conferences, and lectures. Over time, parents thus became a strong and self-reliant base of support for educational reform, the bilingual movement, and school decentralization.[40]

Professionally organized in SPRAT (the Society of Puerto Rican Auxiliary Teachers), Puerto Rican educators paved the way for creating numerous associations, including PREA (the Puerto Rican Educators' Association) and bilingual chapters of the United Federation of Teachers. These served as vehicles for solidarity, support, and advocacy. The professional associations argued for increased visibility at all professional levels and permanency as regular teachers in the system. SPRAT, in particular, was at the forefront of the movement for licensure in the permanent position of Bilingual Teacher in School and Community Affairs, a feat that was accomplished with the first competitive examinations held in February 1962.

Organizing for Advancement

The organizations founded by Puerto Ricans following the Great Migration reinforced the efforts of those compatriots who had emphasized education. To facilitate the work and adjustment experience of the migrants, the Puerto Rican legislature established the Bureau of Employment and Migration in 1947; the bureau was renamed the Migration Division of the Department of Labor of Puerto Rico in 1951. The Migration Division, officially headed by the Puerto Rican Secretary of Labor, was under the direction of the sociologist Clarence Senior from 1951 to 1960. Joseph Monserrat, a Puerto Rican activist, directed the New York City office throughout the fifties and served as national director from 1960 to 1969. Among the Migration Division's primary responsibilities was the organization and monitoring of the general migratory stream from Puerto Rico, including seasonal agricultural migration; its overarching goal was to minimize "the natural problems of adjustment that are produced in all migrations of this type."[41] As late as 1967, however, at the peak of the Civil Rights Movement and community efforts toward self-determination, the Migration Division defined *adjustment* as the adoption of mainstream U.S. mores and middle-class values.[42]

The Migration Division served as a clearinghouse for employment, housing, welfare, health, and educational needs, and attempted to steer nonseasonal migrants to various regional destinations. In addition to providing social service referrals and educational counseling, the Migration Division also represented Puerto Rican interests at local, state, and federal levels. In a bid to lessen the strain on New York's social service agencies, resources, and institutions, the Migration Division encouraged and counseled Puerto Ricans to settle outside of New York and the Northeast.

Throughout the fifties and sixties this agency continued to be the primary arbitrator between the community and stateside government units. But as more Puerto Ricans focused on internal issues in New York, as opposed to island concerns, they began to question the agency's ties to island politics. The director of the Migration Division—or Office of the Commonwealth, as it came to be known—was appointed by the governor of Puerto Rico. Political and financial dependency on either government, that of the island or of the United States, was viewed as counterproductive to the development of an independent homespun leadership in the New York Puerto Rican community.[43]

Despite the political connections between the island and the Migration Division, however, the agency played an influential role in the affairs of New York's Puerto Rican community. Its origins were not universally viewed as contradictory, especially by the many migrants who expected to return to Puerto Rico at some point. For them, the agency counterbalanced an inhospitable, bigoted American society and, perhaps because of its quasi-political visibility, the agency became an acceptable broker. In addition, the agency had the distinction of being Puerto Rican–operated and connected to the island. Others who were committed to the advancement of Puerto Ricans on the mainland did not object to the agency's role precisely because one of its mandates was to work with existing community groups and to encourage the development of leadership among stateside Puerto Ricans.

The Hispanic Young Adult Association (HYAA) exemplifies the kind of group engendered by the Migration Division. Focused on the interests of young professionals and college students, HYAA advanced the assimilationist paradigm that it believed had worked so well for other ethnic groups. Ascribing to the notion that "science and effective social intervention would eventually solve society's ills," many among the HYAA leadership were college-trained social workers.[44] Among the first of organizations to base its mission on the culture and ideology of stateside Puerto Ricans, particularly those in the New York metropolitan area, HYAA aspired to create a leadership committed to integration, rather than concerns of the island. But by 1956 the commitment to issues of identity motivated the HYAA to reject assimilation, define itself as Puerto Rican, and rename itself the Puerto Rican Association for Community Affairs (PRACA). The group's primary objective, however, remained the evolution of a grass-roots leadership corps for the stateside Puerto Rican community.[45]

The *Desfile Puertorriqueño* (the coordinating council for the Puerto Rican Day Parade) and *El Congreso del Pueblo* (the Council of Hometown Clubs) also worked closely with the Migration Division. Unlike PRACA, however, these two organizations drew support from a working-class base and stressed the need to confront the immediate socioeconomic problems facing Puerto Ricans. *El Congreso del Pueblo*, led by community activist Gilberto Gerena Valentín, represented some eighty clubs in 1956, the year of its incorporation. The hometown clubs, maintaining the same active level of sophistication prevalent in the period between the world wars, provided shelter, jobs, emergency financial help, and other social benefits. But under the umbrella of *El Congreso,* the clubs took a broader, more militant stand and led mass demonstrations against injustice, racism, police brutality, and discrimination. The most significant display of Puerto Rican solidarity, however, was a cultural one, the Puerto Rican Day Parade. Here the organizations secured a visible foothold in the affairs of the city, and proudly unfurled the full vitality and potential power of the community.

The following year, in 1957, the Puerto Rican Forum, Inc., surfaced to challenge the domination of the Migration Division.[46] Patterned after the NAACP and the American Jewish Committee, the Forum aimed for citywide recognition as the power broker for the Puerto Rican community. Under the talented leadership of Antonia Pantoja, the Forum pursued its own agenda, promoted community enterprises, and provided funding for other local organizations to develop their own programs. The Forum relied on private internal funding and a cadre of community volunteers prepared to advance the mission of the organization.

Antonia Pantoja, a woman of boundless vision and leadership, had come to New York City in 1944, armed with a normal school diploma and experience as a rural teacher and union organizer. Her first encounters with the depressed economic conditions of New York Puerto Ricans aroused in her a commitment to dedicate her life to organizing the community and harnessing its strengths. Pantoja understood the effects of racism and discrimination, and she knew that political powerlessness coupled with limited access to education and economic opportunity would keep her community poor. She earned a bachelor's degree at Hunter College of the City University, and proceeded to a master's degree and a doctorate in social work. While an assistant professor at Columbia University, Pantoja served on the Bundy Panel, charged with the decentralization of the New York public schools.[47]

Throughout her career, Pantoja recognized the value of education while never forgetting that "first of all, we were and are a people of color, who would not be easily accepted into the mainstream. Secondly, the city had already been made by others. We had no skills to speak of, and the modern city has no place for unskilled people."[48] Her overriding objectives, to provide her people with the necessary skills and knowledge to solve their own problems and restore the well-being of her community, led to the founding of numerous organizations and institutions. A founding member of PRACA, Pantoja also organized the Puerto Rican Forum, and created and directed ASPIRA—three of the most influential Puerto Rican organizations in the city. Pantoja also established a research and resource center, the *Universidad Boricua,* in Washington, D.C.; the Graduate School for Community Development in San Diego; and *Producir,* an economic development project in Puerto Rico. The quintessential leader, Antonia Pantoja has been a teacher, social worker, factory welder, community activist, organizer, and president and chancellor of a college.

During the 1960s, organizations like PRACA and the Forum were encouraged and empowered by the anti-poverty programs inaugurated by the federal government under the banner of the Great Society. But even as the federal programs gave Puerto Rican organizations access to outside funding and avenues for expansion, the anti-poverty funding compromised the organization's independence. Voluntary work became salaried, and organizational structures became more bureaucratic. Nonetheless, the Great Society provided unique opportunities for dozens of local groups— such as the *Instituto de Puerto Rico,* United Bronx Parents, the *Agrupación Femenina Hispano-Americana,* and *Organizaciones Unidas del Bronx*—to work separately or collectively on community projects eligible for federal funding.

For example, in 1964 the Puerto Rican Forum, building on the organizational strengths of the community, proposed a comprehensive Puerto Rican Community Development Project.[49] This project was envisioned as a clearinghouse for numerous self-help programs that could join forces to combat socioeconomic strife and stabilize the Puerto Rican community. Some sixty organizations, including ASPIRA, PRACA, and the Puerto Rican Family Institute, took part in the initial planning, which cited the goals of increasing family income, reducing poverty, raising educational levels, and generally strengthening the family through the creation of cultural and other institutions. An extensive assessment of the mid-sixties New York Puerto Rican community, including its history, geography, demography, educational attainment, employment patterns, and health status, framed the core of the proposal.

Despite the plan's attention to housing, jobs, health care, and education, the proposal failed to attract community consensus on all of its components.[50] Within the ranks of the Puerto Rican Community Development Project, disagreements began to surface over the priorities, mode of operation, disbursement of funds, and directorship. Should the project stress long-range planning and education, or should the social service component and more immediate problems such as employment, health, and housing take precedence? In 1965, after a year's delay, the U.S. Office of Economic Opportunity funded the proposal, but by then the project had modified much of its broad range of concerns, emphasizing instead job training, substance abuse, tutorial programs, and the creation of a neighborhood youth corps.[51]

The real significance of the impasse, however, was that it signaled two alternatives for community advancement, and most of the associations would subscribe to one or the other. The first course of action consisted of immediate efforts to counter the devastating social and economic problems facing the community. The second rested on the premise that the Puerto Rican community was very young, and that long-range educational and professional advancement were necessary if a high level of competency and future leadership were to be engendered among the youth. Organizations like ASPIRA, the Puerto Rican Educators' Association, and the Society for Auxiliary Teachers, among others, best understood this aspect of community formation.

The Puerto Rican Family Institute, founded in 1963, exemplified an association that dealt with the immediate needs of the community. Headed by Agustín González and a staff of volunteer social workers, the Family Institute received anti-poverty funding in 1965 as a citywide agency responsible for serving the Puerto Rican and other Latino communities. Its primary objective was to recreate the traditional support system of an extended family network for the newcomers, facilitate their adjustment, and provide for their basic necessities—all within a familiar, nonthreatening, and non-bureaucratic context. For these purposes the Family Institute identified a cadre of "settled" families who were asked to serve as *padrinos* (godparents) to newly arrived families. Matched by the Family Institute, the godparents would broker for the newcomers, serve as role models, and advise them about the intricacies of urban living, schools, health, and occupational opportunities. The Family Institute also provided referrals, social service counseling, and tutorial programs.

In 1978 the association opened its doors in Puerto Rico, in recognition of the effects that the return migration was having on the island. Many of the families who were returning to Puerto Rico found themselves in need of the same basic orientation that the Family Institute had provided in New York City. Children returned to Puerto Rican schools without an adequate foundation in the Spanish language, and adults, grown used to a more aggressive style of life, needed to learn about island resources. The Family Institute provided a wide range of programs and support to accommodate them.

In contrast, ASPIRA emphasized long-range planning and education as the vehicle for social change. The future of the community, ASPIRA argued, depended on preparing young Puerto Ricans to assume leadership roles at all types of private and public institutions. Thus ASPIRA advocated on key issues, laws, and services affecting stateside Puerto Ricans, and it established chapters in high schools with significant Puerto Rican concentrations. At the local and national level, the association aspired "to guide Puerto Rican youth towards professional, business, and artistic fields . . . towards fields with promise and employment opportunities."[52]

At the time of ASPIRA's founding in 1961, few Puerto Ricans were graduating from secondary schools, and among graduates, few earned academic diplomas. In New York City, for example, only 331 of 21,000 Puerto Rican high school graduates received academic diplomas in 1963. In Boston, there were years in which no Puerto Ricans received academic diplomas, despite the city's significant migrant population.[53] Alarmed by such measures of the Puerto Rican community's vulnerability, ASPIRA pledged itself "to pressure official bodies and mount campaigns" that focused on educational issues. The agency specifically committed itself to helping Puerto Rican youth "relate, identify, and function in the Puerto Rican community of New York," noting that

> Young people who would never have taken an interest in the Puerto Rican community can come together here to learn, by doing, the techniques and methodology of social action for change. At the same time as they develop into politically active and effective people, through the fight for better housing, employment, better education and fight against discrimination, they are recruited and motivated to further their personal educational goals.

Finally, ASPIRA sought "to bridge the gaps for older Puerto Rican migrants [by] helping them to understand the learning problems of their children."[54]

The failure to educate stateside Puerto Rican students became the focal point (and subsequent challenge to American pedagogical institutions) of the ASPIRA conference of 1968. Set against heated struggles for community control and decentralization of the New

York public schools, this historic gathering brought together Puerto Ricans, Mexican-Americans, and non-Latino educators to discuss the special educational needs of urban Puerto Rican youth. After two days of intense deliberation, the Puerto Rican educators had defined their agenda for reform and began planning how best to work together for meaningful change. To those in the educational establishment who would view the conference's manifesto as seg-regationist, Antonia Pantoja replied, "To hell with that. These are the same people who think that somehow segregation is OK because it is imposed from without, but separation is all wrong when it is sought within."[55]

At the close of the conference, participants pledged to renew their campaign for bilingual education and claim the rights of Puerto Ricans within the political and educational spheres of urban America. They knew that the political and institutional establishment had backed bilingual programs for Cuban refugees in Miami—a move prompted by Cold War politics—and now they wanted similar educational alternatives to be available to Puerto Rican children. So ASPIRA and the Puerto Rican Legal Defense and Education Fund launched a class-action suit on behalf of the non-English-speaking children in New York City public schools against the Board of Education. The result was the ASPIRA Consent Decree, issued in 1974, which guaranteed bilingual education to all public school students who needed it.[56]

In struggles that paralleled those of the African-American and Chicano communities, Puerto Ricans also claimed their rights to university educations, advocating for open enrollment and relevant academic programs. The intellectual agenda that emerged went far beyond mere inclusiveness, however. It called for alternative modes of research, multiple and comparative perspectives, accountability to the community, and a radical interpretation of dominant-subaltern relations. As scholar-activist Frank Bonilla stated:

> I am affirming that our struggle in the university is not merely for a better education for young Puerto Ricans or for an intellectual base in the academy or greater tolerance from colleagues. Not only contrary political projects but contrary

world views are in confrontation. It will perhaps come as a surprise to many that so much is in fact at issue in what they may choose to view as a simple assault by primitives on an institution these intruders do not understand. Were the matter as simple as some would like, the sense of threat to the established orders of disciplines, research domains and lines of organization would, of course, not be so deeply felt.[57]

In 1969 the Board of Higher Education of the City University of New York established an open admissions policy. Shortly thereafter, City University campuses, led by Brooklyn and City College, met the demands of students and progressive faculty for the creation of Puerto Rican studies departments and programs. Interdisciplinary in approach, these innovative programs generated new insights into the Puerto Rican experience. Their missions rested upon a firm commitment to bridge the gap between the barrios and the academy, and to combine knowledge, research, and praxis with community empowerment. Representing the voices of the marginalized, the programs and departments brought a strong dose of diversity to the university, even as they fought continuous battles for survival and legitimacy. With the creation of the prestigious research center *El Centro de Estudios Puertorriqueños* in 1972, the migration experience emerged as a focal point of intellectual discourse and scholarship.

Yet in spite of the inroads made by students and activists into the City University system, the major site of academic contestation in New York, the fiscal crisis of 1973–1975 exacerbated conditions for Puerto Ricans. In 1975 Puerto Rican undergraduates in the City University system numbered some 18,570, or 8.3 percent of the total population, an increase from 5,425, or 4 percent, in 1969.[58] Historian Carlos Rodríguez-Fraticelli notes that approximately 35 percent of the Puerto Rican student body in CUNY would not have been admitted before activist struggles forced the implementation of open admissions in 1969.

Although the numbers of Puerto Rican and African-American students in CUNY increased dramatically during the period of open enrollment, in fact white students were the major beneficiaries of the program; the white CUNY population grew by more than 10,000 between 1969 and 1970 alone.[59] However, largely due to the steadily eroding economic situation of the city and the state, open admissions were phased out within seven years, and tuition fees comparable to those of other public institutions throughout the nation were imposed. The effect on the advances made by Puerto Ricans at CUNY was disastrous: faculty and administrative lines were cut, many programs and support services were eliminated, and the number of Puerto Rican undergraduate students diminished. Nonetheless, CUNY's diverse and multicultural nature, initiated in the turmoil of the sixties and seventies remained intact. In the 1990s over 75 percent of graduating high school seniors in New York City are students of color. This diversity is represented and continues to flourish in the enrollment of the City University system.

Politics in the Barrios

During the sixties, the fervent struggles for self-definition and determination in the educational arena were complemented by a resurgence of radical politics not seen since the days of Marcantonio and progressive socialist elements in the Puerto Rican barrios.[60] Throughout the city, young men and women mobilized to "right the wrongs of the community" in organizations like Students for a Democratic Society, the Puerto Rican Students' Union, the Puerto Rican Socialist Party, *El Comité,* and the New York chapter of the Young Lords. Testing their newly formed solidarity, barrio youth challenged established leadership both within and outside the community. For the most part, they rejected conventional party politics, with its characteristic plodding through a cumbersome and conservative system.

By now, Puerto Rican political figures had achieved a degree of citywide and statewide recognition. Many, among them Gilberto Gerena Valentín and Ramón Vélez, had risen to prominence through organizational connections developed through the anti-poverty programs. Gerena Valentín, a long-time activist, represented a pro-active militancy that demonstrated concern both for the social and political struggles of diaspora communities and for island independence. His base of support incorporated massive groups like *El Congreso del Pueblo* and the Puerto Rican Day Parade Committee.

Others, among whom Herman Badillo and Roberto Garcia are the best known, came through the ranks of traditional party politics. Badillo was elected Bronx Borough President in 1965, four years after serving as Commissioner for the Department of Relocation. In 1968 he was elected to the U.S. Congress, and in 1978 he was appointed New York City Deputy Mayor. Garcia entered the U.S. House of Representatives by winning the special election to fill Badillo's seat in 1978. Before that, he had spent thirteen years in the New York State Legislature. Also in 1978, Olga Méndez was elected to the New York State Senate, thus becoming the first Puerto Rican woman legislator in the continental United States.[61]

The radical groups of the late sixties and seventies challenged what they perceived to be the outdated and ineffective political hegemony of Puerto Rican politicians. Their concerns centered on the most basic and immediate necessities: poverty, substandard sanitation conditions, inadequate daycare programs, insufficient health clinics, and unemployment.[62]

In 1969 the New York Young Lords Party, patterned after the Chicago Young Lords Organization, appealed to a broad-based political constituency that included college students of working-class backgrounds and also members of neighborhood gangs and social clubs. From its inception, the Young Lords was representative of those groups that aimed to organize the barrios and bring about justice and social change. Blending political theory with civic activism, the group initiated free breakfast and lead-detection programs, joined in support of welfare mothers, and helped organize hospital and health care unions. They took to the streets to protest wretched and marginal living conditions. The group staged sit-ins, denounced police brutality, and closed down key institutions.[63]

While differences in strategy and tactics existed among the various groups, they coalesced around essential beliefs concerning the impact of racism, capitalist exploitation, and forced migration on the Puerto Rican community. They also viewed independence for the island as nonnegotiable.[64]

The activities of these Puerto Rican groups reinvigorated and elevated barrio consciousness at a highly charged political and historical juncture. As their reputation spread throughout the barrios, urban sectors of the Northeast, and eventually across the nation, the Lords and other such groups sparked the imaginations of young Puerto Ricans and Latinos.

Conclusion

Much of the scholarly literature about Puerto Rican communities in New York City and elsewhere focuses on the deficit model, the "problems" of Puerto Ricans, rather than on their pro-active role in shaping the cities of this nation. But by placing events into historical perspective, we continue to find a people who have nurtured a strong sense of self and who have also come to terms with the impact that sociocultural and political factors have had on Puerto Ricanness. Their struggles in the diaspora have produced continental communities that maintain integral connections with Puerto Rico and that bind the history of the United States with that of the island.

As Puerto Rican communities within the United States have reached maturity, an overwhelming preoccupation with the conditions affecting the lives of Puerto Ricans in the diaspora signaled a shift in perspective. Since the 1960s, in particular, migrants have felt an urgent need to forge national interconnections, build coalitions with other ethnoracial groups, and reaffirm their solidarity with Puerto Ricans in the island. Such solidarity might lead to an equitable relationship between the two and an understanding that Puerto Ricans on the mainland could be instrumental in playing a role in the island's future. Such was clearly the case in 1993, when the three Puerto Rican members of the U.S. House of Representatives—José Serrano (D-NY), Luis Gutierrez (D-Ill.), and Nydia Velásquez (D-NY)—supported island interests in the debate over IRS Section 936, which regulates the taxation of U.S. corporations in Puerto Rico. It was, after all, these elected officials who had the vote in this matter, and not their compatriots from the island.

Some of the Puerto Rican associations that have emerged over the last three decades advocate for specific community concerns, but others concentrate on national affairs and perspectives. The Institute for Puerto Rican Policy, for example, seeks to provide "effective policy analysis" through research, advocacy, and networking; the National Puerto Rican Coalition in Washington, D.C., promotes Puerto Rican interests on the island and the continent; the National Congress for Puerto Rican Rights, a coalition of community groups, is pledged to confront discrimination against Puerto Ricans wherever they reside; and ASPIRA International, also in Washington, D.C., coordinates activities and pursues its national educational agenda.

In the 1990s socioeconomic indicators continue to underscore the increase in the number of Puerto Rican households below the poverty line. However, we must not lose sight of the gains that have been secured. Educational attainment has improved, and Puerto Rican representation in politics, the corporate world, and the professions, as well as in music, literature, and other creative arts is impressive. The challenge will be to recognize and continue to build on those achievements as we direct these resources toward the empowerment of all of our stateside communities.

Notes

1. The 1990 Census counted 22,354,059 Hispanics or Latinos in the United States, or 9 percent of the total population. Of these, 60.4% were Mexican-Americans, 12.2% were Puerto Ricans, 4.7% were Cubans, and 22.8% were other Hispanics.

2. Frank Bonilla, "Beyond Survival: Por que seguiremos siendo puertorriqueños," in Iris M. Zavala and Rafael Rodríguez, eds., *The Intellectual Roots of Independence* (New York: Monthly Review Press, 1980), p. 365.

3. U.S. Bureau of the Census, *U.S. Census of Population, 1960, Subject Reports: Puerto Ricans in the U.S.*, PC(2)-ID (Washington, D.C.: U.S. Government Printing Office, 1963).

4. The Puerto Rican Forum, Inc., *A Study of Poverty Conditions in the New York Puerto Rican Community*, 3d ed. (New York: Puerto Rican Forum, Inc., 1970), pp. 16–18.

5. Joseph P. Fitzpatrick, *Puerto Rican Americans: The Meaning of Migration to the Mainland* (Englewood Cliffs, N.J.: Prentice-Hall, 1987), pp. 39–40.

6. Ibid., p. 25.

7. Michael Lapp, "The Migration Division of Puerto Rico and Puerto Ricans in New York City, 1948–1969" (Johns Hopkins University, Immigration Lecture Series, 1990, unpublished manuscript).

8. Fitzpatrick, *Puerto Rican Americans,* p. 15.

9. Ibid.

10. A great deal of research exists on the loss of unskilled and semi-skilled jobs in New York City during the '70s and '80s. For example, Clara E. Rodríguez, *Puerto Ricans: Born in the U.S.A.* (Boston: Unwin Hyman, 1989), chapter 4; Edwin Meléndez, "Vanishing Labor: The Effects of Industrial Restructuring on the Labor Force Participation Rate of Puerto Rican Women in New York City" (MIT, 1987, unpublished manuscript) and "Los que se van, los que regresan: Puerto Rican Migration to and from the United States, 1982–88" (MIT, 1991, unpublished manuscript); Andrés Torres, "Human Capital, Labor Segmentation, and Inter-Minority Relative Status: Black and Puerto Rican Labor in New York City, 1960–80" (Ph.D. diss., New School for Social Research, 1988) and "Explaining Puerto Rican Poverty," *Centro de Estudios Puertorriqueños Bulletin* (Winter 1987–88), pp. 9–21; and Fitzpatrick, *Puerto Rican Americans,* p. 101.

11. Meléndez, "Los que se van," p. 12.

12. Ibid., p. 32. Meléndez estimates that 285,787 Puerto Ricans age 16 or older left the island between 1982 and 1988. Another 134,587 returned to Puerto Rico during that same period.

13. Marcia Rivera, "The Development of Capitalism in Puerto Rico and the Incorporation of Women into the Labor Force," in Edna Acosta Belén, ed., *The Puerto Rican Woman* (Westport, Conn.: Praeger, 1986), pp. 30–45; Arturo Morales Carrión, *Puerto Rico: A Political and Cultural History* (New York: W.W. Norton, 1983), pp. 256–307.

14. Ibid. See also James L. Dietz, *Economic History of Puerto Rico: Institutional Change and Capitalist Development* (Princeton: Princeton University Press, 1986); Raymond Carr, *Puerto Rico: A Colonial Experiment* (New York: New York University Press, 1984). In 1993 a proposal to reduce the federal budget deficit by reforming, among other things, the tax laws that regulate industries in Puerto Rico, IRS Section 936, was subject to intensive lobbying in Washington and Puerto Rico. Representatives Gutierrez, Serrano, and Velásquez, who defended the importance of protecting jobs in Puerto Rico, used their votes on the Clinton budget as leverage, and the plan to alter Section 936 was shelved.

15. Morales Carrión, *Puerto Rico,* chapters 14 and 15.

16. Fitzpatrick, *Puerto Rican Americans,* p. 35.

17. Morales Carrión, *Puerto Rico,* p. 313.

18. Rodríguez, *Puerto Ricans,* p. 6.

19. Ibid.

20. Ibid., p. 86; Torres, "Explaining Puerto Rican Poverty."

21. Rodríguez, *Puerto Ricans,* pp. 9–21.

22. Ibid., p. 101.

23. Ibid., p. 92.

24. Fitzpatrick, *Puerto Rican Americans*, p. 98.

25. U.S. Department of Labor, *A Socio-Economic Profile of Puerto Rican New Yorkers* (New York: Bureau of Labor Statistics, July 1975), pp. 64–77.

26. Deborah Menkart and Catherine A. Sunshine, eds., *Caribbean Connections, Puerto Rico* (Washington, D.C.: EPICA and NECCA, 1990), pp. 70–75. On the restructuring of the garment industry, see the work of E. Meléndez, C. E. Rodríguez, and J. Barry Figueroa, *Hispanics in the Labor Force: Issues and Policies* (New York: Plenum Press, 1991); Altagracia Ortiz, "Puerto Rican Workers in the Garment Industry of New York City, 1920–1960," in Robert Asher and Charles Stephenson, eds., *Labor Divided: Race and Ethnicity in United States Labor Struggles, 1835–1960* (Albany, N.Y.: State University Press, 1989); Alice Colón, "Competition, Segregation and Succession of Minorities and Women in the Middle Atlantic Central Cities Labor Market, 1960–1970" (Ph.D. diss., Fordham University, 1984); Andrés Torres, "Human Capital, Labor Segregation and Inter-minority Relative Status: Black and Puerto Rican Labor in New York City, 1960–1980" (Ph.D. diss., New School for Social Research, 1988); Palmira Rios, "The Puerto Rican Woman in the United States Labor Market," *Line of March*, vol. 18, (fall 1985); among others.

27. Fitzpatrick, *Puerto Rican Americans*, p. 47.

28. Rodríguez, *Puerto Ricans*, p. 99.

29. Fitzpatrick, *Puerto Rican Americans*, p. 179.

30. Interview with María E. Sánchez, professor emeritus, Brooklyn College, January 1992. See also V. Sánchez Korrol, "Towards Bilingual Education: Puerto Rican Women Educators in New York City Schools, 1947–1967," in Altagracia Ortiz, ed., *Puerto Rican Women in the Twentieth Century: New Perspectives on Gender, Labor and Migration* (Philadelphia: Temple University Press, forthcoming).

31. Francisco Cordasco and Eugene Bucchioni, eds., *The Puerto Ricans, 1473–1973* (Dobbs Ferry, N.Y.: Oceana Publication, Inc., 1973), p. 113.

32. Sánchez Korrol, "Towards Bilingual Education."

33. *Interim Report of the Mayor's Committee on Puerto Rican Affairs in New York City*, September 1949 to September 1953.

34. Ibid., p. 43.

35. J. Cayce Morrison, *The Puerto Rican Study, 1953–1957* (Board of Education of the City of New York, 1957), part 3, chapter 16.

36. *A Brief Study of Questionnaires Submitted by Puerto Rican Teachers Available for Elementary and Secondary School Positions in the N.Y. Metropolitan Area* (New York: Migration Division, Department of Labor, Commonwealth of Puerto Rico, September 1957). See also Patria C.

de Crespo, *Puerto Rican Women Teachers in New York: Self-Perception and Work Adjustment as Perceived by Themselves and by Others* (San Juan: Department of Education, Commonwealth of Puerto Rico, 1969).

37. Sánchez Korrol, "Towards Bilingual Education," table 1.

38. *The Bilingual Teacher in School and Community Relations Pamphlet*, Special Circular no. 64 (New York: Board of Education of the City of New York, 1968).

39. Rafael Vega, *The Bilingual Teacher in School and Community Relations* and *Children of Puerto Rico*, and with Theresa Rakow, *Puerto Rico Today* (Multimedia Production Unit of the Bureau of Audio Visual Instruction, Board of Education of the City of New York).

40. Interview with María E. Sánchez, January 1992.

41. Legislature of Puerto Rico, Law Number 25, December 5, 1947, cited in Lapp, "The Migration Division of Puerto Rico," p. 6. See also José L. Vázquez Calzada, "Demographic Aspects of Migration," in Centro de Estudios Puertorriqueños, *Labor Migration Under Capitalism: The Puerto Rican Experience* (New York: Monthly Review Press, 1979); Luis Nieves Falcón, *El Emigrante Puertorriqueño* (Rio Piedras, P.R., 1975).

42. Lapp, "The Migration Division of Puerto Rico," p. 12.

43. The election in 1992 of Nydia Velásquez, the first Puerto Rican woman to serve in the U.S. House of Representatives, reignited this issue. Velásquez had been director of the Commonwealth Office, now called the Office of Puerto Rican Affairs, in New York. Her ability to adequately represent New York Puerto Ricans was questioned in light of her island connections.

44. Carlos Rodríguez-Fraticelli and Amilcar Tirado, "Notes Towards a History of Puerto Rican Community Organizations in New York City," *Centro Bulletin* (Centro de Estudios Puertorriqueños), vol. 2, no. 6, p. 38.

45. Ibid.

46. Allan S. Kullen, *The Peopling of America: A Timeline of Events That Helped Shape Our Nation* (Americans All, The Portfolio Project, Washington, D.C., 1992), p. 305.

47. Aurea E. Rodríguez et al., "Antonia Pantoja on ASPIRA's Thirtieth Anniversary," in *A Guide to Celebrate Puerto Rican Heritage and Culture* (New York City Public Schools, 1991).

48. The Aspira Association, Inc., *The Aspira Story, 1961–1991* (Washington, D.C.: The Aspira Association, Inc., 1991), p. 2.

49. Puerto Rican Forum, Inc., *Study of Poverty Conditions*; see also Kullen, *The Peopling of America*, p. 318.

50. Rodríguez-Fraticelli and Tirado, "Notes Towards a History of Community Organizations," p. 42.

51. Ibid.; see also Fitzpatrick, *Puerto Rican Americans*, pp. 56–57.

52. ASPIRA, Inc., *Hemos trabajado bien*, A Report on the First National Conference of Puerto Ricans, Mexican-Americans, and Educators on "The Special Educational Needs of Urban Puerto Rican Youth," New York, May 14–15, 1968, p. 34.

53. Ibid.

54. Ibid.

55. Ibid., p. 59.

56. Kullen, *The Peopling of America*, p. 331.

57. Frank Bonilla, "Cultural Pluralism and the University: The Case of Puerto Rican Studies," p. 7, expanded version of opening remarks at an April 1972 session of a faculty seminar on cultural pluralism sponsored by Columbia University and the City College of New York.

58. Carlos Rodríguez-Fraticelli, *Education and Imperialism: The Puerto Rican Experience in Higher Education, 1898–1986* (Centro de Estudios Puertorriqueños, Hunter College, CUNY, New York, 1986), p. 26.

59. City University of New York, *One University for Many Cultures*, p. 4, proceedings of a December 6, 1991, university-wide conference co-sponsored by the Academy for the Humanities and Sciences and the University Faculty Senate.

60. Gerald Meyer, "Marcantonio and El Barrio," *Centro Bulletin* (Centro de Estudios Puertorriqueños) vol. 4, no. 2 (1992), pp. 66–87. See also Peter Jackson, "Vito Marcantonio and Ethnic Politics in New York," *Ethnic and Racial Studies*, vol. 6, no. 1 (January 1983), pp. 50–71.

61. A longtime activist, Méndez became a district leader in 1973 and was reelected to six consecutive terms. In 1992 Nydia Velásquez (D-NY), the first Puerto Rican woman elected to sit in the U.S. House of Representatives, joined José Serrano (D-NY) and Luis Gutierrez (D-Ill.), the two other Puerto Rican representatives.

62. Pablo "Yoruba" Guzmán, "Puerto Rican Barrio Politics in the United States," in Clara E. Rodríguez, V. Sánchez Korrol, and José Oscar Alers, eds., *The Puerto Rican Struggle: Essays on Survival in the U.S.* (New York: Waterfront Press, 1984), pp. 121–128. See also Sherrie Baver, "Puerto Rican Politics in New York City: The Post World War II Period," in James Jennings and Monte Rivera, eds., *Puerto Rican Politics in Urban America* (Westport, Conn.: Greenwood Press) 1984.

63. Young Lords Party, "Palante," in Francesco Cordasco and Eugene Bucchioni, *The Puerto Rican Experience* (Totowa, N.J.: Littlefield, Adams, 1973), pp. 247–48; Frank Browning, "From Rumble to Revolution: The Young Lord's Party," in Cordasco and Bucchioni, *The Puerto Rican Experience*, pp. 242–244.

64. Guzmán, "Puerto Rican Barrio Politics," p. 123.

Appendixes

APPENDIX I:
Organizations in Operation in Puerto Rican Communities, 1900–1950

NAME	PURPOSE FOR ORGANIZING	MEMBERS OR TYPES OF MEMBERSHIP
1900–1919		
Unión Internacional de Tabaqueros	union activity	tobacco workers
La Resistencia	union activity	tobacco workers
Asociación Latino-Americana	fund raising for needy Spanish-speaking families	Dr. Antonio González Dr. Manuel Castillo Vilar Dr. Arturo Font Sr. Alberto León Sr. Francisco L. Pla Sr. Ricardo E. Manrique
Unión Benéfica Español	unknown	unknown
La Aurora, La Razón, El Ejemplo	Mutual Aid Societies	tobacco workers
El Tropical	social activities, fund raising for membership	Gonzalo Torres
Club Ibero-Americano	social activities, cultural purposes	Dr. Henna

NAME	PURPOSE FOR ORGANIZING	MEMBERS OR TYPES OF MEMBERSHIP
1920–1930		
Trabajadores Amalgamado de la Industria del Tobaco	educational; published newspaper *The Tobacco Worker*	Non-Puerto Ricans and Puerto Ricans: W. Rico, Sam Sussman, Cayetano Loria, Bernardo Vega, J. Brandon
La Asociación Puertorriqueña	unknown	Manuel Negrón Collazo
Club Caborrojeño	neighborhood social club; provided meeting grounds for migrants from Cabo Rojo	Ramón Pabón Aviles
Casa de Puerto Rico	to promote Hispanic culture, customs and traditions	Dr. Ruiz Arnau, Martin Travieso, R.M. Delgado, Manuel Argueso, Dr. Lopez Antongiorgo, F. González Acuna, Dr. Janer, Ulises García Sandov, Gonzalo O'Neill, Ledo. Pedro Rodríguez, Dr. Arturo Martínez
Puerto Rico Literario	literary, cultural and social. Promoted desire to learn among Puerto Rican youth.	Pura Belpré, Francisco Acevedo, Lorenzo Pineiro, Max Vázquez, Bartolo Malavé, Rafael Mariotta, René Jimenez Malaret, Juan Bautista Pagan, Luis Hernández Aquino, Erasmo Vando

Organization	Purpose	Members
Liga Puertorriqueña e Hispana	unite Hispanics regardless of national origins. Cultural, educational and mutual aid.	Juan Villanueva, Blas Oliveras, J.V. Alonso, Pedro San Miguel, J.M. Vivaldi, José González Benítez, J.M. Antonmarchi, Tomás Gares, Carlos L. Fernández, Cayetano Arieta, Rafael Pérez
La Alianza Obrera	sponsored syndicalist ideas; a common center for defense of Puerto Ricans regardless of political affiliations.	Lupercio Arroyo, Jesus Colón, Eduvigis Cabán, Guillermo Vargas, Catalino Castro, Luis Muñoz Marín
Porto Rican Brotherhood of America	promoted sociability and friendship; social and intellectual advancement; sponsored civic, social, cultural and educational activities; represented Puerto Ricans.	Antonio Dávila, Eusebio Cruz, Juan Carreras, Aurelio Betancourt, Jacinto Paradis, Faustino Dorna, Juan I. Mares, A. Rivera Hernández
Junta de Defensa de Puerto Rico	attempted to safeguard legal rights of Puerto Ricans	Domingo Collazo, J. Monge Sánchez, Ernesto Andino Cespe, Luis Battistini, J.A. González, Antonio Gotay
Ateneo Obrero	cultural, literary and educational. Promoted the needs of second generation	Bernardo Vega, Sabino Vázquez, Juan Rovira, Manuel Flores Cabrera, Juan Bautista Pagán, Emilio Fariza

NAME	PURPOSE FOR ORGANIZING	MEMBERS OR TYPES OF MEMBERSHIP
Club Videro	social and political	unknown
New York Sporting Club	sports, recreational and social activities	unknown
Club Esperanza	benevolent and charity	unknown
Puerto Rican Employee's Association	social, cultural, athletics and recreational	Carmelo Colón, Bide Jesus, Rafael Rivera, Tomás Gares, Ruperto Ruiz
1930–1940		
Comisión Pro Centenario de Hostos	cultural and social	unknown
Club Claridad Humanitaria	charity	women's group
Club Eugenio María de Hostos	cultural, political and educational	Jesus Colón, Alberto Rivera, Manuel Flores Cabrera, Bernardo Vega, Isabel O'Neill, María Alamo Cerra, Juan Rovira
International Ladies Garment Workers Union, Local 22	union activity	Spanish-speaking workers
Liga Anti-imperialista Puertorriqueña (Centro Obrero Español)	attempted to organize against U.S. imperialism in Latin America	unknown

Organization	Purpose	Members
La Confederación de Sociedades Puertorriqueñas	alliance of all community groups; social and cultural	José Camprubi, J.M. Vivaldi, Oscar García Rivera, J. Cabán Soler, Cesar G. Torres, José Santiago, Laura Santiago, Isabel O'Neill, Tomás Gares, Angel Vidal, García Angulo
Círculo Cultural Cervantes	cultural and literary	unknown
Pan American Women's Association	social and cultural	Latin women
Emergency Unemployment Relief Committee; South Harlem Committee Headquarters	welfare, political and civic	unknown
Spanish Association for the Blind	charity	unknown
Asociación de Empleados Civiles de Correo	civic and social	Postal workers
Sociedad de Mujeres Puertorriqueñas	cultural and social	women's group
Hispanic Merchants' Association	social, commercial	small businessmen
Asociación de Escritores y Periodistas Puertorriqueños	literary, cultural and social	Rafael Torres Mazzor, Angel M. Arroyo, Gonzalo O'Neill, Antonio J. Colorado, Erasmo Vando, Jose Enamorado Cuesta, Max Vázquez, Max Ríos, María Mas Pozo, Clotilde Betances

APPENDIX 1 (continued)

NAME	PURPOSE FOR ORGANIZING	MEMBERS OR TYPES OF MEMBERSHIP
Puerto Rican Civic Club	civic, social, and mutual aid	Joseph R. Pacheco, Pedro Vega, Jr., Octavio y Garavídez, Prudencio L. Vicente, Joseph Hoppe, Sr.
1940–1950		
Porto Rican Athletic Club	social, recreational, athletics	unknown
Puerto Rican Cultural Society, Inc.	welfare, civic and political	Manuel Torres, Cesar Gouverniuer, Eusebio Pérez
Puerto Rican Veterans Welfare Postal Workers Association, Inc.	social, cultural and civic	Juan I. Matos, Luis J. Ramírez, Darío González, Luis A. Vidal, Rafael Villalobas, Angelo Becerra, James A. Figueras, Gerardo Torres, Luis Castro, Miguel Bisbal
Club Artes y Letras	cultural and literary	Josefina Silva de Cintrón
Spanish Correspondence for Soldiers	civic and patriotic	unknown
Comite Hispano-Americano Pro Defensa de America	civic and patriotic	unknown

Sources: Certificates of Incorporation
Memorias de Bernardo Vega, César Andreu Iglesias (ed.)
Group Participation of Migrants as related in interviews

APPENDIX II:
Political Organization Chart, 1900–1930

POLITICAL CLUBS AND ORGANIZATIONS	MEMBERSHIP AND FUNCTIONS
1900–1919	
Club Demócrata Puertorriqueño	J.V. Alonso and Joaquin Colón Puerto Rican Local of New York City–Democratic Party
Harlem Branch	J.C. Cebollero and Domingo Collazo
Puerto Rican Committee of the Socialist Party	Lupercio Arroyo, Jesus Colón, Bernardo Vega, Eduvigus Cabán, Valentin Flores – founding members
Asociación Nacionalista	Vicente Balbas Capo; organization pledged to secure Puerto Rican independence
El Corserio	Anarchist. Some Puerto Rican membership. Mostly Merchant Marines. Published a newspaper.
Alianza Puertorriqueña	Composed of Puerto Rican intellectuals. Founding members: Gonzalo O'Neill, Rafael Torres, Luis G. Muñiz, Domingo Collazo, Fiol Ramos, J. Curzado, Radeo Pico
Club Latinoamericano	J.J. Henna
Club Betances	Tapia and Weber; Democratic Party Local

APPENDIX II (continued)

NAME	MEMBERSHIP AND FUNCTION
Liga Puertorriqueña	A federation of Latin societies. Founding members: G. O'Neill, J. Rodríguez Sanjurjo, R. Pabón Aviles
Club Demócrata Hispanoamericano	unknown
Federation of Puerto Rican Clubs in New York City	Joaquin Colón and J.V. Alonso
Alianza Obrera Committee to Support Robert M. La Follette	Presented activities in support of candidates. Fiorello La Guardia, Jesus Colón, Luis Muñoz Marín, Bernardo Vega, Lupercio Arroyo, Felix León, Valentin Flores, Cabán
El Caribe Democratic Club	Carlos Tapia and Luis Weber
Brooklyn Democratic Club	Founding members: Jesus Colón, Ramón Colón, Julio Díaz, Luis Weber. Active in legal aid and social work.
De Hostos Democratic Club	Functions similar to Brooklyn Dem. Club
Baldorioty Democratic Club	same as above
Guaybana Democratic Club	same as above
Guarionex Democratic Club	same as above
Puerto Rican Republican Organization	Founding members: R. Villar, Juan B. Matos, Fernando Torres, Frank Torres, F.M. Rivera, F. Gómez

1920–1930

Legión de la Flor Roja	Clandestine Cuban and Puerto Rican organization to combat Machado regime in Cuba
Hispanic Branch – Fusionist Party	Founding members: J.M. Vivaldi, Enrique Torregrosa, Victor Fiol, Antonio González, Florencio Ruiz, Felix Caro, J.D. López, Miguel Collazo, Luis Caballero, Salguero Font
Puerto Rican Political and Social League	membership unknown
League of Spanish Speaking Democrats	Chairman: Dr. J.A. López, Secretary: Adelia Pérez Ravelo
Brooklyn Branch of the Puerto Rican Republican Club	Founder: Ramón Colón
Puerto Rican Democratic and Social Union	membership unknown

Sources: César Andreu Iglesias, (ed.) *Memorias de Bernardo Vega*
Ramón Colón, *A Puerto Rican Hero in New York City*
Certificates of Incorporation
Personal Interviews

	1923	1925	1927
President	Rodrigo del Manzano	Blas Oliveras	Carlos L. Fernández
Vice-President	Tomás Gares	Carlos L. Fernández	Rafael Pérez
Secretary	Juan Carreras	Román Mínguez	Antonio González
Treasurer	Vincente Rolón	Julio Delgado	Fernando Navas
			Samuel Roig
Under-Secretary	Julio Pietratoni	Antonio González	José González Benítez
Auditor	Felipe Gómez	Juan A. Natali	Juan A. Natali
Voting Members	Antonio Dávila	Guillermo Patino	William L. Martínez
(Vocales)	Eusebio Cruz	Antonio Mark, Jr.	José M. Vivaldi
	Juan Valderrama	Jaime Gutierrez	Cirilo Pérez
	Aurelio Betancourt	Alfonso R. Quinones	Felipe Gómez
	Jacinto Paradis	Felipe Gómez	Jaime Gutierrez
	Juan I. Matos	Jorge L. Oller	Blas Oliveras
	Faustine Dorna	José R. Silen	Erasmo Vando, Jr.

Sources: César Andreu Iglesias, (ed.) *Memorias de Bernardo Vega*, p. 178.
Souvenir Program, Porto Rican Brotherhood of America, June, 1926
Certificate of Incorporation, Porto Rican Brotherhood of America, #05660-27C, March, 1927

Note: The exact posts held by Julio Pietratoni and Felipe Gómez in 1923 are not known but Vega declares both officers succeeded del Manzano as president.

Glossary

agregado	landless peasant, sharecropper
arroz	rice
barato	cheap, inexpensive
barrio	district or neighborhood, ward
bodega	grocery or general store
bolita	numbers racket or numbers game
bolitero	one who takes bets, numbers runner
Borinquen	indigenous name for Puerto Rico
botánicas	stores specializing in religious articles or plants
campesinos	rural, rustic, a countryman or woman
chiripeo	marginal employment
colmado	grocery or general store
colonia	subdivision of a city, colony, neighborhood, settlement
colonia hispana	Spanish settlement
comadre	godmother
compadrazgo	ritual kinship, the relationship between the natural parents and the godparents of a child
compadre	godfather, benefactor or protector
conjuntos	instrumental musical group
costura	sewing or needlecrafts
cuñha	a bed, a niche or a nest (Portuguese)
curandera	healer
empanadas	breaded meats or vegetables, meat pies
fíjate	observe, take notice
gandules verdes	pigeon peas

hacendado	landowner, owner of an hacienda
hacienda	landed property, large, self-sufficient farm
hijos de crianza	foster children
ingenio	sugar plantation
jaranas	a party, spree or scuffle, binge or revelry
juegos florales	dramatic or poetic competitions for troubadours
marqueta	market
maví	Puerto Rican drink made with fermented ginger root
mofongo	appetizer made with plantains, pork rind and spices
mozón	waiter, male attendant at a restaurant
mujeres	women
pernil	roast ham
personalismo	patron-client relationship based on personal contact
piragua	scraped ice drenched in sweet syrup
piraguero	one who sells piraguas
plátanos	fruit of plantain tree
se cuidan niños	children cared for
tostones	plantain fried chips
trio	musical group composed of three individuals
velada	evening party or gathering, conference
yautía	root vegetable

Bibliography

Books

Braverman, Harry. *Labor and Monopoly Capital: The Degradation of Work in the Twentieth Century.* New York: Monthly Review Press, 1974.

Buitrago Ortiz, Carlos. *Los orígenes históricos de la sociedad precapitalista en Puerto Rico.* San Juan: Ediciones Huracan, 1976.

Brooklyn Daily Eagle Almanac. Brooklyn: Brooklyn Eagle Press, 1926–1939.

Carroll, Henry K. *Report on the Island of Porto Rico.* Washington, D.C.: Government Printing Office, 1899.

Centro de Estudios Puertorriqueños. *Documentos de la migración puertorriqueña, 1879–1901.* New York: Centro de Estudios Puertorriqueños, Graduate Center, CUNY, 1977.

_____. *Taller de migración, conferencia de historiografía.* New York: Graduate Center, CUNY, Centro de Estudios Puertorriqueños, 1974.

Chenault, Lawrence R. *The Puerto Rican Migrant in New York City.* New York: Columbia University Press, 1938; reissued, Russell and Russell, 1970.

Colón, Jesus. *The Puerto Rican in New York and Other Sketches.* New York: Arno Press, 1975.

Colón, Ramón. *Carlos Tapia, A Puerto Rican Hero in New York.* New York: Vantage Press, 1976.

Erickson, Charlotte. *American Industry and the European Immigrant, 1860–1885.* Cambridge: Harvard University Press, 1957.

Ernst, Robert. *Immigrant Life in New York City, 1825–1863.* New York: Kings Crown Press, 1949.

Figueroa Mercado, Loida. *Breve historia de Puerto Rico.* 2 vols. Rio Piedras: Ediciones Edil, 1970.

Fitzpatrick, Joseph P. *Puerto Rican-Americans: The Meaning of Migration to the Mainland.* Englewood Cliffs, N.J.: Prentice-Hall, 1971.

Glazer, Nathan, and Moynihan, Daniel. *Beyond the Melting Pot.* Cambridge: MIT Press, 1970.

Green, Constance M. *The Rise of Urban America.* New York: Harper & Row, 1965.

Gutman, Herbert C. *The Black Family in Slavery and Freedom, 1750–1925.* New York: Pantheon Press, 1976.

Handlin, Oscar. *The Newcomers: Negroes and Puerto Ricans in a Changing Metropolis.* Cambridge: Harvard University Press, 1959.

History Task Force, Centro de Estudios Puertorriqueños. *Labor Migration Under Capitalism: The Puerto Rican Experience.* New York: Monthly Review Press, 1979.

Howe, Irving. *The World of Our Fathers.* New York: Harcourt, Brace, Jovanovich, 1976.

Iglesias, César Andreu, ed. *Memorias de Bernardo Vega.* Rio Piedras: Ediciones Huracan, 1977.

Jennings, James. *Puerto Rican Politics in New York City.* Washington, D.C.: University Press of America, 1977.

Kanrowitz, Nathan. *Ethnic and Racial Segregation in New York Metropolis.* New York: Praeger Publishers, 1973.

La Gumina, Salvatore. *The People's Politician.* Iowa: Kendall Hunt Publishing Co., 1969.

Laslett, Peter. *Household and Family in Past Time.* Cambridge: Cambridge University Press, 1972.

López, Adalberto, and Petras, James, eds. *Puerto Rico and the Puerto Ricans: Studies in History and Society.* New York: Schenkman Publishing Co., 1974.

Maldonado-Denis, Manuel. *Puerto Rico: A Socio-Historic Interpretation.* New York: Random House, 1972.

Mann, Arthur. *La Guardia—A Fighter Against His Times, 1881–1933.* New York: J.B. Lippincott, 1959.

Manning, Caroline. *The Employment of Women in Puerto Rico.* Washington, D.C.: Government Printing Office, 1934.

Mills, C. Wright; Senior, Clarence; and Goldsen, Rose. *The Puerto Rican Journey: New York's Newest Migrants.* New York: Harper & Bros., 1950.

Morales Carrión, Arturo. *Puerto Rico and the Non-Hispanic Caribbean.* Rio Piedras: University of Puerto Rico, 1952.

Morrison, Samuel Eliot. *The Oxford History of the American People. Vol. 3.* New York: New American Library, 1972.

Moscow, Warren. *The Last of the Big-Time Bosses.* New York: Stein & Day, 1971.

Nieves Falcón, Luis. *El emigrante puertorriqueño.* Rio Piedras: Editorial Edil, 1975.

Padilla, Elena. *Up From Puerto Rico.* New York: Columbia University Press, 1958.

Peel, Roy V. *The Political Clubs of New York City.* New York: G.P. Putnam & Sons, 1935.

Perloff, Harvey S. *Puerto Rico's Economic Future.* Chicago: University of Chicago Press, 1950.

Picó, Fernando. *Libertad y servidumbre en el Puerto Rico del siglo XIX. Rio Piedras: Editorial Huracon, 1979.*

Rodríguez, Clara E. *The Ethnic Queue in the United States: The Case of Puerto Ricans.* San Francisco: R.&E. Research Associates, 1973.

_____; Sánchez Korrol, Virginia; and Alers, José Oscar, eds. *The Puerto Rican Struggle: Essays on Survival in the U.S.* New York: Puerto Rican Migration Research Consortium, 1980.

Rubenstein, Annette, et al. *I Vote My Conscience—Debates, Speeches and Writings of Vito Marcantonio, 1935-1950.* New York: The Vito Marcantonio Memorial, 1956.

Sayre, Wallace S., and Kaufman, Herbert. *Governing New York City.* New York: W.W. Norton & Co., 1965.

Senior, Clarence. *Puerto Rican Emigration.* Rio Piedras: Social Science Research Center, University of Puerto Rico, 1947.

_____. *The Puerto Ricans: Strangers then Neighbors.* Chicago: Quadrangle Books, 1965.

Shorter, Edward. *The Historian and the Computer.* New York: W.W. Norton & Co., 1971.

Smith, Page. *The Shaping of America. Vol. 3.* New York: McGraw-Hill Book Co., 1980.

Stewart, Donald. *A Short History of East Harlem.* New York: Museum of the City of New York, 1972.

Swierenga, Robert P. *Quantification in American History.* New York: Atheneum, 1970.

Toro, R. de Jesus. *Historia Económica de Puerto Rico.* Cincinnati, Ohio: South-Western Publishing Co., 1982.

Wagenheim, Kal. *A Survey of Puerto Ricans in the U.S. Mainland in the 1970s.* New York: Praeger Publishers, 1975.

_____. *Puerto Rico: A Profile.* New York: Praeger Publishers, 1975.

Wakefield, Daniel. *Island in the City: The World of Spanish Harlem.* Boston: Houghton Mifflin Co., 1959.

Articles and Periodicals

Alexander, Jack. "District Leader: Profile of James J. Hines." *The New Yorker,* vol. 12 (1936).

Berrol, Selma C. "School Days on the Old East Side: The Italian and Jewish Experience." *New York History.* New York Historical Association (April 1976).

Bone, Hugh A. "Political Parties in New York City." *American Political Science Review,* vol. 40 (April 1946).

Boorstein, Daniel J. "Self Discovery in Puerto Rico." *Yale Review* (1955).

Campos, Ricardo, and Bonilla, Frank. "Industrialization and Migration: Some Effects on the Puerto Rican Working Class." *Latin American Perspectives* vol. 3, no. 3 (1976).

_____ and Flores, Juan. "National Culture and Migration: Perspectives from the Puerto Rican Working Class." *Centro Working Papers.* New York: Centro de Estudios Puertorriqueños, Graduate Center, CUNY (1978).

Cintrón Fernández, Celia, and Rivera Quintero, Marcia. "Bases de la sociedad sexista en Puerto Rico." *Revista/Review Interamerican,* vol. 4, no. 2 (summer 1974).

Citizens Union. "Party Organization in New York City." *The Searchlight,* vol. 41 (May 1951).

Dyos, H. J., and Baker, A.B.M. "The Possibilities of Computerizing Census Data." In H. J. Dyos, *The Study of Urban History,* London: Edward Arnold Publishers, Ltd., 1968.

Estades, Rosa. "Symbolic Unity—The Puerto Rican Day Parade." In Clara E. Rodríguez, Virginia Sánchez Korrol, and José Oscar Alers, eds., *The Puerto Rican Struggle: Essays on Survival in the U.S.* New York: Puerto Rican Migration Research Consortium, 1980.

González, Nancie L. "Multiple Migratory Experiences of Dominican Women." *Anthropological Quarterly,* vol. 49, no. 1 (January 1979).

Gráfico, 1926–1928.

Gray, Lois. "The Jobs Puerto Ricans Hold in New York City." *Monthly Labor Review,* no. 46 (October 1975).

Hernández Álvarez, José. "The Movement and Settlement of Puerto Rican Migrants Within the U.S., 1950–1960." *International Migration Review,* no. 2 (spring 1968).

Hill, Herbert. "Guardians of the Sweatshop: The Trade Union, Racism and the Garment Industry." In Adalberto López and James Petras, eds., *Puerto Rico and Puerto Ricans: Studies in History and Society.* New York: Schenkman Publishing, 1974.

Kazin, Alfred. "In Puerto Rico." In *Contemporaries.* New York: Little, Brown & Co., 1960.

King, Lourdes Miranda. "Puertorriqueñas in the United States." In Commission of Human Rights, *Civil Rights Digest*. Washington, D.C.: U.S. Commission of Civil Rights, spring 1974.

La Correspondencia de Puerto Rico, 1901.

La Prensa, 1919–1924.

López, Adalberto. "Vito Marcantonio." *Caribbean Review,* vol. 8, no. 1 (January–March 1979).

————. "The Puerto Rican Diaspora." In Adalberto López and James Petras, eds., *Puerto Rico and Puerto Ricans: Studies in History and Society.* New York: Schenkman Publishing, 1974.

————. "Some of the Literature on Puerto Rico and Puerto Ricans in English." In Adalberto López and James Petras, eds., *Puerto Rico and Puerto Ricans: Studies in History and Society.* New York: Schenkman Publishing, 1974.

Maldonado, Rita M. "Why Puerto Ricans Migrated to the United States in 1947–73." *Monthly Labor Review,* no. 9 (September 1976).

McCoy, Terry L. "A Primer for U.S. Policy on Caribbean Emigration." *Caribbean Review,* vol. 8, no. 1 (January-March 1979).

Morley, Morris. "Dependence and Development in Puerto Rico." In Adalberto López and James Petras, eds., *Puerto Rico and Puerto Ricans: Studies in History and Society.* New York: Schenkman Publishing, 1974.

New York Times, 1926–1955.

New York World Telegram, 1945.

Pantoja, Antonia. "Puerto Rican Migration." Preliminary Report to the U.S. Commission on the Civil Rights of Puerto Ricans (1972).

Picó de Hernández, Isabel. "Estudio sobre el empleo de la mujer en Puerto Rico." *Revista de Ciencias Sociales,* vol. 19, no. 2 (June 1975).

Quintero Rivera, Angel. "Background to the Emergence of Imperialist Capitalism in Puerto Rico." In Adalberto López and James Petras, eds., *Puerto Rico and Puerto Ricans: Studies in History and Society.* New York: Schenkman Publishing, 1974.

Revista de Artes y Letras, 1934–1946.

Rinker, Buck. "The New Sweatshops: A Penny for Your Collar." *New York,* vol. 12, no. 5 (January 1979).

Rodríguez, Clara E. "Economic Factors Affecting Puerto Ricans in New York." History Task Force, Centro de Estudios Puertorriqueños. *Labor Migration Under Capitalism: The Puerto Rican Experience.* New York: Monthly Review, 1979.

————. "Puerto Ricans in the Melting Pot." *The Journal of Ethnic Studies,* vol. 1, no. 4 (winter 1974).

Salazar, Max. "The Perserverance of a Culture." In Clara E. Rodríguez, Virginia Sánchez Korrol, and José Oscar Alers, eds., *The Puerto Rican Struggle: Essays on Survival in the U.S.* New York: Puerto Rican Migration Research Consortium, 1980.

_____. "Latin Music's Rivalries and Battlers." *Latin New York,* January
    1975.
Santana Cooney, Rosemary, and Warren Colon, Alice. "Work and Fam-
    ily: The Recent Struggle of Puerto Rican Females." In Clara E.
    Rodríguez, Virginia Sánchez Korrol, and José Oscar Alers, eds.,
    The Puerto Rican Struggle: Essays on Survival in the U.S. New
    York: Puerto Rican Migration Research Consortium, 1980.
Senior, Clarence. "Migration as a Process and the Migrant as a Person."
    Population Review, vol. 6, no. 1 (January 1962).
_____, and Watkins, Donald. "Toward a Balance Sheet of Puerto Rican
    Migration." In U.S.-Puerto Rico Commission on the Status of
    Puerto Rico, *Status of Puerto Rico: Selected Background Studies.*
    Washington, D.C.: Government Printing Office, 1966.
Shedd, William B. "Italian Population in New York." Bulletin No. 7,
    Casa Italiana Educational Bureau. New York: Columbia Univer-
    sity, 1930.
Smith, Estelle M. "Networks and Migration Resettlement: Cherchez la
    Femme." *Anthropological Quarterly,* vol. 49, no. 1 (January 1979).
Stevens-Arroyo, Anthony. "Puerto Rican Struggles in the Catholic
    Church." In Clara E. Rodríguez, Virginia Sánchez Korrol, and José
    Oscar Alers, eds., *The Puerto Rican Struggle: Essays on Survival in
    the U.S.* New York: Puerto Rican Migration Research Consortium,
    1980.
Vázquez Calzada, José. "Demographic Aspects of Migration." In History
    Task Force, Centro de Estudios Puertorriqueños, *Labor Migration
    Under Capitalism: The Puerto Rican Experience.* New York:
    Monthly Review Press, 1979.
Wagenheim, Olga Jimenez de. "Prelude to Lares." *Caribbean Review,*
    vol. 8, no. 1 (January-March 1979).

Documents and Reports

Cayce Morrison, J. *The Puerto Rican Study, 1953-1957.* New York: Board
    of Education, 1957.
Evans, W.D. "Effects of Mechanization on Cigar Manufacturing." Works
    Progress Administration, Report No. B-4. Washington, D.C.: Gov-
    ernment Printing Office, 1934.
New York State Manuscript Census, 1925. New York City Municipal
    Archives.
Octavo informe anual del negociado del trabajo. San Juan, 1920.
The Porto Rican Brotherhood of America. Annual Report, 1926-1927.
Puerto Rican Forum. *A Study of Poverty Conditions in the New York*

Puerto Rican Community. New York: Puerto Rican Forum, Inc., 1964.

U.S. Commission on Civil Rights. *Puerto Ricans in the United States: An Uncertain Future.* Washington, D.C., 1976.

———. *Civil Rights Digest,* vol. 6, no. 3 (spring 1974).

U.S. Department of Labor, Bureau of Labor Statistics. "The New York Puerto Rican: Patterns of Work Experience." Regional Report no. 19. Poverty Area Profiles. New York, 1972.

———. "A Socio-Economic Profile of Puerto Rican New Yorkers." Regional Report no. 46. New York, 1975.

U.S.-Puerto Rico Commission on the Status of Puerto Rico. *Status of Puerto Rico.* August 1966.

Welfare Council of New York City. *Puerto Ricans in New York City.* New York: The Welfare Council, 1948.

Welfare and Health Council of New York City. Population of Puerto Rican Birth or Parentage. New York City, 1950.

———. Brooklyn Council for Social Planning. "Report on Survey of Brooklyn Agencies Rendering Services to Puerto Ricans." (June 1953).

Unpublished Materials and Dissertations

Amaral, Daniel Joseph. "Family, Community and Place: The Experience of Puerto Rican Emigrants in Worcester, Massachusetts." Ph.D. Dissertation, Clark University, 1978.

Estades, Rosa. "Patterns of Political Participation of Puerto Ricans in New York City." Ph.D. Dissertation, New School for Social Research, 1974.

Gittell, Marilyn. "Administration and Organization of Political Parties in New York City." Master's Thesis, NYU, 1953.

Gotsch, John W. "Puerto Rican Leadership in New York." Master's Thesis, NYU, 1966.

Gray, Lois. "Economic Incentives to Labor Mobility: The Puerto Rican Case." Ph.D. Dissertation, Columbia University, 1966.

Quintero Rivera, Angel. "Puerto Rico, 1870–1940: From Mercantilist to Imperialist Colonial Domination." CEREP, Rio Piedras, Puerto Rico, 1979.

Rivera Quintero, Marcia. "Capitalist Development and the Incorporation of Women to the Labour Force." CEREP, Rio Piedras, Puerto Rico, 1979.

Sánchez Korrol, Virginia E. "Settlement Patterns and Community Development Among Puerto Ricans in New York City, 1917–1948." Ph.D. Dissertation, SUNY at Stony Brook, 1981.

Additions to the
Bibliography, 1994

Acosta Belén, Edna, Bose, Christine, and Rochelle, Anne R. *Albany–P.R. Womenet Database: An Annotated Bibliography on Puerto Rican Women*. New York: Center for Latin American and the Caribbean and the Institute for Research on Women, State University of New York, Albany, 1991.

———. *The Puerto Rican Woman*. Westport, Conn.: Praeger Press, 1986.

Aliotta, J. J. *The Puerto Ricans*. New York: Chelsea House Publishers, 1991.

Burgos, W., Rodríguez-Vecchini, H., and Torre, C. A. *The Commuter Nation: Perspectives on Puerto Rican Migration*. San Juan: University of Puerto Rico Press, 1993.

Carr, Raymond. *Puerto Rico: A Colonial Experiment*. New York: New York University Press, 1984.

Colón, Jesús, Acosta Belén, E., and Sánchez Korrol, Virginia, eds. *The Way It Was and Other Writings*. Houston: Arte Público Press, 1993.

Díaz-Stevens, Ana María. *Oxcart Catholicism on Fifth Avenue*. Notre Dame, Ind.: University of Notre Dame Press, 1993.

Dietz, James L. *Economic History of Puerto Rico: Institutional Change and Capitalist Development*. Princeton: Princeton University Press, 1986.

Fernández, Ronald. *The Disenchanted Island: Puerto Rico and the United States in the Twentieth Century*. Westport, Conn.: Praeger Press, 1992.

Figueroa, J. *Survival on the Margin: A Documentary Study of the Under-*

ground Economy in a Puerto Rican Ghetto. New York: Vantage Press, 1989.

Flores, Juan. *Divided Borders: Essays on Puerto Rican Identity*. Houston: Arte Público Press, 1993.

Iglesias, César Andreu, ed. *Memoirs of Bernardo Vega: A Contribution to the History of the Puerto Rican Community in New York*. Translated by Juan Flores. New York: Monthly Review Press, 1984.

Jennings, James, and Rivera, Monte. *Puerto Rican Politics in Urban America*. Westport, Conn.: Greenwood Press, 1984.

Levins Morales, Aurora and Morales, Rosario. *Getting Home Alive*. Ithaca: Firebrand Books, 1986.

Meléndez, Edwin, Rodríguez, C. E., and Figueroa, J. Barry. *Hispanics in the Labor Force: Issues and Policies*. New York: Plenum Press, 1991.

_____ and Meléndez, Edgardo. *Colonial Dilemma: Critical Perspectives on Contemporary Puerto Rico*. Boston: South End Press, 1993.

Morales Carrión, Arturo. *Puerto Rico: A Political and Cultural History*. New York: W. W. Norton & Co., 1983.

Morales, Julio. *Puerto Rican Poverty and Migration: We Just Had to Try Elsewhere*. Westport, Conn.: Greenwood Press, 1986.

Ortiz, Altagracia, ed. *Puerto Rican Women in the Twentieth Century: New Perspectives on Gender, Labor and Migration*. Philadelphia: Temple University Press, forthcoming.

Padilla, Felix. *Latino Ethnic Consciousness: The Case of Mexican-Americans and Puerto Ricans in Chicago*. Notre Dame, Ind.: Notre Dame University Press, 1985.

_____. *Puerto Rican Chicago*. Notre Dame, Ind.: Notre Dame University Press, 1987.

Pérez y Mena, Andrés. *Speaking with the Dead: Development of Afro-Latin Religion Among Puerto Ricans in the U.S.* New York: AMS Press, 1991.

Rodríguez, Clara E. *Puerto Ricans: Born in the U.S.A.* Boston: Unwin Hyman, 1989.

Rodríguez de Laguna, Asela. *Images and Identities: The Puerto Rican in Two World Contexts*. New Brunswick, N.J.: Transaction Books, 1987.

Sánchez, María E. and Stevens-Arroyo, Antonio M., eds. *Toward a Renaissance of Puerto Rican Studies: Ethnic and Area Studies in University Education*. Highland Lakes, N.J.: Atlantic Research and Publications, 1987.

Torres, Andrés. *Between Melting Pot and Mosaic: African Americans and*

Puerto Ricans in the New York Political Economy. Philadelphia: Temple University Press, forthcoming.

Wagenheim, Kal and Jiménez de Wagenheim, Olga, eds. *The Puerto Ricans: A Documentary History.* Princeton: Markus Wiener Publishing, Inc., 1993.

Index

$$\begin{array}{r} 900 \\ 12 \\ \hline 1800 \\ 900 \\ \hline 10800 \end{array}$$